Francis Morrissey.

Fintan.

LESTER PIGGOTT

DOWNFALL OF A LEGEND

LESTER PIGGOTT

DOWNFALL OF A LEGEND

Roy David

HEINEMANN KINGSWOOD

Heinemann Kingswood
Michelin House, 81 Fulham Road, London SW3 6RB

LONDON   MELBOURNE   AUCKLAND

Copyright © 1989 Roy David

First published in 1989

0 434 98178 8

Printed and bound in Great Britain by
Richard Clay Ltd, Bungay, Suffolk

Contents

Acknowledgements

The author would like to thank the following for their invaluable assistance in the preparation of this book: Don Mackay, Brian Radford, Graham Bell, Howard Wright, Sam Smyth (from Ireland), Charlie Rose (from New York), Dan Liebman (from Kentucky), Adrian Maxwell, Margot Richardson, and all those who for reasons of confidentiality cannot be named. The author would also like to thank the official shorthand writers Miller, Beak and Ley.

The photographs in this book are reproduced by kind permission of Anglia Press Agency (nos 8 and 9), Keystone Press Agency (nos 1, 2, 3 and 4) and the Press Association (nos 5, 6, 7, 10, 11 and 12).

1. Clouds on the Horizon

It was Derby Eve and the telephone rang, rudely interrupting the quiet dinner Lester Piggott and his wife Susan were enjoying at the London home of their long-time friend, racehorse owner Charles St George. He had set aside tonight with the sole aim of relaxing. Tomorrow was another big day and he would be taking the usual helicopter from Battersea Power Station to the famous Downs and the racecourse he knew so well. He didn't particularly care for the track with its idiosyncratic undulations and cambers. But Epsom? Hell, it had still provided him with many of his finest moments, and had helped make him a very rich man indeed.

Moments later St George returned to the table. 'It's someone for you, Lester,' he said. Piggott got up and strolled to the phone wondering who, outside his family and one or two close associates, could have known he was here. He had also left strict instructions not to be bothered unless it was an emergency.

'Mr Piggott?' the voice enquired. Piggott replied with that barely audible grunt many people have taken for rudeness but which is a legacy of a speech impediment and slight deafness at birth.

'You're going to be shot dead tomorrow,' the caller said in a chilling tone, replacing the receiver before Piggott could respond.

Piggott announced the message to his startled wife and friends, then continued his meal as if nothing had happened. To him it was just another crank. There had been similar times when he had received such threats. Sometimes it was one of the prices for being right at the top.

And if there were any nervously cast glances in the Derby itself, they were simply at the opposition as he rounded Tattenham Corner and galloped on to yet another Classic victory. Lester Piggott, the man of stone, the unflappable, had shrugged off the death threat as he had a thousand other worrying moments throughout his most distinguished 37 years as a jockey.

But now, at the start of 1987, there was no dismissing a new cloud on the horizon. There could be no shrug of the shoulders or wave of the hand over this latest matter. This cloud was black and full of foreboding. Lester Piggott, OBE, probably the greatest and most respected jockey of all time, certainly the most famous sportsman in the world, was facing the ultimate disgrace – that he was a cheat. His well known love of money, a trait Piggott always played up rather than down, that butt of racecourse humour which kept grandstand bars roaring until the champagne ran out, had finally caught up with him. Piggott was facing charges of cheating Her Majesty's taxmen out of their share on undisclosed earnings of more than £3 million. That love of money had turned to greed.

Money, in fact, became so obsessional to him that not only did meanness become his trademark but, rather like a drug, the more he got, the more he wanted. And, like the addict, ultimately, he would cheat and lie to satiate the craving. Therein lies a great irony, for Piggott was proud to call himself an Englishman. He loved his country and strove to make the point whenever possible. On his visits to the dozens of countries he visited throughout the world he acted as unpaid ambassador, flying the flag at every opportunity. On numerous occasions Piggott had proudly pulled on the Royal colours, the purple, gold braid and scarlet sleeves of the Queen. He had shared many private moments with Her Majesty, received her praise, laughed and joked with her. That he should systematically be cheating his Queen and country on such a vast scale at the same time is surely the sting in the tale, indeed, the saddest paradox.

When Piggott retired from the saddle in the October of 1985, exactly a week before his fiftieth birthday, he had amassed a personal fortune of more than £12 million. If to remain at the top of one's sporting profession means self-sacrifice, then Piggott deserves to stand head and shoulders above the rest. For in no other sport, especially one requiring the fitness of an athlete and that physical resilience against advancing age and injury, can a man stay at the pinnacle for so long. Much has been said of Piggott's amazing will-power; the ability to eat just sufficient to provide the energy to ride a half-ton horse maybe six races, sometimes twice that, a day, to say nothing of the early-morning work on the gallops, the 300,000 miles a year of travelling. Yet to do that and remain able to ride at perhaps a good one and a half stone below his natural bodyweight required a motivation verging on martyrdom.

But then, the financial rewards were quite significant too.

Of course, when Piggott did ride his last racehorse on the track, unbuckled the girth strap around trainer Pat Haslam's miler Wind From The West on a cold and dull Tuesday at Nottingham, and carried the saddle to the weighing room for the last time, there were no thoughts of an easier life; a new career was beckoning as a trainer, something to which few former jockeys ever make the successful transition.

It was a decision Piggott had made much earlier, preparing for the day by shrewdly purchasing Eve Lodge stables next door to his Newmarket bungalow in the late Seventies. A considerable sum was spent modernising the complex so that by the start of the 1986 season it had room to house more than 80 horses in the American-style barn.

Eve Lodge had been let in the meantime to a succession of trainers; Bill Marshall, Michael Hinchcliffe and Michael Albina. And when neighbouring trainer Derek Weeden decided to put his Calder Park stables on the market in 1981, Piggott bought them too, so that he now had yards on both sides of his home, housing 120 horses with facilities as good as any in the town.

The year 1985 was a watershed in Piggott's life for a variety of reasons. The Flat season kicked off in March at Doncaster as normal, but this time Piggott was riding once more as a freelance, having been obliged to quit his retainer with the champion trainer Henry Cecil and hand over the reins at Warren Place to Steve Cauthen.

It was an enforced move on Piggott's part. He had planned to end his career at the same yard where, 30 years earlier, he had become first jockey to Cecil's father-in-law, Noel (later Sir Noel) Murless, following the retirement of Sir Gordon Richards. Those dozen glorious seasons with Murless struck one of the best partnerships in racing history. When Piggott decided after 1966 not to accept the Murless retainer, the racing public thought him quite mad. But they were on the outside looking in. Despite a partnership that had provided Piggott with seven English Classics and the jockeys' championship three times, he knew there was more money to be made outside the stable. After all, Murless was one of the old school and did not care much for some of the methods jockeys were beginning to employ to boost their income. Piggott would later seek, and find, those fortunes with the Robert Sangster–Vincent O'Brien syndicate, a partnership that revolutionised the world of bloodstock, racing, and jockeys' rewards.

The ending of the association with Cecil at the end of 1984, came as a personal blow to Piggott. He had just finished four marvellous seasons with the champion trainer, the first two, 1981 and 1982, providing him with his tenth and eleventh jockeys' titles, riding a total of 617 winners.

We have to look back to the September of 1983 to find the roots of this unwelcome split, the cause of which was brought about by one of Piggott's famous 'musical chairs' acts over the riding of a horse in a big race. Parisian Daniel Wildenstein, one of the world's largest fine art dealers, was chief patron in the Cecil stable and, naturally, had first claim on Piggott to ride his Warren Place-based string. But his top-class filly All Along, who was quietly fancied to land the Prix de l'Arc de Triomphe at Longchamp in the first week of October, was based at Lamorlaye, near Chantilly, with trainer Patrick Biancone, a young man who was quietly making a name for himself, not least with several other good horses belonging to Wildenstein.

The 'English' version of events surrounding the row over the booking of Piggott for All Along – which ultimately led to the Cecil–Piggott split – is far different from the 'French' version. Piggott's version is that Biancone telephoned him from Lamorlaye to offer him the ride and that he explained to the Frenchman that he would only be able to take it if his original booking, Sheikh Mohammed's filly Awaasif, worked badly in her final gallop.

Observers later suggested, in support of Piggott, that a misunderstanding could have arisen because Biancone's slender grasp of English coupled with Piggott's indistinct speech meant there were crossed wires, and that Biancone was at fault for announcing to the press that Piggott would be aboard All Along. Biancone speaks very good English, sprinkled with Americanisms, following his two years in the US as assistant to several top trainers including Leroy Jolley and Angel Penna. Perhaps they were unaware, too, that the booking was made in the jockeys' changing room at Longchamp the Sunday before the race when Piggott was riding at that meeting. Biancone has long maintained, to those willing to listen, that he was sitting next to Piggott in the jocks' room when he made the request and that Piggott's reply left him in no doubt that he had just booked the best jockey in the world for his filly.

If, as I am led to believe, Piggott was offered all the Arc-winner's prize money if he won, then fate stepped in to cast the final decision; the ride on All Along went to Walter Swinburn and they won the richest race in Europe with Awaasif trailing down the field. All Along then went on to win $1 million prize money, plus $1 million bonus for winning two major turf races in the US and one in Toronto. Piggott's decision had cost him dear.

But it had not only lost him perks and percentages worth around $250,000, for Wildenstein, incensed at what he saw was a Piggott rebuff, declared that Piggott would no longer ride any of his horses with Henry Cecil. So, for the whole of the following season, 1984, British racing witnessed the peculiar sight of a top stable's number one jockey not being allowed to ride the horses owned by the stable's chief patron. Piggott was forced to stand down whenever the royal blue Wildenstein colours were taken out of the Warren Place laundry room, and Steve Cauthen became the wearer.

Obviously, it was an untenable position for Henry Cecil by the start of the 1985 season. He and Piggott parted company, with Cauthen becoming the new stable jockey. As if to pile on the agony, Piggott then missed out on his tenth Derby-winner, the Lord Howard de Walden-owned and Cecil-trained Slip Anchor, which Piggott would automatically have ridden had he not been forced to quit Warren Place. Instead, he finished seventh on the Dermot Weld-trained Theatrical, who made no show. And from Henry Cecil's point of view, the whole affair had a sorry ending when, just before that Derby, Wildenstein decided to have all his horses based with Biancone in the future, and withdrew his two dozen horses from Newmarket.

Disenchanted with the British scene in his final season, Piggott spent a lot of time in France riding more winners there – including the French Oaks on Lypharita – than his tally of 34 at home.

He would have been totally sickened had he known that for most of 1985 he was a marked man, for a massive VAT fraud enquiry into Piggott's missing millions was already under way. Quite surreptitiously, Customs and Excise officers from the, Investigation Division had begun stalking their prey.

Wednesday, 23 April 1986, was a day that L. Piggott, trainer, will not forget. He ran his fancied three-year-old Northern Baby colt, Geordie's Delight, at Epsom in a seven-furlong maiden race, and the 7–4 favourite won by four lengths to give the master of Eve Lodge his first winner. Piggott had passed his first test. Of course he could train winners. But how many in a season? Bookmakers saw the chance for a little sport and they laid the odds in a match between the two headline-grabbing new trainers, Piggott and Michael Dickinson. Dickinson was a former jumps-trainer who had become the man behind Robert Sangster's powerful team at the famous Manton stables near Marlborough, Wiltshire.

By the end of the season, those who had backed Piggott, the outsider of the two, were counting their winnings – he had saddled a highly respectable tally of 30 winners. He had cleared the hurdle, silenced the sceptics, and, above all, proved to himself he could make the grade as a trainer. The season wasn't all plain sailing, however, and Piggott's credibility was in danger when he announced in April that he might bring his riding boots out of mothballs and ride in the 2,000 Guineas, the first of the colts' classics. Not surprisingly, there were a few stern words in his ear. High-profile owners such as Sheikh Mohammed wanted a full-time trainer, not someone who would take to riding whenever the fancy took him. Like the boxer who announces his retirement and then makes a comeback, for Piggott to have started riding again would have been tinged with vulgarity, almost a besmirching of the vision we had all seen and wished to lock away as a hallowed memory.

In addition, Piggott had signed several lucrative contracts with manufacturers of artefacts and memorabilia so that both could cash in on the wave of sentiment and interest in the retirement of a great jockey. Angrily, they pointed to the small print – and Piggott was forced to put thoughts of returning to the saddle right out of his mind.

Winter is an exciting time for the Flat trainer. By November most of the yearlings are in the yard and have been broken and ridden away. Eve Lodge and Calder Park stables were going through a busy period now. The yearling intake was almost double that of the first season – 62 in all. This was when each would come under the Piggott microscope, his gaze and all those years of experience transfixed on a young horse's conformation, the walk, did he throw his off-fore out? Would it affect the horse next year, as a two-year-old, at the gallop? This new batch of raw recruits, which Piggott and his staff, under the watchful eye of head lad Joe Oliver, would turn into racing machines, first had to be put to the walk, then the trot. In another month they would all be two-year-olds, the bells of New Year's Day heralding another birthday for all racehorses irrespective of the foaling date.

Piggott watched for the sharp types, those precocious on looks and breeding who could be hacked and walked early to muscle them up. When that New Year came they would be cantering by February, brought into full training by March, and running on a track for the first time in their lives by the April.

But first it would be Christmas, a quiet family affair, with Lester and Susan and their two daughters, Maureen and Tracey. Piggott's mother, Iris, and father, Keith, lived next door in the bungalow their son had had built for them. They were both in their eighties. Iris was not in the best of health, and they would look forward to the occasion when they could all be together. For Lester and Susan too, it would be a day or two of peace and quiet; the reflective contemplation of a successful year, with an optimistic eye on the new season.

That really very ordinary Christmas, one shared by millions of families throughout the land, would not, however, come to the Piggott household. Soon, Piggott would find himself in serious trouble. This time the famous cool of the maestro would be shaken and tested like never before.

The message came through to the CID at Newmarket police station at 11.23 a.m. on Friday, 19 December 1986. It was from the Inland Revenue in London. The gist of it was simple enough: Arrest Lester Piggott.

It was common knowledge by then that Piggott was up to his neck in trouble with the taxmen. They had raided his home in the

February of that year, which was reported widely in the press. But it was not public knowledge, nor did Piggott know, that the Customs and the Inland Revenue's massive and far-reaching investigation was already twelve months old by the time that raid was carried out. Throughout the 1985 season, Customs special investigators made Lester Piggott their number one target. Never before would they go to such lengths to probe the affairs of one individual. His movements were closely monitored. Using all the expertise and cunning of a department with undercover specialists and powers even greater than the police, Piggott was tailed, watched and reported on as his dossier began to grow.

Sometimes the undercover men posed as ordinary VAT inspectors and Customs officers so that their prey would not suspect anything when he was questioned in what he thought were normal enquiries, far removed from the probe into the missing millions he had stashed away. But they were well on their way to cracking the financial affairs he had kept secret for all these years. He was well and truly in their sights, and they were just waiting for the right chance to pull the trigger.

By the August of 1986, Piggott, like many other top jockeys, trainers and owners, was hoping he would be allowed to pay up what he owed and let the matter end there. It was not to be, however, certainly not in Piggott's case, and the reasons for this will be fully dealt with later. Suffice it to say that the Revenue were now aware of a series of secret bank accounts belonging to Piggott which had been uncovered by Irish Special Branch while investigating suspected IRA laundered funds. And Piggott had not even told his own accountants about the money in the accounts – over £2 million – or declared it to the taxman at this late stage.

To the detectives on the arresting party this was just another job, even if they were dealing with the most famous man in town. One or two of them knew him too, had met him over the years and always got a smile or a wave in acknowledgement whenever they saw him in and around Newmarket.

By the time the officers had assembled, got into an unmarked police car, and driven off towards Piggott's bungalow on the Hamilton Road, it was nearly midday. Piggott came to the door dressed casually in slacks and a dark blue shirt. Minutes later he was arrested, cautioned, and speeding off in the back of the police car to a special sitting of Newmarket magistrates called for the hearing. He had only had time to put on his favourite camel over-coat.

Newmarket Magistrates' Court is an old Victorian building with high ceilings and booming corridors. Piggott was ushered into the courtroom to face the three magistrates under the chairmanship of John Moore who was, ironically, a former bookmaker. Although further and much more complicated charges would follow, at this stage the proceedings were kept to a simple specimen charge; namely that Piggott had, on or about 29 April 1983, given the Inland Revenue a false statement relating to his affairs. He had told them he possessed only one bank account – at the National Westminster Bank in Newmarket. He had omitted to tell them about the money in the Cayman Islands, or an account in the Isle of Man, the one in Jersey, some in Ireland and several in London.

Piggott sat impassively throughout the short hearing, even when prosecutor Norman Phillips told the court that the Inland Revenue alone were claiming £2 million owed to them in tax, plus a further £800,000 in interest. It would be another three months, he said, before the other charges were laid and the case would reach the committal stage – where the prosecution would be seeking to have Piggott committed to the Old Bailey.

Then came a further bombshell. Mr Phillips, although raising no objection to bail, stunned even the most hardened of courtroom observers when he asked for the bail to be set at £2 million and for Piggott to surrender his passport.

Piggott's solicitor, Newmarket-based Jeremy Richardson, who has other top jockeys among his clients, often representing them in Jockey Club disciplinary hearings, objected strongly to the amount. The intimation had been that, with £5 million sitting pretty in a Cayman Islands bank account, Piggott might just flee Britain never to be seen again. Mr Richardson, however, pointed out Piggott's success in his first season as a trainer, adding that Eve Lodge and Calder Park stables now housed 120 horses in training for the new season with some 50 employees involved in the operation.

Chairman of the bench Mr Moore, the former bookie, hedged his bets after listening to both pleas, and he called for a 45-minute adjournment. On their return, the magistrates announced that bail would be set at £1 million – an all-time British record – plus two sureties of £100,000 each as well as demanding the surrender of Piggott's passport and ordering him to report to the police once a week.

Pressmen had been tipped off about the hearing and some had dashed up the M11 from London. Outside, camera crews and radio reporters waited for Piggott to emerge. They were in for quite a wait. Piggott's nightmare had only just begun.

To raise £1.2 million on the afternoon of the Friday before Christmas was no easy matter. It wasn't a question of Piggott taking out a cheque book and simply writing a draft for that amount. After all, which account would he use? Piggott's humiliation was only just beginning too. While his solicitor went off to make frantic attempts to raise the money, Piggott was unceremoniously taken down to the cells below the courtroom and promptly locked up.

The National Westminster Bank on Newmarket's High Street is the type found in many a small town, friendly and efficient and where most of its customers are known personally to manager Bob Tanner and his staff. In all Mr Tanner's years of banking, however, he had never been asked for £1 million before and when that request came from Piggott's solicitor, with the emphasis on an expeditious transaction, Mr Tanner could be forgiven for thinking he had just become embroiled in a scenario for a thriller. Mr Tanner did not have the authority to issue a banker's draft for £1 million and, when he contacted officials at the bank's regional head office in Norwich, neither did they. By now, time was pressing and Piggott was still in his cell. A call to NatWest in London brought no joy either because no senior director could be found. For them, naturally, so late on the Friday before Christmas, the weekend had already started.

Outside the court, the press posse was getting restless. Newsmen were conscious of the state of play and the probable obstacles in raising so much cash so quickly. But time was not on their side either. They all had deadlines to keep and the way things were going early editions might miss the outcome of today's drama. And this was an important story too. Every national newspaper in the country, the television news, and radio, all wanted to lead with the day that Lester Piggott was arrested and thrown in jail.

It was more than three hours before Piggott's advisers came up with a solution to put before the court; if they could get magistrates to accept the deeds to Eve Lodge and Calder Park and to Piggott's home, secured at a value of £950,000, then the court might just let Piggott free. The deeds to the properties were hurriedly obtained, so too was the signature of Piggott's wife Susan who signed her full name, Susan Elna Piggott, in her capacity as secretary and director of their company, L. K. Piggott Limited.

In the meantime, urgent calls had gone out to Henry Cecil and Charles St George to see if they would be prepared to stand the £100,000 sureties. Cecil was contacted at Warren Place and had only a short distance to travel to the court. St George, though, was in London at his West End office and was obliged to make the car journey to Newmarket. Both men had long-standing friendships with Piggott and, now, the ultimate test of friends would prevail; they were being asked to back their loyalty with hard cash. Because there was a £50,000 shortfall on the bail amount, Cecil and St George were each required to deposit a surety of £125,000 to make up the total of £1.2 million.

With the logistics finally resolved, Piggott was brought up from his cell to appear before the bench once more. The chairman sternly warned Piggott and his solicitor that, satisfied as they might be for the moment with the deeds to the Piggott property being lodged with the court, they had better turn up with the cash after the weekend. He therefore gave them until 5 p.m. on Monday to return to the court with £1 million, otherwise Piggott would be arrested again – with the prospect of facing Christmas behind bars.

That weekend was a miserable one for Piggott, his family, and friends. It had given them time to digest the full implications of Friday's court case, the full-blown headlines and intensive media coverage, the pressure to raise £1 million cash by Monday, the telephone calls of support, but, above all, the public disgrace of having been arrested and thrown into a cell like a common criminal.

With 25 minutes to spare before the Monday deadline, Piggott's solicitor arrived at Suffolk's Shire Hall in Bury St Edmunds and handed over a bank draft for £950,000. That particular race would not go down in the racing record books, but it was one of the most important in which Lester Piggott had ever participated.

The following day, after an application by Piggott to the High Court, the bail was reduced to £500,000, Piggott's passport was returned, and he was allowed to report to the police once a month instead of weekly. It was some consolation, if not much, and at least Piggott could return to the business of training racehorses until the next court date, the resumption of the magistrates' hearing on 19 March.

Until then the messages of support and sympathy would continue to flow in. Some, touchingly, even included offers of money from his legion of punters; the housewives, the pensioners, and the racegoers whom Piggott had thrilled through the years with his great skill. But no amount of artistry, courage or determination – attributes the maestro had displayed constantly throughout his career – was going to extricate him from this mess. He was in at the deep end.

2. Traits of a Champion

In the words of the great English poet William Wordsworth: the child is father of the man. Therefore, it must be to Lester Piggott the child we turn in order to discover some of the characteristics of Lester Piggott the man, traits that in the end brought about his downfall.

Piggott arrived relatively late in the marriage of his parents, Iris and Keith. By his birth, on the Bonfire Night of 1935, they had been married more than six years and Iris, from the famous Rickaby racing family, was approaching 30. She was a practical, no-nonsense woman, an accomplished horsewoman who twice won the Newmarket Town Plate as an amateur. Keith Piggott also came from a distinguished racing family. He was a tough, uncompromising jockey.

Both parents desperately wanted their only child to be a successful adult in the only life they knew – the world of racehorses. Their intensity and passion for horses may have been responsible for casting the Lester Piggott mould prematurely. For, by the age of five or six, they had not a child on their hands but a young adult; the childish things had already been put away. Consequently, Piggott grew up possessing a great deal of self-sufficiency. He has never been an outwardly confident person, preferring not to deal with people if he can help it. This has often been passed off as shyness, but Piggott is not shy: it takes more than a glass or two of champagne for a shy person to dance on the table at The Minstrel's Derby celebration party as he did. Rather he is an insular person, content with his own company as he was as a child, playing alone and not caring for the company of other children.

Education, as for many children during the war years, was

uninteresting. But Piggott also was born with a hearing handicap – deafness to sounds of a high frequency – which must have made many lessons arduous. Giving this, and his growing impatience because he already knew where his future lay, it is not surprising that schooling was seen as a necessary evil.

So the only people the young Piggott really listened to were his mother and father. Intensive coaching in all aspects of jockeyship was a daily routine, and when that first winner came at the age of twelve at Haydock it was no great surprise, rather a progression of all that had gone on before. It was not natural, however; precocity in man or horse does not always lead to greatness or fulfilment. Those qualities are only seen retrospectively, when maturity has helped nurture the initial spark and prolonged it with consistency over a period. Piggott, of course, achieved that greatness as a jockey. But, as a man, did that early 'forcing' carry a price? And was Piggott now paying the penalty for that?

The late Bill Rickaby, a very good jockey who won three Classics, and who was Piggott's cousin, did not let family ties muddle his appraisal of the Boy Wonder. In fact, Rickaby was always quick to point out that Piggott truly was the product of his parents; a menace on the track, with a preoccupation for money off it.

Iris Piggott had known jockeys who were successful, seen them come up from nothing to a position where they now had plenty of money – and lots of 'friends'. She had also seen them mismanage their new-found wealth and eventually hit the ground with a thump, penniless and friendless. She was most concerned, therefore, to ensure that her son would not end up the same way, constantly reminding him how a jockey's life could be a short one, how racing was a business of highs and lows, how today's success could be tomorrow's failure. So she drummed into him the need to be careful with his money, to treat it with respect and to save for the rainy day.

It was advice many a mother might give her son in similar circumstances. And it might explain why, in spite of the vast amounts he was earning, his mother's words acted as a governor to any thoughts of rashness, quashed the impulse while it was still that. He never skimped with his own family, although his daughters Maureen and Tracey were never spoiled. They never got everything they wanted nor, when they got older, did they expect it. But he provided for his parents in their old age, built them a bungalow next to his own, and always made sure they were never wanting. He and Susan always had a nice car, a BMW or Mercedes, and they travelled the world. They had a good home and spent money on the clothes they liked.

This could well be seen as a form of selfishness, though, when it is compared to Piggott's general level of generosity or reciprocation in today's society. The stories of Piggott's meanness, his distinct ability to keep his hand in his pocket when it was time to pay a bill, expansive gestures with all but his own money, were not born from some nebulous Chinese whisper. This was part of the Piggott make-up and people made allowances like they always do – out of respect or out of sycophancy, or maybe a little of both.

Fellow jockeys put up with it because they had to like it or lump it. Piggott would sometimes tap them for small change to buy an ice-cream or a newspaper. Sometimes it was a fiver – 'I've left home without my wallet' – and those who'd wised up would tell him rudely where to go. Often it was all in fun, although at the end of the day, and as Bill Rickaby once said, Piggott relished each crisp fiver like it was a precious jewel. Waiters and taxi-drivers never got a tip; to part with money, whatever the social grace or common practice, was, to him, painful. Quite plainly, he was a Scrooge.

On the racecourse too, as an emerging rider of talent, Piggott was extremely economical with the largesse. True, Piggott entered the game when the old boys' network was still in evidence, and Sir Gordon was at the top. But it was time for change, not merely a new generation of jockeys with new habits to upset the tradition. That had been happening every 20 or 30 years; each new wave of riders blending into the scene with as little fuss as possible, treating their seniors with due respect, listening to their advice, perhaps, after a while, even becoming friends and earning mutual admiration. Piggott, though, was different. Impatient for success and oblivious to any advice save that from his father. If he saw a gap during a race, he went for it. Of course, it brought him not only many a brush with his fellow and more senior jockeys but also with authority.

To a large degree it was water off a duck's back. He treated his peers with disdain on and off the track. Determined not to be intimidated as was the wont of more senior riders to a young upstart, he gave as much, sometimes more, than he got. Unseen by the stewards in one race at Sandown, Piggott hit Doug Smith over the head – with the heavy end of his whip – when the five-times-champion jockey tried to move out into a challenging position. Smith never reported the incident to the stewards but simply reflected just how ruthless the young Piggott could be.

There were aspects of riding that, some felt, Piggott would have been better learning for himself than having been drilled in by his father. As a teenager, he was pulling off tricks on the track that only Keith Piggott would have done. There was a feeling, too, that Piggott would have been better off learning for himself, without having his parents around him at the track, acting as his mouthpiece when the going got rough, often on hand to prompt him this way or that. Being left to fight his own way out of a corner earlier in life might have been much more beneficial.

The ruthless streak was never curbed. But then, if it had been, Lester Piggott would never have been at the top for so long. Even the stewards of the Jockey Club, alarmed at the strength of this hurricane and anxious to tame it, tried hard – some would say excessively – to bring the young Piggott to heel. Eventually, frustrated at the lack of success fines and minor suspensions were having, the stewards banned the 18-year-old Piggott for six months. This came after riding Never Say Die (his first Derby-winner) in the King Edward VII Stakes at Royal Ascot in 1954.

One of the stipulations of the ban, and by this time those in power felt the father–son relationship was not 'healthy' from the sport's point of view, was that Piggott be sent away from Berkshire where he was apprenticed to his father, and placed with the veteran Newmarket trainer Jack Jarvis, a noted disciplinarian with a temper to match. Piggott served half the ban but, unfortunately Mr Jarvis was ill for most of that time, and so he was unable to exert much influence over the 'wayward' young Piggott.

While he was at Newmarket it was suggested that he stay with Bill Rickaby's mother – Piggott's aunt – and that she should charge him for the use of the 'digs'. If the people of the town where Piggott would later become the most famous resident didn't know of the mean streak already, then it would not be long before they did. Piggott had not been staying with his aunt more than a few weeks when, one day, to her surprise, there was a bunch of flowers on the hall table, courtesy of her nephew. Well, she thought, after all I'd been warned, he's not such a mean young man after all. It was only when he later knocked the cost of the flowers off his weekly boarding bill that the truth dawned. On another occasion he tried to deduct the cost of one night's accommodation because he had only spent two hours in his bed following a late-night party.

To his legions of admirers all over the world, such stories have provided much humour and, no doubt, Piggott has tried to live up to the reputation despite his many unpublished donations and good deeds for charity. But against events which, much later in his life, were to bring such serious charges against him, the youthful flirtation with Scrooge was a dangerous field in which to play. For it would be littered with mines – many of them laid by himself.

The most relevant advice Keith Piggott passed on to his son, certainly that which had the most influence, was to try to win at all costs and if he did win then never to question why. Questions were only about why he didn't win. Child psychologists studying the effects of indoctrination might, one day, care to take a closer look at the Piggott father and son apprenticeship.

Surely they would find good reason for believing it was this unique relationship which spawned the streak of ruthlessness, the single-mindedness and the will to win that made Lester Piggott one of the greatest jockeys in the world. The effect on Piggott the person, too, would make equally intriguing study.

Before Piggott reached the age of 22, he had ridden 642 winners, 16 of them over hurdles. He also had two Derbys, a 2,000 Guineas and an Oaks to his credit. It was no wonder the British racing public knew they were witnessing something special, hardly surprising he had already carved a niche in their hearts. By now, having completed his third season with Noel Murless, it seemed this man Piggott only needed to sit on a horse for it to win.

A further 1,130 winners in Britain were amassed by the time the 1966 season started when Piggott was 30. For this season, though, he decided not to take up the retainer with Murless, feeling that, should the opportunity arise of a better outside ride in any of the big races, then he would have no qualms about taking it. That situation did arise in the June at Epsom when Piggott turned down the ride on the Murless-trained Varinia in the Oaks in favour of the Vincent O'Brien runner Valoris. It was a decision which caused much acrimony. Murless thought loyalty the highest form of integrity. Piggott saw the chance of another big winner. He rode Valoris to victory and Varinia was five and a half lengths back in third. It was the beginning of the end of the famous partnership. Piggott's eyes were roaming. The jockey's life was fraught with ups and downs, his mother had told him that. He had to make more money now, while the going was good.

Murless was quite uninterested in gambling and hardly encouraged his owners to participate either. Piggott felt he was losing out financially, and that he could get better presents from grateful owners and other perks elsewhere. He knew he was the best jockey in the country, but just how long it would all last even he didn't dare to think. He was married now as well, and had two daughters. It wasn't just a case of thinking about himself. He had responsibilities, plans for the future.

The victory on Valoris forged a new partnership with Vincent O'Brien, one that over the next eleven years would provide Piggott with another nine English Classics, including four Derbys. It would also see his earnings rise sharply, for O'Brien had owners who were new to the sport. They could understand the realities of business. Times were changing. It was no longer good enough to get a pat on the back from one of the 'old school' owners after just riding the Derby-winner. If they were making vast sums from a Classic-winner's subsequent stud potential, then Piggott felt he should be in on that too. In the harsh new world of Flat racing, sport was taking a back seat to business. And there were many who knew Piggott was shrewd, no pushover. They didn't blame him for wanting a bigger slice of the action.

O'Brien himself had been a brilliant trainer of National Hunt horses, sending out the winners of all the major English races from his County Cork base, which later switched to Cashel in Tipperary. In a space of three years in the mid-Fifties he won three Grand Nationals with different horses; Cheltenham, the Mecca of jump racing, held no fears for him either and in 1949 and 1950 he captured remarkable Champion Hurdle – Gold Cup doubles.

While O'Brien was reaping rewards on the racetrack, he was establishing himself as a very shrewd gambler too. By 1951 he had earned enough money at both to decide to buy his present training establishment, Ballydoyle, a sumptuous Georgian mansion set in more than 300 acres of parkland. He then made the decision to switch to Flat racing, gradually running down the National Hunt side of the operation until he was soon on the way to becoming one of the most successful trainers of all time.

Two years after Valoris, Piggott again teamed up with O'Brien to land the 2,000 Guineas with Sir Ivor, a horse that became one of Piggott's favourites, especially after the combination went on to land the Derby five weeks later, then crowned a glorious season by winning the Champion Stakes at Newmarket and the Washington International in America.

When a Derby-winner like Sir Ivor goes to stud, he is literally worth a small fortune. Although he might have one owner as a race-horse, the horse will be syndicated as a stallion into 40 shares, each shareholder buying into the horse and thereby obtaining the right to send a mare to be covered by the stallion each year, or, alternatively, selling that right to another breeder.

In the United States, capital value on a top-class stallion can be anything up to $40 million-plus, with a nomination fee of perhaps $200,000. A shareholder in that stallion could therefore either sell the share for $1 million and have no further connection with the animal, or sell his nomination each year for $200,000, producing a regular annual income. Of course, if the stallion proved successful, its popularity boosted by the exploits of its offspring on the race-track, the cost of an annual nomination would be increased.

While this description of the logistics of buying into a top stallion is a simplification, it is still the basis for all dealings in such animals in the multi-million dollar world of bloodstock. Naturally, not every top racehorse makes a good stallion. It is a high-risk business, one where a multitude of complications arise. Stallions can prove infertile, their stock might be moderate thereby reducing the stud fee, disease of one form or another is never far away, and horses can die from a simple colic. Shareholders thought they were on to a good thing with Shergar until he was stolen, and later killed. Many of the syndicate found their hefty insurances did not cover theft.

It certainly is a fraught business when your £500,000 investment in a share in the latest stallion is only worth a fraction of that amount for whatever reason. Mind you, it's a little less worrying when that share cost nothing in the first place.

Lester Piggott soon latched on to the vast amounts good racehorses were fetching as stallions and he became determined to have his share – literally. Before long, he was stipulating in his contracts with top trainers like Vincent O'Brien that he wanted a share or a breeding right in colts he rode to a success in the top Group One races like the Derby, the Oaks and the St Leger. If in some cases the agreement was not for a whole fortieth-share, then a lesser percentage was still a good deal in some of the high-flyers. It meant that, all of a sudden, Piggott had created a breakthrough in the amounts a jockey could earn.

Only the idealist would disagree Piggott had a right to stake such a claim. After all, he was playing a most important part in making the racehorse what it was now worth as a stallion. For without the Piggott expertise, that unique skill in a driving finish, many of the big-race short-head winners would have been losers – and had millions wiped off their potential value at the same time.

It was not surprising, therefore, that pragmatists such as O'Brien, and a little later, Vernons chief Robert Sangster, the man whose high-powered syndicates transformed the international bloodstock industry, were willing to set up a package valuing a jockey of Piggott's stature in more realistic terms. Some of the old-school jockeys still living might have had other views, but, Piggott had seen poorer days too. He was fortunate that he was able to prolong his career over two generations, and had seen the heralding of the new, rich dawn.

But, to the racing industry, and the world at large, there were no real complaints about the amazing amounts of money Piggott was now in a position to earn, although even they could only half guess at the sums involved. It was what he would do with it that would later cause incredulity.

3. A Share of the Profits

Before Robert Sangster teamed up with Vincent O'Brien and founded his international syndicates of multi-millionaires from various parts of the world, Lester Piggott had already ridden three Epsom Derby-winners for the County Tipperary stable. Following Sir Ivor's win in 1968 came Nijinsky, one of the most famous racehorses of the century, in 1970. Nijinsky was also ridden by Piggott to win the 2,000 Guineas and the St Leger and so became the latest horse to win the colts' Triple Crown.

Then, in 1972, Piggott was aboard O'Brien's Roberto, though not before a certain amount of controversy over his booking for the ride. Australian Bill Williamson was to have ridden American owner-breeder John Galbreath's colt after having finished second on the bay in the 2,000 Guineas five weeks earlier. Williamson, however, hurt a shoulder in a fall at Kempton ten days before the Derby and, although he declared himself fit two days before the race, O'Brien and Galbreath decided not to take any chances and to book Piggott for the ride.

There followed a public outcry with the sympathy on Williamson's side amid accusations of disloyalty by Galbreath and opportunism by Piggott. In fairness to Piggott, Williamson would have done exactly the same thing had the boot been on the other foot and it has to be remembered that Piggott was a freelance, without a Derby ride until this offer arose. Sure, Piggott often angled for rides and his expertise on the telephone – in spite of his hearing problem – became renowned. Even so, unless he staked his claim and used his elbows a little, he would find himself on the wrong horse – or no horse at all.

Piggott's 29 Classic victories constituted a British record, one that had stood since Frank Buckle rode Zinc to win the Oaks at the age of 57 in 1823 to record his twenty-seventh Classic. Of all, the win on Roberto is one that has given him the most pleasure. Some jockeys, like the very horses they rode, loved to taunt the opposition and win by the biggest margin possible. It became fashionable with one or two of the leading jockeys in the Eighties to look round disdainfully at the rest of the field during a race and delight in their struggling before letting the mount have its head and galloping on to victory with a great air of superiority.

Such wins, while very welcome, were not what made the Piggott blood stir. He reckoned any good jockey aboard such a horse could ride it home first. No, the supreme test of jockeyship was when two horses were evenly matched, when they were racing for that winning post giving their all, in line and with neither giving best. That was when the world knew that to have Piggott on your side was the best ally in racing, where his strength in the saddle would more often mean victory, not defeat.

And so it was with Roberto. With two furlongs left Piggott began to make his challenge. He had been lying just behind the leaders and now he moved Roberto up to race with Rheingold on his outside and Pentland Firth towards the rails. As with many a horse on that rolling Epsom camber, Rheingold began to hang left and on to Roberto, pushing Piggott's horse towards Pentland Firth as all three galloped at full stretch for the line. This was racing at its very best, real blood and thunder, sweat, cursing, the power of half-ton beasts pounding the turf almost deafeningly.

From the stands and the crowded Downs it was a graceful spectacle. Three jockeys in perfect harmony with their mounts and the roar, that roar as a quarter of a million voices reached crescendo, filling the jockeys' ears and blotting out the staccato snorting rasps of the animals underneath them.

Soon, Piggott had pushed Roberto clear of Pentland Firth but Rheingold was still upsides and still rolling. The two horses touched, then bumped, and again. Piggott was desperate with his whip and used it as he so often did, seemingly unmercifully and with great rapidity, as Roberto and Rheingold sprinted for the line inside the final furlong. The winning post loomed but neither horses nor jockeys would give way and the shrieks from the enthralled masses reached fever-pitch as the two horses, almost inseparably, flashed past the line.

Piggott unsaddled his horse on the course, not daring to enter the winner's enclosure. He walked towards the weighing room, his face unsmiling, still set with the grim determination which, although he did not know at that moment, had won him the race.

The crowds were silent. There would be no cheers for the maestro this day. They had not forgotten Bill Williamson. To many of them the Australian should have been aboard Roberto. To some extent, the reaction of the crowd was overplayed by the media because many spectators stayed quiet out of the doubt over the result. There were still some cheers, albeit muted, when the photo-finish showed that Roberto had prevailed by what the French call a nose, what the British call a short head, but what was, in fact, a nostril – reckoned to be no more than four inches.

The Piggott power had reigned supreme and no other jockey, including Williamson, could have ridden a finish like him. Those four inches in that Derby and in subsequent big races were worth millions of pounds. Piggott revelled in those nip-and-tuck finishes, just loved to get there literally in the nick of time.

And that was precisely why a jockey like Lester Piggott was worth paying what he asked.

As will be discovered later, however, his timing over his financial affairs and, even when he was rumbled, his attempts at a last-minute bid to keep himself out of court were to prove a sorry failure.

When they each retired to stud at the end of their careers as three-year-olds, Sir Ivor, Nijinsky and Roberto were syndicated for a total of approximately $10 million. A fortieth-share in each represented a total of about $250,000 capital value, at late Sixties/early Seventies prices. But that was small compared to the values being put on stallions after the Sangster régime took over the world bloodstock scene. By the early Eighties, for instance, a nomination in Nijinsky, the most successful stallion of the trio, was fetching at least $200,000. A shareholder of that horse, therefore, was on a very nice annual income indeed if the nomination was sold each year.

Robert Sangster's first big success was in the Derby of 1977 when Piggott powered home The Minstrel. In the same year Alleged also boosted the coffers by winning the Prix de l'Arc de Triomphe, Europe's richest race, a feat Piggott repeated on the same horse the following year. The Minstrel was retired to stand at his breeder, E. P. Taylor's Windfields Stud in Maryland, USA, at a valuation of $9 million. At the end of his career as a four-year-old, Alleged also went back to the US to begin his stud career in 1979 at Walmac Farm in Lexington, Kentucky, at a European record value of $16 million. A fortieth-share in the two at that time would have been worth more than $625,000 capital value. And by the December of 1986, nominations in both totalled something like $150,000 for the year.

It can be seen quite clearly that by selling those nominations each year, the income figures run into mind-boggling millions over the ensuing years.

Lester Piggott not only had shares in the likes of Sir Ivor, Nijinsky, The Minstrel and Alleged, but literally dozens of other top horses he rode over the years.

For he had it written into his contracts that he wanted similar perks for all Group One winners he rode to victory.

And soon he was earning more money than he ever dreamed possible.

Robert Sangster is the son of the late Vernon Sangster, founder of the pools empire which subsequently stretched from finance houses to car sales. He bought his first horse for fun in 1968 regarding the sport as little more than a pleasant pastime. But his analytical mind and business acumen soon began to set out a masterplan for revolutionising the racing game. To him it seemed that, so far, to be successful, an owner first had to have the money, then the luck. Then, somewhere along the line, a decent horse or two might come along.

There was no guarantee, however, and if that champion did not materialise, well it was all viewed as good fun, the proverbial rich man's hobby.

Sangster, though, was used to getting a return on his capital. He was interested in percentages and margins, low downside risk and the possibility of making a killing.

Viewing the industry through the eyes of a newcomer, he began asking questions where, perhaps, tradition demanded silence; he was not a traditionalist, for to him that meant throwing money away. In his international business dealings too, he could see the world was becoming a smaller place. Communications in this new sphere of technology were drawing countries closer. And he foresaw that the future chief influence on the European bloodstock market was going to come from the US.

There are few races in America run over the one and a half miles' distance of the Epsom Derby, Europe's premier race. The accent in America is on speed and Sangster could see that American-bred horses were beginning to make their mark on the domestic scene; it was a blend of their speed with our stamina.

When he initially started out as a breeder he began to encounter a string of frustrating obstacles; the 'closed shop' network of breeders and owners, the traditionalists, were not enthusiastic about doing business with this newcomer. Consequently, many of his applications to send his mares to the top stallions were shunned. He made up his mind quite quickly that there was only one course of action to take. He would turn out his own stallions and breed from them – something the Arabs and other astute owners are now copying.

Recognising Vincent O'Brien as perhaps the world's greatest trainer of racehorses, Sangster then invited wealthy friends, business associates and successful owners to join a syndicate headed and run by him. They all had to be like-minded people or those who could be persuaded to see that the future of the international bloodstock and racing business was in their hands.

It was a gamble that paid off handsomely.

But if the likes of Californian millionaire Danny Schwartz, French Jean-Pierre Binet and Greek shipping magnate Stavros Niarchos were going to join this exclusive club, the team of experts they would want around them would have to be first-class.

Sangster, of course, had already thought that out thoroughly too. The idea was to buy stock from the premier US sales, sons and daughters of the stallions to which he had been refused access.

To make inroads into the fiercely competitive premier horse sales of the world requires a great deal more than the basic raw commodity of money. It takes cunning, sharp thinking, expertise, and a thick skin. Sangster already possesses the latter. He is a gentleman, extremely courteous, friendly and helpful. But he was a fairly decent amateur boxer in his day, still loves the sport now, and is not averse to taking the gloves off when the situation demands getting down to a scrap. Instead, he was soon to analogise between the opulent and highly charged competitiveness of the sales ring and the streets of Liverpool where the Vernons organisation is based and which he knows so well.

Ultimately, he would put his success at the sales down to the fact that he was a good street-fighter. He even had the sense of humour to call one of his horses by that name too.

And he called upon those tactics time and again in the multi-million dollar bid battles with adversaries who, in the early days at least, were not quite sure how to handle the aggression, or the guile.

Sangster had assembled a good team. Along with Vincent O'Brien came his son-in-law, John Magnier, respected as one of the best stallion men in the world. The three men were soon visiting the likes of Keeneland sales in Kentucky, leaving Ireland in their Lear jet and arriving in the Bluegrass State, if not at first to the red carpet treatment, then certainly a little later when their reputation was established. There they would pore over the sales catalogue, discarding horses on pedigree. Some of those would have made good racehorses, they were sure of that. But as a stallion? There were often others with more fashionable bloodlines, better propositions commercially.

Having selected perhaps six horses, maybe ten, on pedigree alone, they then had to bring in their team of equine medical experts to thoroughly examine the real product; veterinarian specialists in heart and lungs, knees and feet. X-rays would be taken, horses were walked, trotted, stethoscopes were produced, notes taken. The reports would be collated and, back at their hotel on the eve of the sale, Sangster, O'Brien and Magnier would thrash out exactly which colts interested them most. Several others would now have been discarded to leave three or four 'naps' – their racing certainties. But how much should they bid? Each man wrote out what he thought each blue-blooded colt was worth, tossed the estimate into a hat, and they then compared the prices settling on a top and bottom bid, their strategy for bidding, and which 'reserves' to go for if some of their bids were unsuccessful. Sometimes the competition meant they would pay well over their original estimate – other times they felt they had got a bargain.

Several years on, when the sight of Sangster and his syndicate at a particular sales ring would create much excitement, auctioneers could virtually bank on new records being set. It would soon become commonplace for the Sangster entourage to leave Kentucky having spent upwards of $10 million, sometimes double that.

But with the syndicate's rise to prominence and subsequent success both on the racetrack and later in the stud farms of the world with their 'home-grown' stallions, another problem occurred when they visited the sales. The prime consideration now: just how to avoid being run up in the auction.

When Sangster, O'Brien or Magnier gave the final nod to that bid of $3 million for the colt with the fine conformation, the intelligent head and loppy ears and the first-class pedigree, who had been the underbidder? For it was just as important to know that the bidding had been straight, that the underbidder was bona fide and the price was a fair one, given the circumstances, as to be pleased at having secured the right yearling.

Several years later on when the wealthy Arab families turned their gaze on British horseracing in particular, Sangster's grip on the world of bloodstock would be prised open. Backed by a seemingly bottomless well of oil-dollars, the Arabs moved into the market with ruthless determination and intent on buying the best bloodstock available – no matter what the price. They were attempting to do what smaller breeders had taken a generation to achieve: find successful formulae and stick to them. But to do that required haste and, in the hurry, mistakes were bound to happen.

Being run up at the sales is not very pleasant. It hurts the pocket less when a million or two either way does not really matter. The Arabs, however, were not going to be taken for fools. Though there is no doubt there have been occasions when they have been run up in the earlier days of their rise to prominence, there is now a strict code employed that sees them drop out of the bidding at the slightest hint of any impropriety.

There are many versions of the yearling sales sting. The most obvious is for the unscrupulous owners of a yearling to employ someone to enter the bidding, perhaps at the half-way stage, and leave near the top end – without having had the slightest intention of buying the colt or filly.

With so many bloodstock agents, racing managers, trainers, breeders and private individuals coming in and dropping out of the bidding at various stages it is not always clear to the auctioneers, despite maintaining the highest integrity, whose bid is 'for real'.

There have been stories on both sides of the Atlantic of sharp practice directed particularly at the Arabs. By the early Eighties bloodstock prices in America were going through the roof anyway;

crazy prices in a crazy world. Sheikh Mohammed, the most active of the spend-spree Maktoum brothers of Dubai, paid $10 million in 1983 at the Keeneland sales for a son of Northern Dancer, the most influential sire of modern times, only to subsequently discover the horse was near to useless. Later named Snaafi Dancer, it was trained by John Dunlop at Arundel in Sussex but never took part in a race. It was packed straight off to stud as a three-year-old in the hope its progeny, two-year-olds in 1989, might prove a little better and therefore help recoup some of that massive expenditure.

With competition between Sangster and the Arabs at such a fierce level, new world records were bound to be set. In 1985 the Sangster syndicate paid a world record $13.1 million for a yearling colt, a son of US champion racehorse Seattle Slew, named Seattle Dancer. Although it turned out a reasonably decent horse in the 1987 Flat season, it was far from the top-class colt connections hoped for when shelling out that much money. Still, with its first-class bloodlines, Seattle Dancer may well make the grade as a stallion. It will be another commodity for exploiting in some country or other, another one in the 1,000-plus Sangster empire of foals, broodmares and racehorses with 50 trainers and a dozen or more stud farms around the world.

The basic concept of the Sangster operation has been emulated by the Arabs successfully. Sangster, though, runs his business on a global scale so it is unfair of the critics who claim he has lost his grip and been toppled from Britain's top-owner spot by the Arabs. In 1986 Sangster won 268 races worldwide collecting more than £2.5 million prize money, a figure that was well up on the previous year.

Sangster's great gift is to recognise the potential for exploiting his horses throughout the world. Having bought a yearling on breeding and handing it to O'Brien to turn into a decent racehorse, the only ingredient the syndicate now needs is a touch of luck. There is absolutely no guarantee that a Derby-winner mated with an Oaks-winner will produce a son or daughter of equal merit. But with a worldwide organisation, a half-decent colt or filly with the right breeding can be sent to stand as a stallion in any one of a dozen other countries should it not appeal to breeders in the US, Britain, Ireland or France.

When he first set up his famous syndicate, it was such a

professional operation that he almost engineered that Fortune would smile sooner rather than later. It meant the downside risk was minimal.

Sangster's success was also Piggott's way to riches – with Vincent O'Brien as the catalyst. All of them became wealthier than before. And with Piggott the success snowballed. The more top-class colts he rode, the more big races he won. There was rarely an important Group One race in the racing calendar in which he did not have a ride.

In the comparatively short period of six years, Piggott's income had rocketed. He became the pace-setter for his profession in the earnings stakes. Soon other top jockeys such as Pat Eddery (who subsequently took Piggott's place with Sangster and O'Brien), Steve Cauthen, Willie Carson, Joe Mercer and Greville Starkey were in the big-money league. To be given shares or breeding rights in a multi-million dollar Group One-winning colt was no longer a rarity, more the norm. Paradoxically, this new-found wealth among jockeys had, at this stage, been given little publicity; tennis, golf and boxing were always the domains of the high-earners. While jockeys might have made a decent living, not too many people inside the sport, never mind the casual observer, knew the height to which the new pay-scales had leapt.

If some men got rich, or maybe richer, there were others casting covetous eyes on the whole business and especially in the area of bloodstock where, ostensibly, crazy sums were being paid for American-bred yearlings transcending anything ever seen before and heralding a new approach to commercial breeding of the thorough-bred. To the uninitiated it could have all seemed like money for jam, particularly at the sales when the Arabs were bidding. What were a couple of hundred thousand dollars to the oil-rich men from the Middle East whose participation in British racing was increasing by the month? A run-up at the yearling sales would hardly cause a ripple on that oil lake but its perpetrators would indeed land rich pickings.

To some people this bloodstock game was almost like playing Monopoly, only this money was real – and plentiful. It was a foolish and dangerous assumption, however, an amateurish view of a business entered into by professionals playing for high reward. Running up a yearling at the sales was not always going to be so easy as it might have appeared, especially when those doing it were not very adept.

Lester Piggott's downfall, however sad, might well be perceived in the final analysis as being self-inflicted, but the greatest irony is that the ultimate discovery of his wrong-doings would arise out of this new climate of wealth that he helped create. It would be brought about by a yearling sales run-up with which Piggott had no connection whatever. It would turn out to be a curious runaway course of events over which even the mighty Piggott had absolutely no control.

4. Spilling the Beans

The several million pounds that Lester Piggott had been secretly salting away through a myriad of offshore companies and clandestine bank accounts (some of which had been in false names) might always have remained *terra incognita* to the tax authorities but for one man, Melvyn Walters. It was the bloodstock agent Walters who publicly shopped Piggott, alerting the Inland Revenue and Customs and Excise to cash payments that he, among others, had been asked to make to Piggott when he was riding for the Henry Cecil stable.

Ostensibly, Walters was given a better start in life than most people, being sent by his parents to Carmel College, a fee-paying Jewish independent boarding school in Wallingford, Buckinghamshire, which he left in 1956 at the age of 17. Although his future working life would see him in a variety of occupations, his first job on leaving the college was to work for his uncle, Norman Walters, as a £25-a-week clerk to the on-course bookmaker at London dog tracks. There followed a series of misadventures, particularly in the used-car trade, which culminated in his setting up as a second-hand motor dealer in London. From 1973 to 1976 he was co-director of two firms which went into liquidation. It was a year later that the dark-haired, brown-eyed Walters made an appearance at the Old Bailey and was given a six-month prison sentence for acting as a company director and obtaining credit while an undischarged bankrupt. More problems ensued and subsequently he was sentenced to three years in prison on a number of charges relating to high-priced motor cars and including obtaining pecuniary advantage by deception.

As someone who had taken a keen interest in horseracing and betting it was not surprising that Walters should enter the professional side of the business and this he did in 1980 after he had met Frenchman Maurice Lidchi, a friend of Walters's second wife, Barbara. Lidchi was a wealthy international businessman with interests in art (particularly Persian carpets), and owner of several thoroughbred stud farms which were under the umbrella of a company called the Alchemy, based in Kentucky, America's most prestigious horse-rearing state. It was at this time that Lidchi was leaning towards adopting a London representation of his bloodstock company to exploit the expanding business between Britain and the US. Walters, with his contacts in the world of racing already established, appeared the ideal candidate and, on 1 December 1980, Lidchi bought himself an off-the-shelf limited company in order to achieve this new aim.

The original company's name was Avriland Limited, bought by Lidchi for a little over £200 and changed into Alchemy Farms of Kentucky (International) Limited and registered at offices at 144–6 New Bond Street, London. The primary business use (known as the Memorandum of Association) was for general import and export, but this was changed to include livestock.

On 17 February 1981, less than two months after the Lidchi 'takeover', he officially appointed himself a director of the £100-capital company with a 75 per cent holding. Walters became the other remaining shareholder a month later with a 25 per cent share. Being a £100-capital company meant that Alchemy Farms of Kentucky (International) Limited was only liable up to £100. As we shall discover, when the company ran into trouble, following a court case that shook the bloodstock auctioneering world, it was left with substantial costs, and was wound up without paying its debts.

For many years Lidchi was adviser and supplier of various artefacts to several American establishments, including the Los Angeles County Museum, the Boston Metropolitan Museum of Art, and the Washington DC Textile Museum as well as owning a thriving art business on New York's Madison Avenue. It was, however, as someone connected with horses as an owner and breeder for two decades that he wanted to establish a British side to the business. Alchemy's core business in Kentucky is run from a 440-acre farm in Versailles, where six large horse-barns, a stallion complex and foaling barn (with 150 heated stalls) form a modern thoroughbred breeding estate standing seven stallions, broodmares, horses at boarding, and yearlings being specifically prepared for the sales.

But, in addition to the Kentucky operation, Lidchi also owns stud farms in Normandy, France, and Cape, South Africa, where he once served as a consultant in the arts field to the South African government.

Melvyn Walters, as a director of Alchemy's newly acquired London company, was able to use his position to further the relationships he had made with many of the top names in racing. Towards the end of his first year representing Alchemy, a yearling filly was bought at the Keeneland fall sales in Kentucky for $62,000 and sent to the stable of Henry Cecil at Newmarket. She was named Bright Crocus and, as a two-year-old the following season, ran in the colours of Barbara Walters.

Barbara's husband, Melvyn, had therefore cemented his contact with Britain's top trainer. Soon, he would also do the same with the world's greatest jockey, Lester Piggott.

Bright Crocus was an attractive filly and, once in full training, Cecil reckoned she would prove quite useful. On her first appearance on a racetrack she showed plenty of promise. Ridden by Piggott, as she would be in all her eight races as a two-year-old, she was beaten by a short head in a five-furlong maiden race at Windsor in the May of 1982. She then went on to win her next two races, including a valuable listed event at Newbury, and later in the season took the Group Three May Hill Stakes at Doncaster by an easy five lengths. On her final outing, though, she was tailed off and later found to have broken a blood vessel after being made favourite for one of the best staying events of the season for juveniles, the Hoover Fillies' Mile at Ascot. In the International Classification for two-year-olds published at the end of the season, Bright Crocus was rated just 10 lbs below the top-rated juvenile in Britain, France or Ireland, another Henry Cecil-trained horse called Diesis.

In the autumn of 1982, around the same time that Bright Crocus was being sent to race in America in the hope that the Florida sun would help her bleeding problems, Walters was setting up one of his first deals for Alchemy. Anthony Cherry-Downes, commonly known by his nickname 'Tote', is a bloodstock agent of repute with a good reputation for spotting bargains at the sales. Among the many low-priced Group-winners he has bought are horses like Mecca-Dante Stakes-winner Be My Native, a $45,000-yearling buy, and Mattaboy, a 10,500-guinea yearling at the Tattersalls sales who went on to land the Group One Middle Park Stakes. He bought Bright Crocus too.

Cherry-Downes has Henry Cecil, his friend of more than 20 years, as a partner in his bloodstock business.

Alchemy (International) Limited, the New Bond Street side of the company, were the buyers of a colt foal by Riverman at the Fasig-Tipton Kentucky Fall Sale. Cherry-Downes completed the transaction, paying $95,000 for the American-bred colt.

The business of buying foals to keep for almost a year then selling them as yearlings is known as 'pin-hooking', the object being to pick a nice foal that will sell better next year. Many a fine profit has been made by the 'pin-hookers' – it cuts out the cost of breeding from a broodmare, the cost of the nomination to a stallion, and the cost of keeping the broodmare during the eleven months' gestation until the cycle is completed when she visits another stallion.

'Pin-hookers' arrange for a stud to keep the foal and prepare it for the sales, keeping their fingers crossed that the market will still be buoyant and that their estimates of a decent profit will be realised when it is eventually auctioned.

In the case of the Riverman foal, the $95,000 still provided a decent profit for the breeders, Royal Broodmares USA, while the new owners, Alchemy, set their sights on sending the animal to the following year's Tattersalls Highflyer sales at Newmarket with the aim of making a nice profit for themselves.

Henry Cecil and his twin-brother David are also partners in the Cliff Stud at Helmsley, north-east of Thirsk in North Yorkshire. The Cliff Stud is just a stone's throw from Hambleton where Cecil's father-in-law, the late Sir Noel Murless, started training in 1935. Sir Noel and Lady Murless also ran the stud for more than 30 years before giving up the lease at the end of 1980. Henry and David took over the lease, expanded the stud to 250 acres, and brought in Cherry-Downes to help in the aim of producing top-quality yearlings for the sales.

And so it was to the Cliff Stud that the Riverman foal went at the end of 1982 and there, under the watchful eye of David, the stud manager, it was raised and cared for until being prepared for the Highflyer sales the following September when it was a yearling.

Having a yearling accepted for these particular sales is not that easy, however. Its credentials have to be first-class; pedigree, conformation, habits, all have to be checked. In the Riverman yearling's case this was done by Richard Mildmay-White of Tattersalls and further consideration of the colt's eligibility was made by the Tattersalls Catalogue Committee – no use them passing a yearling who crib-bites, whistles or roars in his wind at the trot or on a lunge rein and may be subsequently returned by a disgruntled buyer.

Tattersalls are the biggest and most renowned bloodstock auctioneers in Britain having been established in 1766. Operating from Park Paddocks, Newmarket, the company reached a turnover aggregate of 79 million guineas for the year ending December 1986.

On Sunday, 25 September 1983, Alchemy's Riverman yearling arrived at Park Paddocks in preparation for being put up for sale on the Tuesday, the first day of the four-day Highflyer Premier Yearling Sale, known as the Select session.

In the sales catalogue, the Riverman yearling, a bay or brown colt out of a Dancer's Image mare called Celerity, attracted quite a lot of pre-sale attention. There was a certain amount of novelty value in the colt too, because he was the only Riverman progeny in the catalogue (Riverman being a Kentucky-based stallion). There was even a paragraph noting that fact in the *Daily Telegraph* – the only newspaper in Britain to make mention of the colt.

The vendor was listed as the Cecils' Cliff Stud in reports following the sale. The colt, however, was consigned from Cliff Stud, the vendors being Alchemy (International) Limited – Lidchi and Walters.

Many of the top names in British racing were in attendance when the sale got under way at 2 p.m. and there was an air of excitement that the Tattersalls record for a yearling – 640,000 guineas in 1981 – would be broken. The fifth of the 126 specially selected lots gave a hint of what was to come. A bay filly by Robert Sangster's 1977 Derby-winner The Minstrel was knocked down to Royal trainer Ian Balding, with Sangster the underbidder, at 310,000 guineas.

By the time the Riverman colt entered the sales ring as Lot 116, two colts had already smashed the million-guinea barrier. A son of the 1979 Derby-winner Troy was sold to Her Majesty's chief trainer Dick Hern for 1,020,000 guineas and, several lots later, a General Assembly colt went for 1,400,000 guineas.

So it was a heady atmosphere in the sales pavilion as the Riverman yearling – with a reserve of 150,000 guineas – was led round the small sawdust-covered ring and Tattersalls' senior partner, Captain Kenneth Watt, stood on his rostrum to start the bidding.

A few minutes later, Captain Watt's hammer was brought down on a final bid of 430,000 guineas. Melvyn Walters must have been a happy man. Alchemy's $95,000 foal had just realised a profit of something like 500 per cent. Even the 'shilling for the groom' (the extra shilling over the pound which makes up a guinea), part of the final bid in guineas came to £21,500 – enough to pay a fair portion of the total costs such as Tattersalls' commission and the fee to Cliff Stud for the colt's keep and preparation.

In any horse sales, the usual practice is for the final bidder to approach the rostrum and sign the sales slip. What was to happen next, however, was to signal the start of one of the most mysterious and bizarre incidents ever known in the world of bloodstock auctioneering.

Soon after Captain Watt had accepted what was to be the final bid from a man standing with a companion at the back of the sales pavilion, the man denied making the final bid and left without signing the sales slip, or leaving his name and address. A saga that was to inextricably drag Lester Piggott into the machinations of its final outcome had just begun.

Once it had been quickly established that there was a problem over the final bid, Captain Watt informed Henry Cecil and 'Tote' Cherry-Downes of the situation, asking each man if they knew the final bidder or if they were involved in any way in the bidding. Both men stated quite categorically that they did not have anything to do with the bidding and that they did not know the man who had just disappeared. In fact they were both disgruntled at having been asked that question.

But, understandably, Tattersalls were most concerned. Their business is based on integrity. A gentleman's word, or bid, is his bond. In an auctioneering career of more than 40 years, Captain Watt had never come across such a situation. The big question on everyone's lips was: 'Was this a "run-up"?'

It could well have looked that way as the underbidder – and by the time the colt had reached 400,000 guineas there were only two men bidding – was an Arab, Omar Assi, personal secretary to one of the most powerful and wealthy racehorse owners in the world, Maktoum Al-Maktoum, or to give him his full title, Sheikh Maktoum bin Rashid Al-Maktoum, Crown Prince of Dubai and eldest of the four Maktoum brothers.

There might have been a time, in the very early days of the Maktoum brothers' involvement with racing, when they would have been interested in taking a yearling if offered the chance as underbidders following a problem with the final bid. Not these days, however, and certainly not in the case of the Riverman colt – even Cecil knew that himself. He had once bid on behalf of Maktoum Al-Maktoum in Ireland and found himself as the underbidder. But when the final bidder refused to pay and Cecil was offered the chance to buy the yearling at the underbid price, Maktoum Al-Maktoum refused point-blank.

There was also a case at the Keeneland sales when an American seller tried to run up his horse against Arab bids. He ended up stuck with the animal himself after bidding somewhere in the region of $2 million.

The Arabs do not like to come out second-best. They either buy a yearling, confident that the transaction is above board, or they leave it well alone.

Rather than re-submit the Riverman colt there and then, Captain Watt felt that, owing to the lateness of the hour, it was better to contact the underbidders to give them the opportunity of buying at the underbid, Tattersalls then making up the difference to Alchemy – in this case 10,000 guineas. A phone call was made later that evening to one of Maktoum Al-Maktoum's advisers, Michael Goodbody, who was staying at a nearby hotel. Goodbody told Captain Watt he would discuss the matter with his partner, Omar Assi, the underbidder, and contact Tattersalls the following day. Captain Watt got his reply next morning – a firm 'no'.

Goodbody's reasons were part of the policy the Arabs had now adopted. His immediate reaction was that there was something suspicious about the bidding. Add that to the fact they had been run up in the past because of the high prices they were willing to pay, and it was no surprise the answer to Captain Watt was in the negative.

Henry Cecil was most annoyed. He felt the colt should have been put back in the ring as soon as the problem was realised. As far as he was concerned, Tattersalls had sold the horse and the ball was in their court. Captain Watt, however, took a different view. Re-auctioning the colt that night when there were only nine more lots left to pass through the ring and when interest in the remaining lots was waning would have been counter-productive and not in the best interests of the vendor.

So Tattersalls eventually made up their mind to re-auction the colt and, two days after the original sale, and with a new reserve of 200,000 guineas – increased from the original 150,000 guineas by Tattersalls – it was knocked down to an agent acting for Maktoum Al-Maktoum's brother Hamdan Al-Maktoum at an ironical 200,000 guineas, therefore just making its reserve.

The world of bloodstock valuations is a funny one. What one man might give a million guineas for, another man would not take for half that. The fickleness of the business was now being laid publicly for all to see because the Riverman incident had now attracted a certain degree of publicity in the newspapers. Casual observers must have been scratching their heads at how a colt could be knocked down for 430,000 guineas one day, and less than half as much two days later.

Now, there were going to be recriminations. Walters was not a happy man. He had just seen Alchemy's 'profit' knocked for six. Following a great deal of discussion it was decided that Alchemy would sue Tattersalls for the shortfall. And it would be another 20 months before the Riverman case, one unique in the history of British bloodstock, eventually came to court.

5. 'Please Pay in Cash'

Lester Piggott and Henry Cecil are among many people in racing who rue the day they met Melvyn Walters. But for Cecil, when Walters first set foot in Warren Place in the summer of 1981, not long after the Alchemy London company was established, it seemed like the start of a very promising business relationship which would be beneficial to all parties concerned.

Alchemy, for a variety of reasons, was seeking a high-profile presence in Britain so it was no surprise that Walters should aim to do business with the then three-times-champion trainer. Cecil was not only very successful as a handler with one of the biggest and best outfits in the country, but he was also extremely well connected. His owners read like a *Who's Who:* Stavros Niarchos, Daniel Wildenstein, Lord Howard de Walden, Charles St George and soon, Sheikh Mohammed, who would go on to become the world's most powerful owner.

Cecil's bloodstock interests were top-notch too. He often recommended horses and bid for them on behalf of his patrons and on the horizon was the new venture at Cliff Stud with his twin brother David. From Cecil's point of view, Alchemy and Walters seemed just the type of people with whom to do business.

Alas, Cecil, as his friends have often pointed out, is too trusting, too kind, too ready to take people at face value. Sadly in the world we live in today, these attributes are deemed a disadvantage by many other sharper men more ready to exploit situations rather than be exploited.

In part, it was the legacy of a teenage dream that led to Cecil opening up a business relationship with Walters. After leaving Canford Public School in Dorset at the age of 17 with his twin brother David, both boys went to work at Newmarket's Woodland

Stud, owned by Lord Derby. It was there that the twins met 'Tote' Cherry-Downes and became great friends, hoping that, one day, one of them would be the manager of a top stud with an international reputation.

Henry Cecil's link with Alchemy began around the same time that David returned from the US where he had been working at various top stud farms including the world-renowned Spendthrift Farm of Lexington, Kentucky, home of such fabulous stallions as Affirmed, Seattle Slew, Raise A Native and Caro among its 40-odd inmates. Henry was particularly keen to help David and make a success of their newly acquired Cliff Stud. With the Alchemy connection there would be an opportunity to enhance Cliff's reputation, a chance to bring an international flavour into the business. The plan was for 'Tote' Cherry-Downes to buy foals from the States on Alchemy's behalf, transport them to England, and send them to David at the Cliff Stud to prepare them for the top Newmarket sales when they would be sold as yearlings – just like the Riverman colt.

One of the first deals between the two parties was for Walters, on behalf of Alchemy, to arrange the purchase of a three-year-old colt trained by Cecil called Age Quod Agis.

The American-bred grey colt, a $60,000 yearling, belonged to Daniel Wildenstein and in its first season, as a two-year-old, won three races including Newmarket's July Stakes in 1980. The following season when ridden by Piggott it ran only twice before meeting with an accident. Its three-year-old debut ended in a good second in the Clerical Medical Greenham Stakes at Newbury in April, a race often contested by horses with Classic aspirations. The following month it again filled the runner-up spot when beaten one and a half lengths at Haydock by the top-class filly Marwell.

Walters was interested in buying the colt on behalf of Alchemy to stand at stud. In June, however, Age Quod Agis got loose while at exercise on the Newmarket gallops, collided with a car, and injured itself. Subsequently, the deal was called off.

By then, though, Walters had established a relationship with Cecil and there was the promise of further deals as and when the opportunity arose. It was later that year that 'Tote' Cherry-Downes purchased a yearling filly at the Keeneland fall sales for $62,000. She was Bright Crocus.

Although Bright Crocus was initially owned by Maurice Lidchi, through his US Alchemy operation, it is believed he accepted a 15 per cent profit on the filly, plus expenses, the money being put up by Cyril Levan of Miami, a former partner in London's Victoria Sporting Club casino, and London businessman Lenny Weston. When Bright Crocus ran so successfully in that 1982 season, she did so in the colours of Melvyn Walters's wife, Barbara Stanley Walters, although Weston's name and that of Cyril Levan's wife Valerie were also added to the ownership document registered with Weatherbys.

In her only season in England, Bright Crocus won more than £28,000 prize money before being sent to Adrian Maxwell in Florida where she was put on the anti-bleeding drug Lasix which is forbidden in British racing but legal in parts of the US. Maxwell, the Eton-educated Englishman who was a very successful trainer in Ireland before moving to the States, trained Bright Crocus to win the Group Three Fair Ground Oaks worth $100,000 added prize money, and a $75,000 stake at Hialeah – her only two US victories – before running a luckless second in the Kentucky Oaks to the brilliant filly Princess Rooney after jockey Sandy Hawley had dropped his whip at the eighth pole.

While Bright Crocus was in training in the States, she ran in the names of Melvyn Walters, Lenny Weston, and Cyril Levan's wife, Valerie. Soon after the Oaks the filly was taken away from Maxwell's care and placed with Neil Winnick at Aqueduct. She never won again.

One of the benefits of being connected with a top stable, at least from a gambler's point of view, is the amount of inside information that can be accumulated. Of course, the few successful punters there are in Britain are not only armed with the best information regarding a particular horse's fitness and ability, but, more importantly, the self-discipline of a monk under the vow of silence coupled with a cast-iron set of self-imposed rules which are the product of many years' painful experience. Many a person, no matter how well connected, has gone under because he did not possess the latter two attributes. Alcohol and a weak will are the bookmakers' biggest allies. A punter who allows the drink to make him reckless is usually bound for one destiny only – ruin.

Melvyn Walters likes a bet. In fact, since he opened an account with Ladbroke in 1963 he has had credit accounts with more than 20 different firms of bookmakers. In the May of 1981 when the link with the Cecil stable was about to be established, Walters applied to Mecca Bookmakers for a £4,000 credit account giving the address of the newly registered Alchemy company at 144–6 New Bond Street, London, and also an address in his birthplace town of Hove, Brighton. This was 48 Wick Hall, a pleasant two-bedroomed ground-floor flat belonging to his mother and which Walters subsequently sold when his mother died sometime in 1984. For most of the time Walters lived in London and his mail was forwarded at regular intervals.

A month after opening the Mecca account, Walters opened two more; one with William Hill for £4,000 and the other with J. Ward Hill for £5,000. Then in the July he opened another with Tote Credit for £1,500.

So, in the space of little more than two months, Walters had opened credit accounts worth £14,500. But just a couple of weeks later another bookmaking firm, Laurie Wallis of London, registered Walters as a defaulter on losing bets totalling £5,540. This was at a time when William Hill believed he was also owing a 'considerable' sum to yet another firm, Gus Demmy.

Bookmakers tend to be in a cleft-stick position when it comes to credit customers who default because, in law, gambling debts are not recoverable. Defaulters primarily fall into two groups; those who are purely punters and who never go racing, and those who have some involvement in the sport, perhaps as an owner or breeder, and who therefore need to go racing either as part of their business or for pleasure.

Dealing with the first group, a bookmaker will persevere with threatening letters for perhaps the first couple of months. Then the tone might turn to one of a conciliatory nature in the hope both parties can come to an amicable settlement. If there is still no response – and by this time the defaulter might have moved address – a final warning letter is sent before the firm calls in a debt-collecting agency who will aim to track down the customer and make personal representations in the hope they can persuade him or her that it would be advisable to pay up.

In the case of owners, or those professionally involved – indeed they might be smaller bookmakers owing money to a larger firm – the last resort is to report the defaulter to Tattersalls' Committee, an arm of the Jockey Club, racing's controllers and by whose rules everyone who sets foot on a racecourse, in whatever capacity, is bound.

The majority of cases the Tattersalls' Committee-members hear at their irregular secret meetings in a room on the fifth floor of London's Café Royal concern disputes between bookmakers. These sometimes arise from a mix-up in communications during the hurly-burly of the betting ring before a race where a bookie's clerk might have recorded the wrong bet or the wrong amount. Whenever this appears to be the case, the Committee try to act as arbitrators, encouraging a settlement where possible. It is no surprise that the majority of disputes follow on from the three biggest betting meetings of the year – Cheltenham, the Derby, and Royal Ascot.

If the Tattersalls' Committee find a case proven, they have the power to order that the defaulter be 'warned off'. This means they cannot set foot on a racecourse, own a racehorse, or participate in any capacity in any aspect of racing under the Jockey Club's power – and their power is absolute. A person who is 'warned off' is also very unlikely to be able to open a credit account with any bookmaker in the country as a list of all such people is kept by Racecourse Security Service officers – the 'police' of the racing industry – and the Tattersalls' Committee Secretary to whom bookmakers make an enquiry about each credit account application.

The list, however, is secret and never made public, a rule that also applies to the proceedings and the 'verdict' in any case held before the Committee.

In 1987, the Committee's profundity was rather shaken when racehorse-owner Terry Ramsden appeared before them. The 34-year-old London lad-made-good, head of the private investment company Glen International, reportedly worth more than £100 million, and the then-chairman of Walsall Football Club, left the Committee room flanked by Tattersalls' members, only to be besieged by a posse of presspersons, reporters and photographers, expecting a statement from the normally forthcoming Ramsden. But 'Our Tel' was having none of it and tempers got rather heated as the posse pushed forward towards the fifth-floor lift. Committee men shouted, so did the press, and Ramsden escaped, chased by a pack of photographers.

Their presence at the sacred Committee rooms followed news-paper stories from the previous day – hotly denied by Ramsden. *The Times* alleged that the slightly extrovert millionaire and heavy punter had got himself into a spot of bother with the bookies to the tune of £2 million gambling debts owed to Ladbroke. Whatever the reason for Ramsden's appearance before the Committee, all parties concerned were tight-lipped afterwards in the best tradition of the hearings. One thing was for certain, however, he was not warned off at this time for he appeared on a racecourse several days later. But then, with over 100 horses in training at certain times, life would have proved rather difficult had he been. It would be later, in the October of 1988, that events would finally catch up with Ramsden when he was formally declared a disqualified person by the Jockey Club over this dispute and when he threatened to quit racing altogether.

Tattersalls members like to consider themselves conciliators, reaching a settlement in a gentlemanly fashion. After all, gambling is basically all about taking a gentleman at his word. It just so happens that many of the people attracted to the world of horseracing and gambling are gentlemen and women who honour their debts. The minority are those people who renege and cause all sorts of problems. Maybe they think that the likes of Ladbroke, capitalised at something like £1.9 billion and diversified into a range of businesses from hotels to US racetracks, is able to stand the loss. A bit like the Exchequer and tax-dodging really.

If Melvyn Walters was getting good information, then he did not appear to be using it to good effect. The £5,540 debt to Laurie Wallis Bookmakers was still being paid off at the rate of £150 per month some three years later.

His troubles did not stop there, though, for in the February of 1983 he opened an account worth £5,000 credit with Esal Bookmakers. And just a few weeks later they were registering him as a defaulter to the tune of £3,269.

The Esal security department came up with the idea that, since Walters had applied for the account as a director of Alchemy Farms of Kentucky (he was only a director of Alchemy UK), then they should write to the US company. Several weeks after doing this they received settlement for the full amount of the debt.

While Melvyn Walters was having some luck in 1983 with the

partnership filly Bright Crocus in America, events were heading downhill at home. In an effort to repeat the success of Bright Crocus, another US-bred filly was bought in the States as a yearling and went into training with Cecil. She was by the American stallion Run Dusty Run and was again registered in the name of Barbara Stanley Walters, the filly subsequently being named Bright Gemini. A two-year-old in the 1983 season, she never set foot on a racetrack and was eventually shipped back to Alchemy's US operation.

The name Bright Gemini, however, will not just appear at this stage as a filly who flopped in England. For, as we shall learn a little later, she became the centre of a bizarre deal which led to a London company filing a large lawsuit in America against Alchemy.

But if Bright Gemini's failure to run as a two-year-old was a disappointment, the other hammer-blow, of course, came with the débâcle of the Riverman colt sale. Soon after the colt was put back in the ring and sold for 200,000 guineas, Lidchi and Walters, as directors of the Alchemy UK company, decided they would go ahead and sue for the 230,000 guineas' shortfall. Consequently, the legalities were set in motion.

By the time Alchemy (International) Limited – the UK company – had served the writ on Tattersalls the auctioneers, Henry Cecil was beginning to wish he had never become involved with Melvyn Walters. He was now aware that the police were investigating the Riverman colt case and felt there could have been something suspicious about the original 430,000 guineas bid. He decided to have nothing more to do with Alchemy.

Several months into 1984 Walters was anxious to see if Tattersalls would settle out of court and he made frantic attempts to communicate through third parties with Cecil in order to enlist the trainer's help in making representations to the auctioneers for such a settlement to be made. Cecil, though, would have nothing to do with it and this was conveyed to Walters. Undeterred by Cecil's refusal, Walters then began telephoning friends and business associates of the champion trainer asking them to speak on his behalf to get Cecil to change his mind but all these requests fell on deaf ears.

At one stage he also tried to enlist Lester Piggott's help to further this aim. Unfortunately for Cecil – and ultimately for Lester Piggott as well – the teetotal trainer's refusal even to discuss the situation with Walters 'over a cup of tea' was to have dire consequences for both men – especially Lester Piggott.

Because Melvyn Walters acted as administrator of the three-person syndicate owning Bright Crocus and looked after the paperwork for his partners, Lenny Weston and Cyril Levan, such correspondence as training bills and other letters pertaining to Cecil's handling of the filly were sent to Walters from Warren Place. During this time Cecil had sent out a secret letter to his owners, the contents of which were a transgression of Jockey Club rules. It concerned Piggott's retainer for the 1982 season – the money paid by a yard's owners to the stable jockey in order to retain that rider's services for the season. For Piggott to be a retained jockey with any stable it would have had to be worth his while. As stable jockey to the champion trainer, who by his position trained champion horses, any deal with the Cecil owners was going to be a good one.

The letter, which, among other things, asked for certain payments to be made to Piggott in cash, was also accompanied by a note from Cecil advising that the letter should be destroyed once it had been read. Under the strict *Jockey Club Rules of Racing* – a 170-page book containing more than 200 rules with sub-sections and addenda as well as 30 pages of 'instructions' – every retainer shall be registered in full with Weatherbys, the racing administrators.

The exact wording of Rule 75 is thus:

Every jockey at the termination of his apprentice riding agreement or conditional jockey's agreement is free to form engagements for himself irrespective of any which have been made for him during the term of such agreement.

The terms of all agreements must be registered at the Racing Calendar Office and no agreement shall provide for a jockey to ride for a lower fee than laid down in rules 70 and 71.

In the absence of special agreement, a jockey's retainer terminates at the end of the relevant racing season. Half the agreed retaining fee must be paid in advance, and the remainder at the termination of the retainer.

Under the terms of the secret Cecil–Piggott agreement, drawn up in document form, the greatest jockey in the world was demanding a secret cash retainer of £45,000 for the 1982 season. This was on top of the 'official' retainer of £10,000 which was registered with Weatherbys.

Piggott also wanted his own percentage (7.5 per cent in cash) on top of a jockey's normal percentage of the first-prize money, and additional 10 per cent payments on any placed horses he rode over and above the usual percentage as laid down by the Jockey Club. All the percentages were to be based on a race's penalty value, i.e. the amount before any deductions to the trainer, stable, or a jockey's normal percentage are made.

The demands did not stop there, for it was also stated that Piggott would be requiring a share in certain Group-winners he rode. These would be the real big-money earners because Piggott sold most of the stallion shares he was awarded when the horse later went to stud. Over several seasons such a deal would be worth millions of pounds. As we have already seen, a fortieth-share in a Derby-winner is worth around £250,000 and possibly much more.

One of the bills that had been sent to Walters from Cecil's secretary, Ann Scriven, had asked for an outstanding amount to be paid in cash or with a cheque made out to cash. Another bill made a similar request, adding that if it were not possible to make out a cheque for cash then one payable to Lester Piggott would suffice.

In all, such cash arrangements were in force for the four seasons Piggott rode for Cecil as stable jockey – 1981 to 1984.

The letter referring to the 1982 agreement included the following words: 'Lester has asked that for the cash element of the retainer and for the extra percentages, he be given a cheque made out to cash. It looks as if there will be 130 to 140 horses in training here next season so the cost of his retainer will work out at about £392 plus VAT per horse.'

A further note accompanying the document stated that 'perhaps it would be as well to destroy it as soon as you have read it'. As subsequent events were to prove, Walters disregarded Henry Cecil's advice and kept the retainer document and even the note on file. And, following Cecil's severance of their business relationship, Walters took the letter to Fleet Street where it was eventually published in the *Sunday People* after at least two other newspapers had turned down the story – the then-proprietor of one being a racehorse-owner himself.

There is a much-believed myth that the Inland Revenue and

Customs and Excise will pay 10 per cent of any money they recover should anyone act bounty-hunter and inform on someone's tax-dodging activities. If that were so, a reward on the magnitude of Piggott's debt to the government would be rich pickings indeed. In reality, however, the Customs and Excise 'top whack' is about £5,000 – and then only for the likes of information which leads them to a ten-kilo haul of heroin. Despite malicious rumours to the contrary, Walters never sought any payment for what he had done, and instead, when the letter was published, the four-figure sum he received from the newspaper was donated to London's Great Ormond Street Hospital for Sick Children.

With the start of the 1985 Flat season now imminent, all eyes were on Cecil and his new stable-jockey Steve Cauthen. Would this partnership reach the same heights as the Cecil–Piggott association? And how would Lester Piggott fare in his final season as a jockey, back in the role of freelance once more?

These were the sort of questions the racing world was posing as, in the usual atmosphere of anticipatory delight, they heralded the launch of the new Flat season. Melvyn Walters, though, had started his own 'season', a campaign against the racing establishment. He knew that the massive investigation, which had started because of him and on which he would co-operate, would eventually shock the whole of the sport, its jet-set owners, wealthy trainers and star jockeys. And although he may have expected Henry Cecil would be his main victim, events would subsequently show that only one man would feel the real force of the hurricane Walters had started: Lester Piggott.

As far as Walters was concerned, Piggott was not his intended target. He had shopped Cecil. That Piggott would end up the 'victim' of his deeds would be the biggest irony of the whole affair and one over which Walters would later make apologetic noises amid his deep embarrassment.

With the wheels of the tax investigation soon in motion, the full might of the Customs special investigators was focused on Piggott. Unbeknown to him throughout this final season in the saddle, the plainclothes investigators would follow Piggott's every step, watching his movements abroad, checking his rides in Britain, and even travelling to Nottingham races for the day when the greatest jockey this century finally called it a day and rode his last race in this country.

6. Operation Centaur

Operation Centaur is the biggest ever crackdown on the world of British horseracing, one that has caused shockwaves to penetrate areas of the sport previously considered relatively safe from the clutches of the taxmen. On a broader scale this far-reaching enquiry is part of the government's major drive against the thousands of tax-dodgers who, according to official estimates, are costing Britain in the region of £5 billion in lost revenue each year, the equivalent of a reduction of more than 3p in the pound in the rate of basic income tax for the rest of the nation's workers. It is no coincidence, therefore, that Lester Piggott should find himself in trouble at a time when the Exchequer was introducing the most comprehensive measures to stamp out what has been cynically called Britain's most thriving industry, the Black Economy.

Chancellor Nigel Lawson took the first of the new steps in 1985 by allowing the appointment of more Inland Revenue staff and the deployment of hundreds of new inspectors to form special 'hit-squad' units operating on a *carte blanche* basis throughout the country. The Inland Revenue alone had a staff of 850 people in its Black Economy Unit by the time recruitment slowed down in 1988.

At the bottom end of the tax-dodging scale are the handymen, the gardeners, plumbers, painters, small hoteliers and other traders who prefer cash in the hand to cheques. A government survey in 1985 revealed there were more than 700,000 people in Britain with second jobs – many of them thought to be within the realms of the Black Economy. These are the people who pay no income tax or VAT on some of their cash earnings.

The top-end tax fiddlers are no different either: the shopkeepers who falsely register their takings, the companies who falsify expenditure and profits, the company directors and their tax-free perks and, in racing, the jockeys and trainers who do not declare cash 'presents' given by grateful owners.

Such cash gifts are part and parcel of the sport, a tradition dating back to the days when jockeys were treated as little better than villains, and poorly paid ones at that, subservient to their masters and the stables' wealthy patrons and when they did not receive, as today, a percentage of the prize money. Notice, even today, how jockeys returning to the winner's enclosure still touch the peak of their riding caps – a modern manifestation of the forelock-tugging cap-doffing antics of yesteryear. When interviewed on television or radio, too, jockeys still refer to trainers and owners as 'Mister' Cecil, 'Mister' Stoute or 'Mister' Harwood. Lester Piggott was an exception to the rule, for very rarely was he seen touching his forelock to anyone. Henry Cecil's retained jockey, Steve Cauthen, refers to his boss by his christian name in the media, but he too is an exception.

It is true that a great many jockeys in Britain today work extremely hard to eke out a living, risking life and limb, travelling hundreds of miles sometimes for just one ride and spending their £45 riding fee on petrol just to get to the track and be seen, with the added hope of picking up an extra ride. If he receives a 'pony' (£25) for riding a moderate horse to win a handicap worth a couple of thousand pounds, who can blame the grateful owner? Who would begrudge the jockey? Whether the jockey declares that cash or not is up to him.

For the top jockeys, though, it is a different matter. One day a very well-known jockey rode a friend's horse to victory in a five-furlong sprint race at Haydock Park. The owner's small business was going through a rough patch, so much so that he could not afford a bet on his horse. No sooner had the winning combination of horse and jockey returned to the winner's enclosure, however, than the jockey, who must be a millionaire at least twice over, jumped off the horse and demanded £200 in readies. No doubt this was to help pay for the several-hundred-acre estate and stud farm he had just bought. My friend, shocked and also embarrassed that such a big-name jockey had put him in this position, eventually parted with a much-needed £100, vowing that the jockey in question would not ride his horse again.

The Inland Revenue spreads its net far and wide. One squad

now has the responsibility of dealing with visiting show-business stars to Britain thereby closing a loophole through which millions of pounds have been lost. Top performers from overseas used to receive their British earnings in full before leaving and subsequently negotiate on their tax demands once they were back home. Now, however, a new 'withholding tax' means they will have up to 20 per cent of their fees retained by promoters and handed over to the Inland Revenue. This new tax-team, set up in Birmingham and in action since the start of the 1987 tax year in April, expects to collect up to £100 million each year.

Football clubs, too, and the whole area of players' perks have fallen under the Inland Revenue spotlight. The Revenue is convinced there have been hundreds of thousands of pounds going astray, especially in the area of signing-on fees and testimonial games.

Investigators have even turned their eyes on company pension funds they believe may be buying and selling shares for a quick profit – and avoiding the tax due on such transactions by hiding under the exemptions on capital gains and income tax on investments for paying pensions.

Another area to fall under the microscope is the sweat-shop rag trade where thousands of badly paid workers are falling victim to shady contractors who set up a company, then hire equipment in rented premises. They deduct income tax and National Insurance contributions from unsuspecting employees but this money never finds its way into the government coffers. Instead, the company pockets the cash and is then promptly wound up before tax inspectors can claim what is rightfully theirs. Each time a new clothing contract is won, a new company is set up. At a couple of hundred pounds a time to set up an off-the-shelf company, it is an open invitation to the dishonest to exploit and benefit from such a situation.

But it isn't only the employees who suffer in such circumstances. A TUC survey in 1986 revealed that the missing billions from the Black Economy would be sufficient to increase married couples' pensions by £13 a week and provide an extra £8 a week in child benefits, or pay for the construction of 100,000 new homes and create more than 85,000 new jobs over five years.

Even so, one of the biggest problems the Revenue inspectors and senior civil servants face is the general public's attitude. Taxmen have always nestled uncomfortably between 'the wife' and 'the mother-in-law' in the general public's perception. But they find it no laughing matter to win the hearts and minds of a nation more ready to condone, with a nudge and a wink or a cheerful blind eye, than to condemn the shady dealings of the tax-dodgers. Even Lester Piggott himself once admitted publicly: 'So what. Everyone owes tax, don't they?'

The increase in tax-fraud enquiry teams is paying off. Figures show the Inland Revenue collecting £16 for every £1 spent on recovery.

Customs and Excise have among their ranks the 'hard men' of all the government's various tax or fraud-enquiry teams; they are known as the Investigation Department, a highly secretive force about which little has been previously written. Its members are drawn from the ranks of Customs and Excise officers, men and women who have a minimum of two years' service and who are then sent on an intensive two-month training course covering aspects such as law, surveillance, covert operations, and other undercover work. From time to time, ID officers are also sent on specialist courses on subjects ranging from drugs like heroin and cocaine to electronics, and even to learn self-defence. Their work embraces many aspects of the more clandestine divisions of Britain's police service such as Special Branch or Criminal Intelligence (C11). Like the police, they move in areas that are dangerous, secretive, often both.

But whether the Investigation Department officers are on the trail of a major heroin racket or a large VAT fraud, there are some parts of their operation that cannot be compared to police work: the Customs 'hit men' have far greater powers. A facility the police would no doubt like at their disposal, but which is unique to Customs, is a document known as a Writ of Assistance. This is a 'generic' search warrant, which does not even require the signature of a magistrate. In other words it is, as they say in the trade, 'an all-standing season ticket to kick the door down'. And the season is never-ending.

By the time Lester Piggott was starting his final season as a jockey (as previously said, reverting to a freelance, having been forced to leave Henry Cecil's stable), Operation Centaur had already begun. Quite unknown to Piggott, indeed known to only a few people within the Inland Revenue and the Customs and Excise, a team of top operators from the Customs Investigation Department was being assembled. Their brief was to leave no stone unturned. And so surreptitiously would they work that it would be almost another year before Piggott and the rest of the racing world knew that he was being investigated.

The name, Centaur, given to this most intensive operation, was not derived solely out of the irony of the Greek mythical monster who was half man, half horse. Most of the initial ten-strong squad came from the London VAT team 'C'. There are more than a dozen different teams in the capital all designated by a letter and whose various codenamed operations, therefore, start with the same letter as that particular team. London also has teams specialising in drugs: six for heroin, four dealing with cocaine, three for cannabis and one for amphetamines – all highly trained men and women.

The Customs investigators do not mind how long it takes to crack a case, nor how complicated it might be. A nine-strong squad from London's VAT team 'E' spent six years investigating the biggest VAT fraud ever known and which is estimated to have cost the country more than £100 million in lost tax. This was the series of swindles on gold coins smuggled into Britain by a succession of crime syndicates.

In June 1987, three businessmen were convicted in London's Central Criminal Court for their part in a similar sting. To some degree, the opportunity of gold coin swindles was brought about by the government itself. For in 1979, in one of Mrs Thatcher's first Acts, the VAT on such coins was scrapped, while it remained on gold bullion – the bars that normally lie in bank vaults. Soon, syndicates backed by the Mafia, even the IRA, were smuggling gold coins into the country then melting them down into bullion and selling it to legitimate bullion dealers who would pay 15 per cent VAT on top of the purchase price. The fraudsters would then simply pocket the VAT on the millions of pounds' worth of gold involved.

That was the theory of it at least. But so complicated were some of the deals that the Central Criminal Court case took five months at a cost approaching £3 million. Customs investigators had spent years following money-laundering routes through bank accounts from Britain to various parts of the world. Some 84,000 documents were seized and, even though these were reduced to 5,000 at the trial, they still represented a 350 volumes of court exhibits standing over 30 feet high.

Officers had to hire space in London's Lyceum Ballroom during their investigation – to store all the documents. The cost of photocopying alone was said to be £100,000.

Although VAT was reapplied to gold coins in 1983, that four-year spree was an expensive lesson for the government. Very little of the stolen millions has been recovered.

While staffing recruitment among the specialist divisions of Customs and Excise and the Inland Revenue has been increased, the figures have to be seen alongside claims that the government has cut civil servant manpower by 136,000 jobs since it came to power in 1979. And who would be a tax inspector? In a report to the Treasury and Civil Service Select Committee in July 1987, the Council of Civil Service Unions said there were abnormally high levels of anxiety and depression among tax officers.

At Customs and Excise, too, the recent successes have to be seen against figures that show uncollected VAT worth £1.5 billion outstanding at October 1986, and £800 million of VAT written off since 1979. The unions claim that an extra 1,000 Customs staff costing £20 million could bring in an extra £120 million revenue each year.

When the Inland Revenue were tipped off by Melvyn Walters through the Henry Cecil letter to his owners published in the *People*, a communication was passed to Customs and Excise at the highest level. Although this would be a joint operation it was felt that, in the early stages at least, the Customs VAT team 'C' would be in a better position to collate the evidence before passing some of it over to the IR for joint consultation. The consultative role between the two services was conducted 'from the top' and each step was carefully monitored in order that a joint strategy could be achieved. There is little doubt, however, that the Customs VAT people were the most suitable for this operation as they are experts in the field of undercover work.

And, besides, Lester Piggott had already pulled the wool over the Inland Revenue taxmen's eyes a little earlier. In 1979 and in 1983 the IR had several questions over Piggott's tax returns and had accepted from him a signed Statement of Affairs in which he declared he possessed only one bank account – with the NatWest in Newmarket's High Street. At that time, the Inland Revenue had accepted the statement in good faith and settled with Piggott accordingly.

So, by the February of 1985, when Operation Centaur was started, the Customs VAT team 'C' were armed with the allegations that Lester Piggott had been demanding extra cash payments from Henry Cecil's owners plus shares or breeding rights in Group One-winning stallions while he was stable jockey at Warren Place. The 'C' team had to prove Piggott had received the money – millions of pounds of it – and that he had stashed it away without declaring it either to the Inland Revenue or to Customs and Excise. It was going to be no easy task.

Although there is, within the VAT 'hit squads', a great degree of inter-team co-operation with specialists in one area helping out when a particular team's enquiry perhaps overlaps into that specialist field, there was no way this operation could be prejudiced by allowing an 'open' flow of information between several teams. For this enquiry had to be tight with no risk of information leaking out to alert their target. It was for this reason that several hand-picked members of other teams were drafted into the 'C' team – specialists who had previously dealt with betting tax fraud and, although they might not have known a horse's fetlock from its cannon bone, people who knew their way round a form book, knew the difference between a Group One-winner and a selling plater – the lowliest form of racehorse.

They were quite cute in their initial enquiries. Posing as friendly VAT inspectors, the type who make periodic checks on individuals, small businesses and companies, they began a series of visits to Lester Piggott's home, and to Henry Cecil at Warren Place, as well as several other top jockeys and trainers. Under this guise they were freely able to sift through all the paperwork involved in running a business today: invoices, correspondence, files, as well as checking the method by which Piggott and his company were recording transactions for VAT purposes.

Of course, they were not allowed to see all of Piggott's business transactions – just the ones he wished them to see. Even so, the 'C' team officers were already beginning to form a picture of how the situation could develop. Secret visits were also made to the VAT offices at Cambridge where Piggott's quarterly VAT returns were kept and, after sifting through several years of returns and extracting the relevant information, they went back to their London headquarters at the old *Daily Mail* building, Harmsworth House, to start the next stage of their enquiry. As each new stone was unturned, Customs and Excise passed on the relevant information to the woman leading the Inland Revenue investigation team, Freda Chaloner, an experienced and determined senior tax inspector based at head office, London's Somerset House.

Weatherbys are the administrators for the whole of racing. From their headquarters at Wellingborough in Northamptonshire, known as the administrative centre and housed in a light modern office complex, the company looks after most of the administration for the whole of Britain's racing and breeding industries. For over 200 years the company has acted as secretary to the Jockey Club. When racing started emerging as an organised sport some two centuries ago, it was a Northumberland solicitor, James Weatherby, who was asked to work in Newmarket as the Jockey Club's Keeper of the Match Book, Secretary and Stakeholder. Computers now do much of the work required to run such a detailed and highly documented sport; over 12,000 owners on file, 2,000 stallions with details of bloodtyping (something the 'progressive' New York Racing Authority are only just getting round to copying) and more than 20,000 broodmares. There are details of newly born foals, stallion certificates and the general stud book itself to be collated. As the Jockey Club secretary, Weatherbys are also responsible for a vast array of complexities, from fixture compilation, race planning and licences, to running the accounts of jockeys, trainers and owners.

The 'C' team's next move was to pay a visit to Wellingborough and inspect the recorded payments to Piggott and several other leading jockeys. These were riding fees, retainers, and prize-money percentages, all logged by Weatherbys in accordance with the *Jockey Club Rules of Racing*. Before long, the team were in a position to compare information obtained from some of his previous VAT returns with his recorded income as registered with Weatherbys.

Armed with the knowledge that Piggott had been given shares in Group One stallions, team members now set about the task of collating all the Group One horses Piggott had ridden to victory over the past ten years. Racing form books and back copies of the *Sporting Life* were brought into the team's HQ and scrutinised for the results that would tell them just where and when Piggott had been successful.

After several months of investigation, the team were able to compare Piggott's recorded income via Weatherbys and his VAT returns with his annual total number of rides, his winning rides plus win and place percentage prize money and, more importantly, the capital value he received by way of shares in those Group One-winners which had now gone off to stud. Although only estimates were made in these early stages it became evident to the 'C' team that there were discrepancies between Piggott's official and un-official earnings. To them it seemed they had a cracking good case to pursue further. The Inland Revenue were kept abreast of the Customs findings in the top-level communications and, although they were quite happy to allow the 'C' team's investigations to continue, the IR also requested certain information for their files and this was passed over.

By now, the Customs net had been cast wider. After all, if Lester Piggott was earning these incredible sums of money, who else was? Operation Centaur spread to other top owners, trainers and jockeys and the whole method of investigation, as on Piggott, was repeated. And still the racing world and its very wealthy élite did not suspect that it was the centre of the biggest shake-up it had ever undergone.

7. A Dishonourable Bid

Several interesting developments occurred before the now infamous Riverman colt trial finally got under way before Mr Justice Hirst at the High Court in London on Tuesday 4 June, the day before the 1985 Epsom Derby for which the Henry Cecil-trained colt Slip Anchor was favourite. As a consequence of the publicity surrounding the secret letter Cecil had sent to his owners and which Melvyn Walters had disclosed, the Jockey Club began their own enquiry into the affair. This was conducted by Peter Smiles, 'Chief Constable' of the Jockey Club's Racecourse Security Services (RSS), now known as Jockey Club Security. Smiles, a former public schoolboy, has been head of RSS since joining in 1977. Now, with a small team of 'detectives' he investigates hundreds of cases connected with the seamier side of the turf – from non-triers to illegal bookmakers – acting on tip-offs, racecourse gossip, or, as in the Cecil case, on a newspaper source.

Once Piggott and Cecil had been interviewed by RSS, it became evident there had been a clear transgression of the *Rules of Racing*. Subsequently, in the May of 1985, just a few weeks before the start of the Riverman trial, trainer and jockey were called before a meeting of the Jockey Club's Disciplinary Committee, a body of Jockey Club members not known for their leniency.

Indeed just two years earlier the Disciplinary Committee had acted with sharp retribution following the case of Liverpool rider Billy Newnes, first jockey to trainer Henry Candy, and who was found guilty of accepting a £1,000 bribe from professional gambler Harry Bardsley after his riding of a favourite at Royal Ascot the previous year.

The case was not unrepresentative of certain relationships between some jockeys and their 'punters' – the nickname given by riders to gamblers who either pay them for information or place bets on their behalf. In this instance, Newnes was riding that grand stayer Valuable Witness in the Queen's Vase on Royal Ascot's second day. He had been approached by Bardsley, who asked him to 'pull' the horse and stop it from winning. Newnes, who told Bardsley what everyone who read a form book knew – that the horse did not like the prevalent fast ground – finished only fifth behind a horse called Santella Man, an 11–1 long shot ridden by Greville Starkey, and later found £1,000 had been put in his car by Bardsley. Treating it as a 'gift', Newnes pocketed the money.

The Disciplinary Committee banned Newnes from riding for three years, though they accepted he did not stop the horse. It was a savage blow to the 24-year-old jockey who had become the first apprentice to ride a Classic-winner for 29 years when he rode Time Charter to victory in the Oaks the previous year. He eventually got seven months' remission and continued his career in the July of 1986.

So it was with a certain amount of trepidation that Henry Cecil appeared before the Committee charged with a breach of Rule 75 governing Piggott's retainer. Represented by solicitor Jeremy Richardson, the man who later acted for Piggott when he was arrested, Cecil gave evidence to the Committee along with Piggott and, after considering that evidence, the Committee fined Cecil £2,000 having taken into account the breaches for the three other years Piggott was with the stable. It was £1,000 less than the maximum 'penalty' for disregarding the rule.

Piggott did not attend the hearing in any capacity other than a witness because the responsibility to register his retainer lay purely with Cecil. Whatever the moral issue of encouraging his owners to pay Piggott in cash, Cecil made no public comment about that aspect of the affair.

With just a week to go before the Derby and the start of the Riverman case, Cecil then had the misfortune to lose the two dozen top horses owned by Daniel Wildenstein who decided that he was getting too old for travelling from Paris to watch his horses run. The string was then sent to Patrick Biancone at Lamorlaye.

These were not the only developments before the trial opened in Court 22 of the imposing High Court building. The police had been called in to investigate the affair in its early days following the Newmarket sale, and had spent many months interviewing several owners, trainers and businessmen with racing interests. In the March of 1984, Wednesday 28 March in fact, the police received a tip-off that the man who was alleged to have made the bogus bid of 430,000 guineas for the colt was at Heathrow Airport. They swooped and arrested him as he was just about to board a British Airways shuttle to his home town of Belfast.

That man was Jimmy Flood, a professional poker player, dogs and racehorse gambler, on his way back home from the Cheltenham races. He was also someone who knew absolutely nothing about the world of bloodstock, least of all yearling sales. Yet he would be the central character in this bizarre case which, over the next 13 days, would hold the racing world spellbound.

Ostensibly, the case was a fairly straightforward one. Lidchi and Walters's London company, Alchemy, were suing Tattersalls for the 230,000 guineas' shortfall in the eventual Riverman colt sale, alleging that the auctioneers had been negligent in their conduct. There was also a claim against Flood by Alchemy. The defendants, Tattersalls, denied the action and they also took out a third-party indemnity against Flood should they lose the case.

Both sides fielded eleven witnesses each, with Flood calling on just one – his friend Hugh Boyle of Camlough near Newry, County Down, Northern Ireland. Those called for Alchemy included Henry and David Cecil, 'Tote' Cherry-Downes, Omar Assi, Sheikh Maktoum Al-Maktoum's personal secretary, and Michael Goodbody, manager of Newbury's Gainsborough Stud and adviser to the Maktoums. Tattersalls called on Captain Ken Watt, their senior partner who auctioned the colt, David Pym, a freelance auctioneer working for Tattersalls that day, and Detective Chief Inspector Stewart Chapman of Suffolk Police, among others.

It was not Tattersalls' intention to speculate as to why Flood had bid for the colt, nor was it for the court to pursue that motive (this is examined in the next chapter) so consequently there were a great many questions left unanswered with names of various racing people flitting in and out of the proceedings as if dropped teasingly by a butterfly with mischief on its mind. A complication entered the case in the form of a submission from Jimmy Flood, who claimed that he had not made a final bid of 430,000 guineas. This was coupled with a declaration from the underbidder, Omar Assi, that he had not bid 420,000 guineas but that his final bid was 400,000 guineas.

This aspect was enlarged upon at a stage in the trial when various statements Flood had made to the police were read out in court. Flood stated that he had bid 410,000 guineas – there was no dispute about this – but he told Mr Justice Hirst that he refused to sign the sales slip because an underbidder at 420,000 guineas could not be found and he believed he was being 'run up' by Tattersalls themselves. When Captain Watt was cross-examined by Flood's counsel, Peter Martin, QC, he said he was absolutely convinced Mr Assi had bid 420,000 guineas and that Mr Assi must have been mistaken in believing his final bid was only 400,000. Assi's partner, Michael Goodbody, added more confusion to this point when he said they had fixed a 400,000-guinea ceiling on the colt anyway.

Mr Justice Hirst took the view that this aspect of the case had been an honest mistake, made around the 420,000 guineas' bid, and there had been no time during the sale to clarify it because the bidding quickly reached 430,000 guineas – the bid from Flood. Melvyn Walters, not called as a witness in any capacity, occupied a seat in the public benches on all but two days of the 13-day trial.

Cecil, triumphant with Slip Anchor in the Derby, returned to the court the following day to receive the congratulations of Mr Justice Hirst and to amuse the court with a tale of the day he attended a 'resale' of a colt in America. Initially the son of the world's top sire Northern Dancer had made $1.3 million before it was discovered the animal was a crib-biter – one with the bad habit of biting the top of the stable door and usually sucking wind (though this does not, as a rule, affect their racing performance). Put back into the ring, however, the animal went on to fetch the grand sum of $4 million. Cecil told the court he turned to Sheikh Mohammed, who was standing next to him, and told him that the man who had just bought the horse must be mad – only for the Sheikh to admit that he was the buyer.

Tattersalls were basing their defence on three counts: the lateness of the hour, when it would not have been advisable to put the colt back in the ring due to the fact that the sales ring was rapidly emptying of buyers; although Flood had denied making the 430,000 guineas' bid he had admitted to making one at 410,000 guineas which had given Captain Watt hope he might accept the colt at the lesser price; and the chance that the underbidders, once they had been contacted, might be prepared to buy the colt at their last bid.

After Captain Watt had recorded, and discarded, several names in his catalogue as speculation as to the identity of the final bidder, he met with Flood and a companion at the rear of his rostrum and soon afterwards told Cecil and his partners there was a problem. Cecil told the court that Captain Watt had said there was some confusion over the bidding but there was no need to worry as they knew who the underbidder was and Tattersalls would make up the difference. By the time Omar Assi was contacted – through Michael Goodbody at his hotel later that evening – and had come back the next day to say he was not interested in taking the colt at the underbid – Tattersalls had no option but to wait another day before putting the colt back in the ring.

Two pieces of evidence Mr Justice Hirst found remarkable were a video recording of the night of the sale and an audio tape. A television was set up in the courtroom to show the video but the scenes it showed were not conclusive. It showed Flood nodding his bids but the camera pulled away too quickly to ascertain whether Flood had made a perceptible movement when the 430,000-guinea bid was asked for by Captain Watt. Flood was emphatic that the recording showed him shaking his head although Mr Justice Hirst said the audio tape, which clearly revealed the different intonations in Captain Watt's voice when he was asking for a bid or acknowledging one, was a lot more helpful.

Captain Watt explained the technique he used on the bidding. He told Flood's QC, Peter Martin, that he always used the figure he had been bid, never an advancing figure, to signal the next step in the bidding. This was an important point in the proceedings and one on which Flood was basing his defence, for Flood was asking the court to believe he thought the figures Captain Watt was using during the bidding were interrogative – not confirming a bid. This stance was totally dismissed by the judge in his summing up, however, when he said Flood had been telling lies regarding the method of bidding he thought he was using.

There were witnesses for both Alchemy and Tattersalls who showed the differences of opinion about how they would have reacted to the problem facing Tattersalls on the night of the sale. Jonathan Irwin, director of the Irish-based Goffs Sales, said he would always advise a vendor to put a horse back in the ring immediately even though the vendor might be disappointed at the eventual resale figure.

David Pym a freelance auctioneer working for Tattersalls on the day, said he would have done exactly as Captain Watt, adding that to have re-offered the horse that night would have been very doubtful as to the benefit. Another Tattersalls witness, Michael Watt, who is now a senior partner in the firm, told the court it would have been disastrous to have put the animal back in the final three lots of the sale – the only opportunity that night – or at the end. Had this happened, and the reserve of 150,000 guineas been left on the horse, it was doubtful it would even have been sold at all, he said.

Captain Watt also said that one of the considerations Tattersalls had had to discuss after Flood disappeared was, in fact, whether they had a dispute on their hands at all. In his evidence, which lasted a little over seven hours spread over four sessions, he said that a normal dispute in bidding is when two or more people make a claim that theirs was the last bid. If that was ever the case, he would always put the horse back up and sell him. In this case, however, he believed there was no such dispute because the colt had been knocked down to Flood who had bid him the 430,000 guineas.

He said that in all his 40 years of auctioneering he had never come across such a strange, unusual and bizarre situation. He felt he had very few alternatives; there was very little time to put the colt back in the ring, and it would probably have been the final lot had he done so which would not have been fair to Alchemy. In his experience, if a horse was not put back in immediately and came back later, there was always a stigma attached to the animal and very often they never made as much again because potential buyers were then wary.

The opposite view was voiced by Henry Cecil who insisted that, as far as he was concerned on the night of the sale, the horse had been sold. It was Tattersalls' problem and there was no way he wanted it sold under the name of Cliff Stud later in the week when it would be like going to a matinée rather than a gala performance. (Cliff Stud was named as the vendor when the colt was sold two days later.)

Flood himself added his own inimitable version of events prior to the sale, some of which stretched to incredulity the opinions of many of the racing professionals present in the courtroom. Smartly dressed in a grey suit, and with his fair hair cut short, he claimed, in his soft Belfast accent, that on the Sunday before the sales and in the Churchill Hotel almost opposite the London headquarters of the Jockey Club in Portman Square, he and Hugh Boyle, his friend from County Down, met up with racehorse trainer Barney Curley to form a three-man syndicate with the express intention of bidding for three horses at the sales. Boyle, as Flood admitted, was a man whose knowledge of horseflesh was as scant as his own – he too knew nothing. Barney Curley, though, is a different proposition.

Irishman Curley, now training horses in England, is a successful backer and buyer of horses. He once made the non-racing headlines when he auctioned his Irish stately home and raised more than £250,000 in the process although the Irish government, ruling that the auction was illegal, made him pay a percentage of it to charity. He doubled the amount for good measure.

According to Flood (with his and Hugh Boyle's knowledge of bloodstock this might seem much of an understatement), Curley was the brains behind the syndicate. The three men agreed to each put up £150,000 and Curley picked out three possible lots for which to bid: Lot 62, which was sold for 1.12 million guineas; Lot 116, the Riverman colt; and Lot 117, a Hello Gorgeous colt who broke the European record at 1.55 million guineas. Flood claimed Curley had said that any one of these three horses would be a good buy at £450,000 (horses are always sold in guineas). On the night of the sale, however, Curley, the so-called brains behind the syndicate, did not even attend the sales ring. And, significantly, he was not called by Flood's counsel as a witness. He was said to be in America but, as the judge pointed out, he could have been subpoenaed under the Evidence Act and ordered to appear had counsel wanted.

Under cross-examination, Flood was adamant that Curley had left it to him to bid for the horse even when Tattersalls' counsel, Michael Connell, QC, asked him if the court was to believe that, with all Curley's knowledge, he had left it to Flood, who had no knowledge, to bid so much money. Flood also admitted that he had not inspected the colt before it walked into the ring, and he did not know whether or not it had been inspected by a vet.

There were murmurings of disbelief, too, when Flood was asked about his financial status and his ability to pay for the colt had the sale gone through. He was unable to say how much he had received for his Belfast home when he and his wife had gone to live in Marbella in 1983 and he could not remember whether a bank loan against the house was for £30,000 or £13,000.

It was not the only time contradictions entered the hearing. For Flood also said in evidence that a man called Freddie Thomsett, an old friend, had recommended he bid for the colt. He was asked if he knew Melvyn Walters and replied that the first time he had met him was in his solicitor's office in preparation for this case, adding that Walters had given him no reason to believe that Freddie Thomsett was known to him. During his interviews with police, Flood was also asked if he knew a man named Michael Tabor, a bookmaker and racehorse owner with a string of London betting shops. The relevance of these characters to the case and any implications they might have had for the sale of the River-man colt were not raised in court, thereby leaving many teasing questions completely unanswered.

In his four-hour summing up, Mr Justice Hirst made reference to Captain Watt's decision on the night of the sale:

His evidence was that he did think of re-auctioning but concentrated first on pinning Mr Flood to his bid and then finding the underbidder. Re-auction was fairly low on Captain Watt's agenda in favour of the other alternatives. I find it inconceivable that an auctioneer of the acknowledged expertise of Captain Watt would not have considered re-auction. That he strongly disfavoured re-auction is obvious.

The judge's remarks on this issue swept aside the assertion by Alchemy's counsel, Mr Peter Sheridan, QC, that Captain Watt's action had been a wrong one. Mr Sheridan had maintained that Tattersalls had been faced, not with a dilemma, but an emergency. He compared it to a dentist suddenly faced with a patient who had a cardiac arrest, or an aeroplane pilot who had both engines cut out on him. It was an emergency for which the auctioneers should have been prepared, he said.

But, referring to a possible re-auctioning of the colt that evening, Mr Justice Hirst said that Omar Assi, the underbidder, would not have bid and Flood, because of the previous difficulties, would not have been allowed to bid more than 200,000 guineas' reserve. Therefore two other bidders at least would have had to have been found. It was speculative that anyone would have taken bidding beyond the 200,000 guineas for which the colt was eventually sold. As regards Flood and that final bid, the judge said Flood had had the opportunity to deny it by shouting out. He said Flood's explanation was that he was a shy man. But the judge added:

Mr Flood is anything but shy. By his self-assessment he is described as flamboyant. Bombastic would be a better description.

On the question of credibility, I found all Tattersalls' witnesses entirely honest, straightforward and convincing, prepared to make concessions even if it did not advance their claim.

I wish I could say the same about Mr Flood. He has lied on material issues both to the police and to this court.

If Mr Curley was a one-third participant, it is almost inconceivable he would have allowed an inexperienced tyro to bid for him. I strongly suspect that the so-called syndicate is illusory.

Mr Justice Hirst added that there could be no doubt that Flood had bid without the intention of honouring that bid. Flood's bid was therefore fraudulent, he added.

Mr Justice Hirst delivered his verdict; and Tattersalls were cleared of any negligence. The famous auctioneering house had struck a blow for the rest of the industry which would have been in turmoil had the case gone the other way. Correspondingly, the judge then told the court how his verdicts would be imposed.

Alchemy were ordered to pay all Tattersalls' legal costs – a figure in the region of £70,000. Alchemy were awarded the 230,000 guineas (the amount of the shortfall on the colt's sub-sequent sale) – but to be paid by Jimmy Flood with interest from 24 hours after the sale until settlement. Flood was also ordered to pay the costs of Alchemy's case against him plus the costs of Tattersalls' third-party proceedings against him.

According to newspapers, costs of the 13-day trial were estimated at around £250,000, a large part of which was Alchemy's case against Tattersalls. This figure was wide of the mark – they were much nearer £120,000.

The main judgment was dispensed with the wisdom of Solomon, or so it seemed. Lidchi and Walters's Alchemy might have lost their case against Tattersalls alleging negligence, but on the other hand they had been awarded their 230,000 guineas after all in the judgment against Flood. Perhaps, knowing Flood's financial circumstances, however, Mr Justice Hirst was saying something, for it was very doubtful Alchemy would ever see that money.

Conclusions from the case were most difficult to draw, even for the most hardened of professional observers attempting to untangle the web of fact, fiction and insinuation. There were just too many questions left unanswered although, to be fair, it was not the court's aim, nor within its compass, to discover exactly what had been the reason for Jimmy Flood to be bidding for top-class bloodstock at Britain's premier horse sale. It was not the court's responsibility, either, to investigate the 'mystery men' whose names flitted in and out of the case like Banquo's ghost in *Macbeth*.

For Henry Cecil, though, it was the end of an association with Melvyn Walters that had promised much, but which ultimately turned into a nightmare. Exonerated by the judge from any culpability, Cecil was glad to see the back of a court case over a colt in which he had no financial interest other than as any stud proprietor who prepares yearlings for the sales and charges a fee on a commercial basis for doing so.

But Walters felt aggrieved, let down. It was now five months since the *People* had published the letter from Cecil which he had given the newspaper in the hope of setting the record straight regarding the behaviour of some of racing's top names. It was only a month since Cecil had appeared before the Disciplinary Committee, having been fined £2,000. Walters felt that the Disciplinary Committee should have taken much more vigorous action (even though, as we have stated, the maximum fine was £3,000). Now he was going to lose money as a result of this Riverman case and someone in the racing establishment would have to pay. Over the next three years, Walters would wage his own battle against racing's élite, maintaining his contact with the Sunday newspaper and alleging all manner of transgression.

At this moment in time, he was confident they were all in for a major surprise. Soon, he hoped, the Customs men would come knocking on doors. Then the whole can of worms would be opened for the racing public to see.

8. Lowdown on the High Roller

Despite a police investigation which lasted for months and included the quizzing of top owners, trainers and other racing professionals, the Director of Public Prosecutions decided not to bring criminal charges against Jimmy Flood or the people whose names littered the Riverman colt trial. There were a number of reasons for this, not least because, in a way, the private prosecution case of *Alchemy* v. *Tattersalls* and the way in which the case resulted probably was enough – at least in the case of Jimmy Flood who ended up a good several thousand pounds out of pocket.

Flood himself, an ignominious character after the trial, held a somewhat chequered reputation before it. Born in the backstreets of Belfast, he fought his way up the hard way, living off his wits and earning the reputation as a bit of a wide-boy always on the lookout for a killing in one sort of deal or another, and always preferring to conduct his transactions in cash. His love of the 'readies' is not surprising really, for his father and mother owned two second-hand goods shops in Belfast's Smithfield Market.

As the family business began to flourish, they moved out of the distinctly unfashionable Carlisle Circus and down the Antrim Road to a house next door to Gerry Fitt, the former MP for West Belfast and now Lord Fitt. Soon, Flood developed a penchant for gambling – and he became quite proficient at it too. Some days he could clear £10 a day, not bad for someone still under the watchful eye of the Christian Brothers at the nearby St Mary's School which was oblivious to the organised games of pontoon and poker behind the school buildings. When he was twelve he put £1 each way on the 1964 Grand National-winner and won himself £15. But it was while he was sitting for his 'O' level exams that he made his first big killing and simultaneously left school to embark upon a new career.

His lucky break came as he was doing his Geography paper, when his thoughts were more on four horses he had backed in a multiple-bet Yankee than sorting out his coastlines, oceans and continents. From previous winnings he had bought himself one of the latest electronic gadgets, a transistor radio, the type with a small earpiece. Throughout the exam he kept tuning in to the racing results, the radio hidden in his top pocket, the wire of the earpiece running inside his jacket and the earpiece itself secreted in his ear. As soon as he heard the first three horses had won he put down his exam paper and walked out of the school. All four horses – Four Fella, Crooner, Sleeping Partner and Katmandu – had won, netting him £900, sending him on his way to a mercurial career among the professional poker players and gamblers of Belfast, later the world, anywhere in fact where there was some action on the go.

So began the life of living on his wits; of gambling dens and illegal card-schools, of dog tracks and racecourses, of smoky hotel rooms, all-night sessions behind drawn curtains ending only when the rest of the outside world were starting their daily work. He learned his trade in Dublin, winning a few thousand pounds here, losing a couple there, mixing with waiters, restaurant owners, club proprietors who were fanatical gamblers. But the early days also saw his fair share of mug punting, betting every day on the dogs or the horses and playing cards at night in golf clubs and hotels throughout the North of Ireland. He even spent the first night of his honeymoon with his wife Patsy at Belfast's Dunmore Park dog track and continued to live the first couple of years of married life in run-down flats, often skint and subbing from his friends in order to raise the stake for the next big poker game.

Once, he bought himself a Mercedes and drove up to Dublin to take part in a game – he had just £7 in his pocket but returned hundreds of pounds up. In 1976 he went racing to Fairyhouse during the Easter meeting, backed a horse called Lord Hansel, and won £25,000. But it did not last long and he was soon on the way down. On St Patrick's Day in 1978 he collected again – this time £27,000 and to celebrate he flew off to Jamaica only to find there was no casino in Montego Bay. He gave the place a miss and flew on to Antigua to play the tables.

When he wasn't flush he ran errands – sometimes across the border – for Belfast's biggest bookie, Barnie Eastwood, later to receive international prominence as boxing promoter and manager of world champion Barry McGuigan. Wherever Eastwood and his partner, Alfie McLean, were to be found after a big race-meeting, Flood was to be found there too, organising a game, playing the night away while those who dropped out shook their heads half in admiration, half in wonderment at the Belfast boy's stamina, his enthusiasm to split the deck at any opportunity and, above all, his skill as a poker player. There was no doubting that when Jimmy Flood was on song, he was a very good card-player indeed.

He moved to London for a spell doing the rounds of the dogs and racetracks and the poker schools. He moved back to Belfast after a couple of years but had still made many contacts in the twilight world of high-rollers and low-lifers. Back in Ireland, he touched lucky and bought himself a Rolls Royce, paying £1,500 alone for the personalised number plate JF 12. The Roller helped his image and bolstered his growing reputation as a decent card-player. Inevitably there were others who saw him as a challenge, wanted to whup the boy from the backstreets.

One year he staked a small fortune on backing Bjorn Borg and Martina Navratilova to win their respective Wimbledon titles – and collected over £42,000. That windfall gave him enough of a stake to play an Irish millionaire industrialist in a marathon card game in a Dublin hotel. The tycoon left the hotel having lost a reputed £70,000 to Flood. Another big win came when he backed the filly Three Troikas to win the Prix de l'Arc de Triomphe and ended £60,000 the richer.

He lived well during the successful times and for one period in his life he owned a £130,000 home with its own private beach in a secluded cove at Helen's Bay in Belfast Lough. A couple of Rolls Royces were parked in the drive. Often he would only work one day a week. Sometimes he would catch Belfast's evening shuttle to London to take part in card games against Greek and Italian businessmen. He'd arrive back in Belfast on the 8.20 morning flight from Heathrow, red-eyed but thousands of pounds the richer. To his friends and acquaintances it seemed Jimmy Flood would bet on the proverbial two flies crawling up the wall – he was straight out of *Guys and Dolls*.

In the January of 1985, just four months before he was to

appear at the High Court for his role in the Riverman case, he and another professional gambler from County Roscommon teamed up in an ingenious and perfectly legal 'sting' on an Irish nightclub owner. It was a brilliant scheme, a punter-proof system for backing greyhounds at London's Harringay dog track – one in which they could not lose.

They left a £4,000 deposit with the club-owner, saying that they wanted to back every dog returned at a starting price of 11–2 to a set amount whether that dog won or lost. They claimed to have won somewhere in the region of £27,000 before the club-owner claimed foul and accused them of manipulating the odds.

But the scheme worked like this: the Roscommon punter had had the time to spend a year studying the Harringay dogs' results, noting the returned starting prices and also the fact that a pattern was beginning to emerge. There were three meetings each week with ten races a day and the usual six dogs in each race. The Roscommon punter claimed to have noticed that very few beaten dogs were returned at the 'split' odds of 11–2 (the average of one bookie showing 5–1 and another 6–1) but were usually returned at the 5–1 or 6–1 price. The half-point difference was, naturally, of no consequence to anyone because that dog had been beaten.

This was not the case with all beaten dogs at lower prices, though, because they would often be returned at 'split' odds of, say, 5–2, 7–2 or 9–2. So it was just those beaten dogs that really should have been 11–2 shots that were returned at the whole numbers.

But when they won, however, the pattern was that the 5–1 or 6–1 odds – providing the bookies were showing that price for the winner – would be 'split' and the dog would therefore be returned at 11–2. In other words, Flood and his pal from Roscommon could expect their fair share of winners at 11–2 but very few, if any, losers at that price. It was the punter's dream – you could not lose.

The club-owner refused to believe the scheme had been straight. He claimed they must have had inside help at Harringay for outsiders who lost to be always 5–1 or 6–1 while winners were 11– 2. Consequently he refused to pay over any of the 'winnings'.

It was a brilliant scheme if it were true but, perhaps, clumsily executed. If it was such a simple winning scheme, how much wiser it would have been to have set up deposit accounts for much smaller sums with hundreds of smaller bookmakers the length and breadth of Britain. They then could have sat back in crafty retirement – laughing all the way to the bank as they collected their small 'unsuspicious' winnings each month from the unsuspecting bookies.

Retirement, in fact, had been mentioned by Flood to his friends when, in 1980 and at the age of 28, he reckoned he had made enough money out of the gambling game to call it quits and sit back in luxury. Then, he was taking working holidays in the likes of Hawaii and Las Vegas, claiming he had made £500,000, and playing the tables or joining a card-school for the hell of it.

Perhaps the love of the life he was leading was deserting him. Maybe so was his self-discipline, that cold, hard and unforgiving characteristic requiring hours of concentration; an ascetic existence where, pale-faced and drained from the battle, he would emerge blinking in the daylight, his emotionless mask now cast aside to reveal real tiredness in those eyes, bitter disappointment now he was losing.

Jimmy Flood is quite familiar with the decadence of some of the London nightlife and the people who live in the twilight world of the capital's seamier side. Not that he would consider himself one of them, for he always liked to think he had a touch of class. He was proud of the fact that he had never drawn dole or asked the National Health Service for so much as a bandage. But then, he would have trouble with the latter, for he has never had a NH Insurance card.

Two of the people Flood met on his travels were the Thomsett brothers, George and Freddie.

Police investigating the whole area of the Riverman colt case were working on the theory that it had been a 'run-up' against the Arabs – to boost the price of the colt and thereby the profit for its owners at the end of the day.

When Flood was arrested at Heathrow Airport and taken back to Newmarket police headquarters under suspicion of taking part in a criminal conspiracy, Detective Chief Inspector Stewart Chapman told the Irishman that the police suspected Flood's bogus bids were part of a deception to obtain money.

During the court case, DCI Chapman read out his questioning of Flood after the arrest. It went like this:

CHAPMAN: I said we have evidence to suggest that you made the final bid.

FLOOD: No I didn't. I was interested in two horses. One out of Troy and Lot 116 [the Riverman colt]. I bid for the Troy and it went up to over a million.

CHAPMAN: Do you know who owned 116?

FLOOD: Henry Cecil, I think.

CHAPMAN: Do you know Freddie Thomsett?

FLOOD: Yes, I meet him at racecourses – he's into sex shops.

CHAPMAN: What about George Thomsett?

FLOOD: I don't know him too well.

CHAPMAN: What about Melvyn Walters?

FLOOD: I don't know him.

CHAPMAN: Michael Tabor?

FLOOD: I have heard of him. He's a top-level gambler. He's a very shrewd man. They won't accept a bet from him in Ireland because he's so shrewd.

CHAPMAN: What about Alchemy Farms?

FLOOD: That doesn't mean anything to me.

If any clue were needed as to Flood's total ignorance of bloodstock, it came out in that brief session. Referring to the Troy colt, Flood called it a colt *out of* Troy whereas the correct terminology – seeing as the stallion Troy was the sire of the colt – should have been *by* Troy ('out of' referring to the colt's dam).

The Thomsetts are a couple of interesting characters. Both are British, but their respective birthplaces could not be more disparate, nor ironic. Elder brother George was born in Iraq, while Freddie was born in Iran.

After DCI Chapman's first interview with Flood, police believed that Flood's companion at the sales might have been George Thomsett. At a second interview, however, Flood said that the man with him was his friend from County Down, Hugh Boyle. This prompted the question from DCI Chapman: 'Why should we be told it was George Thomsett; does it look like him?'

So what are we to make of this mysterious affair? It is a fact that Freddie Thomsett knew Flood as well as Walters and that Walters knew Michael Tabor. The police have their own theories about the Riverman sale but, as previously stated, it was left to the *Alchemy* v. *Tattersalls* civil case for the matter to be resolved even though that case did throw up some intriguing questions that remained unanswered.

Observers of the Riverman trial, and the police themselves,

asked Flood if he knew Walters, and Flood said that they had not met until six weeks before the case; in this respect Flood was telling the truth. Both men had, coincidentally, had a different horse in training with Adrian Maxwell in New York at one time – Walters had Bright Crocus, of course, and Flood owned a horse called Los Christianos. During the trial, Flood said he had been in dispute with Maxwell about the value of his horse which was subsequently sold by Maxwell. Flood said in court: 'Mr Maxwell says the horse was sold for $40,000 but I think it was nearer $100,000.'

Alas for Jimmy Flood, this is not the case. Los Christianos, an ex-inmate of Irish trainer Michael Kauntze's stable was bought for just a few thousand pounds as a three-year-old gelding by Maxwell who later sold it on to Flood. It ran in claiming races at Hialeah in Miami without success before Maxwell sold it for $1,000 and it went to run in Boston where it never won a race.

As a sequel to one of the strangest cases involving the turf of recent times, Melvyn Walters was virtually out of another job, his aspirations to a business partnership with Henry Cecil dashed.

The Riverman colt itself raced in the colours of Hamdan Al-Maktoum and was named, appropriately, Sulaafah (Arabic for Trouble). Sulaafah turned out to be a useful horse, winning four of his 13 races as a two- and three-year-old and being placed among the top 20 milers in Britain, rated 7 lbs inferior to Oh So Sharp at up to $10\frac{1}{2}$ furlongs in the 1985 International Classification of top European three-year-olds. Retired to stud duties at the Blackdown Stud in Somerset, Sulaafah is now covering mares at 1,500 guineas a time.

After the Riverman verdict the curtains closed on an affair that, years later, is still a most perplexing one for some of those involved. The only certainty arising from the débâcle was that Lester Piggott was now a marked man. He was on the 'wanted' list of the Inland Revenue and Customs and Excise now that Operation Centaur was already four months old. The demise of Lester Piggott had begun because of the Riverman colt row between Henry Cecil and Melvyn Walters and the publication of the now-famous letter requesting those cash payments for Piggott himself.

9. Losses at Lloyd's

Controversy and Lester Piggott have never been far apart. In fact it could be said that the two have ridden upsides each other throughout the great jockey's long and most distinguished career. Officialdom and petty rules have always been one of his great dislikes and those attempting to impose such bureaucratic measures on the maestro have usually ended up feeling his verbal backlash; two or three words in retort, usually delivered with the rapidity with which he often used his riding whip to good measure stretching for the line.

Many of the conflicts have been on the lighter side, an opportunity for the renowned dry wit to sparkle and cause hoots of laughter from his fellow riders, the repartee going into the humorous annals of the weighing room, repeated with relish over the years in racecourse bars all over Britain.

There was the time when he tried to pull the wool over officials' eyes at Doncaster when a medical officer asked him for sight of his medical book. Piggott told him he had already shown it to the officer's colleague, a story he trotted out when that colleague had earlier asked him to produce the book all jockeys are obliged to show each day. If Piggott had simply reported that he had left the book at home he could have got away with a £7 fine. As it was, the two medical officers subsequently checked with each other – and Piggott was fined £100.

He was once fined £280 in South Africa for swearing at a starter who opened the gates before Piggott was ready.

The impetuous Piggott seemed to be at his worst behind the wheel of a car. Sir Noel Murless once said that Piggott drove his cars like he rode his horses – if he saw a gap he went for it. His meanness, too, often infuriated his fellow professionals and is best summed up by a close friend who observed that he thought Piggott did not so much enjoy the money he made as he enjoyed actually making it. If a deal could not be done at the right price then Piggott would simply walk away from the situation. He did just that in his final season when the racing world expected that, out of sentiment, Piggott would have his final ride at Haydock Park, scene of his first winner as a boy of twelve those many years ago. Not so, however, for Haydock would not come up with the necessary cash and so Nottingham – who paid him a fee of £1 a head for every spectator at the track – stepped in readily. Basically, there was no giving way to emotion if the money was not right.

The great picture of Piggott, conjured in the minds of the general public, was of him puffing a giant cigar and with a glass of champagne in one hand and a copy of the *Financial Times* in the other. Charles St George was once asked if he was Piggott's financial adviser. The millionaire owner replied that Piggott was so adept at managing his own affairs that he doubted the champion jockey would take advice even from the Governor of the Bank of England. Fellow world-class jockey Pat Eddery was asked what he would do if he won a million pounds on the pools – he said he would give it to Piggott to invest for him.

Piggott was indeed someone who off the top of his head, could reel off the current prices of shares in most of the major companies and who took a deep interest in international money matters. But the light-hearted quips all began to have a hollow ring about them when it was realised that Piggott's legendary prowess as a shrewd investor did not always pay off.

As Piggott's riches and personal wealth began to grow at a spectacular rate, so too did his choice of investment vehicles to carry the money. There was never a shortage of opportunities, all with their associated degrees of risk. He could not, of course, go far wrong on the shares and breeding rights in the many Group One horses he rode to victory and which later became stallions – he sold most of them before the risk factor associated with highly prized horseflesh came into play; let the breeders and owners worry about infertility, disease, even death. With the money sitting pretty in an offshore company or one of his bank accounts there were other areas into which to channel the millions.

Piggott liked to play the stock market, buying equities off his own bat, sometimes acting on a recommendation. But, like a lot of wealthy people, his eyes turned to one of London's oldest institutions, the insurers, Lloyd's. And this was where his long-time friend, the racehorse owner Charles St George, could be of assistance.

The basic premise by which Lloyd's operates today is little changed from that of three centuries ago. The insurance business of the middle 1600s, centring on London and its unparalleled dominance in the world of shipping and cargo, saw most transactions conducted at the emerging popular coffee houses of the capital. Great store was placed on sobriety. It was time for clear heads and lucid thinking, and the coffee houses took precedence over the inns and taverns which had flourished as business venues up to this time.

Shipping and allied insurance was a straightforward matter. A vessel owner or merchant seeking cover would contact the equivalent of today's broker who would then take his policy to the City for anyone with the private wealth to take a share of the risk in return for a share of the insurance premium.

Ironically, little is known about Edward Lloyd himself, except that the Welshman's Lloyd's Coffee House first appeared in London's Tower Street in 1688. There is no evidence to suggest Lloyd was an insurer or had the means to underwrite the risks on the vessels of the merchants, sea captains, ships' owners or traders who frequented his establishment. He did, however, build up a reputation for being able to supply his many patrons with the latest shipping news. In the days of gossip and misconception it was imperative that those connected with the sea should be able to communicate with each other and make their decisions based upon the reliable information that Lloyd was able to supply. The coffee house, therefore, became one of the centres for all forms of maritime business and, after his death in 1713, the name of Lloyd lived on into posterity.

Lloyd's of today owes its existence to an Act of Parliament passed shortly after the South Sea Bubble of 1720, that curtain-raiser to a new era of eighteenth-century commercialism. The South Sea Company was formed by Tory Ministers of Queen Anne (to whom racing enthusiasts should be indebted for the building of Ascot Racecourse). It had a monopoly on the Spanish slave trade and a large share of the Spanish-American trade in

European goods, and proved the focal point for the speculation fever hitting London. As new speculators were actively encouraged to purchase stock – made available by constant 'new issues' – the holders of original stock bailed out with a handsome profit. As the bubble grew, it encouraged other schemes of a similar ill-founded nature, sucking investors in at ridiculously high prices, until it finally burst, ruining thousands of speculators who had sold land and property in order not to miss out on this exciting new venture.

Among the statutes of the so-called Bubble Act, restricting similar joint stock companies in the future, was the granting of charters to the Royal Exchange Assurance and London Assurance companies prohibiting marine insurance to be conducted by any other business partnership or corporation. But the Act specifically excluded those 'honourable' gentlemen merchants previously prepared to stand 'each for his own part, not for one another' and lay their entire personal wealth on the line, acting as private individuals in order to accept part of a risk in return for part of the premium.

Towards the latter part of the eighteenth century, the establishment known as New Lloyd's Coffee House was opened. This was formed by a breakaway group of customers from the original premises which had also seen the rise of more speculative forms of 'insurance' – the sport of gambling. This new group wanted to concentrate on the interest closest to their hearts, marine insurance, and such was the demand for space in the New Coffee House that further premises were sought and later found in the City's Royal Exchange. A constitution subsequently evolved, so too a committee with regulatory powers. By 1871 a new statute, Lloyd's Act, gave birth to a solid and reliable society which had withstood the ravages of war, famine, and the emergence of the competition from the new insurance companies. And over the next century, the growth and strengthening of the original concept gave way to the Lloyd's of today – where a private individual, or 'name' still is required to put at risk his or her entire personal wealth; personal unlimited liability is the bedrock on which Lloyd's was founded.

It does not always come to that, of course. But someone worth, say, £500,000, who has underwritten only half that amount could lose virtually all his or her estate should calamity strike the insured object – be it a ship, an aeroplane, a car, even a film star's legs.

Becoming one of the near-30,000 'names', or members of Lloyd's, is a relatively simple procedure. The amount of premium income a member may accept is based on a 'means test' with the current minimum standing at £100,000. Next step, having satisfied Lloyd's with a Statement of Means setting out approvable assets, is to hand over a deposit. For someone showing the minimum £100,000 assets, this sum would be £50,000 which is placed on deposit with Lloyd's with the insurers as trustees in the case of property or shares. If the deposit is in cash, then this is held in Lloyd's own deposit account – naturally earning interest, as are the residue assets comprising the 'means-tested' £100,000.

Next step is to find a members' agent to act for them. There is a standard agency agreement setting out the respective rights and conditions for both parties. A Lloyd's members' agency has no direct role in the procedure of underwriting. That agent's responsibility lies in suggesting which syndicates the 'name' should join, delegating that role to a managing agency. In other words, the members' agency is there purely to look after the member's or 'name's' interest, charging a management fee and a percentage of any of that member's profit at the end of each three-year account. The 'second step' managing agency's responsibility is the actual formation of the 370 or so syndicates and the underwriting of each member's risk.

The theory of the whole procedure from an investment point of view is that, while a 'name's' original means-tested money and deposit are untouched and earning a healthy rate of return, he or she can also look forward to an extra profit in the form of insurance premium paid for the amount of risk underwritten on their behalf.

So while we have members' agents to manage the affairs of the 'name', and managing agents skilled in the art of underwriting, and both of which are two separate agencies within Lloyd's, some of the Corporation's firms actually carry out both functions, similar to a firm of stockbrokers which also has a market-making division (something becoming increasingly common since the advent of the Big Bang).

The agency run by Charles St George was just this sort of business. It was called Oakeley Vaughan, based in Fenchurch Street in the City, dealing as managing agents (underwriters) and members' agents, and with a separate insurance-broking company. Lester Piggott was one of St George's most valuable clients. The two men were also very close friends, on and off the track.

When, several years ago, St George made that famous quip about not daring to advise Piggott how to invest his money, it did not tell the whole story. For Piggott did join several Lloyd's syndicates through his friend's Oakeley Vaughan agency. And while Piggott probably made money on some of the deals as a syndicate 'name', he no doubt would quickly like to forget the day he took Oakeley Vaughan's advice to join Syndicate Number 551 or Syndicate Number 420. Both were among those that produced losses totalling millions of pounds and brought a great deal of trouble to Charles St George.

The dashing former Coldstream Guards captain, now in his early 60s, is best known to the racing public as a wealthy owner of top-class horses. A patron of the Henry Cecil stable for more than 17 years, his black with white chevron colours have been carried by such horses as Primera, trained by Cecil's father-in-law Noel Murless, as was the Champion Stakes-winner Lorenzaccio, victor over the mighty Nijinsky. He owned the 1972 Oaks-winner Ginevra and the 1975 St Leger-winner Bruni. In 1973 he won the famous sprint race at York, the Gimcrack Stakes, with Giacometti, and gave the traditional Gimcrack speech in which he far-sightedly called for closed-circuit television in betting shops to produce more revenue for increased prize money – a dream that saw reality in 1987 with the introduction of the SIS satellite broadcasting system of live races beamed to betting offices throughout Britain.

That same year, St George's allegiance to Piggott brought its share of controversy, for as one of the syndicate owing Prix de l'Arc de Triomphe winner Rheingold, he was one of the factions that thought it better if Yves St Martin, France's champion jockey, was replaced on the colt in the Benson and Hedges Gold Cup at York by Piggott. Piggott, who was to have originally ridden Moulton for the late Harry Wragg, jumped off that horse in favour of Rheingold. The race itself provided poetic justice when Moulton won and Rheingold, who went on to win the Arc with Piggott aboard, was third behind runner-up Scottish Rifle. It led to a major row, however, when St Martin complained to the York stewards, who subsequently issued a statement deploring the fact that riding arrangements had been changed at the last minute. Chief shareholder in the colt, Henry Zeisel, said publicly that he was ashamed at the way St Martin had been treated. He claimed he had been outvoted by St George and his partners over St Martin's substitution by Piggott.

More recently St George owned that great horse Ardross who was bought for an undisclosed sum from the estate of the late Paddy Prendergast. The deal, struck on the advice of Cecil and Piggott, was another shrewd investment by St George adding to his reputation with followers of the turf as a rather wise and sporting owner. Ardross was a late-maturing sort who blossomed under Cecil's care at Warren Place where he won eleven of his 14 races for St George and was also beaten by a head by Akiyda in the 1982 Prix de l'Arc de Triomphe. The record included two Ascot Gold Cups, two Yorkshire Cups, the Jockey Club Cup and the Goodwood and Doncaster Cups. For a stayer, Ardross's earnings of £304,000 were a remarkable tally, falling £84,000 short of Shergar's total winnings but a marvellous testament to the skill of Henry Cecil.

Charles Anthony Barbaro St George looks every inch the English gentleman. With his slick-backed grey hair, his panache and charm, the well-dressed and wealthy businessman is seen by racegoers as the epitome of success. In his earlier days he was tagged a leading light in the Mayfair 'Gin and Jag' set. These days, however, he drives a Mercedes with the registration CAB 1. St George was born in Malta, the Baron Zimmerman of St George, of a German father and Maltese mother, later adopting British nationality after spending part of his early education at a military academy in Italy.

Revered as a man with many contacts all over the world, St George acted as a 'half-commission' man in the early days, introducing clients for a percentage of the commission their business would generate with brokers. When he took over the Oakeley Vaughan agency the brokerage side of the business soon had clients from among the world of racing and he was particularly adept at helping to arrange bloodstock insurance on a wide variety of top-class horses.

As business was generated on the underwriting side, St George's high profile in racing and his friendship with Piggott and Cecil helped produce more clients with racing interests and many of the names on Oakeley Vaughan's syndicates were from this sphere.

The St George–Piggott–Cecil friendship goes back many years and their success is intertwined. Cecil's wife, Julie, is godmother to Maureen, elder of the two Piggott daughters. Maureen, a successful horsewoman in her own right as a three-day-event rider, was bridesmaid to Julie when she and Henry married at Newmarket's St Mary's Church in the October of 1966, three years before Cecil began training. St George's connection with the stable goes back to the early days; indeed, in 1971 Cecil saddled his horse, Orosio, to win the Cesarewitch and the following season they won the Group One Premio Roma with Irvine. Of course, whenever the St George colours were carried to success, invariably Piggott would be in the saddle.

When St George is staying at his Newmarket home of Sefton Lodge, the former Jim Joel-owned estate, one of his great pleasures is always to visit the Cecils at Warren Place first thing Sunday morning, and talk racing for a few hours over a bottle of champagne or two. Often he was a constant unannounced visitor at Piggott's home too, sweeping up the drive in the Mercedes, walking in to sit himself down in Piggott's comfortable lounge, his sense of humour delighting in poking harmless fun at his host. Naturally, with Piggott's dry wit, the banter was always exchanged.

St George has many amusing anecdotes to relate about the man who has ridden him so many winners. In fact, in pride of place at St George's former splendid Mayfair home in Brook Street (a house valued at £1 million in 1987) was a portrait of Piggott commissioned from the internationally renowned artist Raymond Skipp, and St George is fond of relating how it took the artist five years to complete the work – he could never pin down Piggott long enough at each sitting.

Married in 1947 to Mary Le Bas of Chobham, Surrey, St George's first union produced two sons: James, who was subsequently to join the board of Oakeley Vaughan, and Mark who also worked for the family firm. St George was married to his second wife, Christine Child, a glamorous showbusiness personality, in fitting style at the Desert Inn, Las Vegas, in 1968, and they have two sons. At one time the couple were widely expected to move into Fort Belvedere, the former home of the Duke of Windsor where, as King Edward VIII, he signed his abdication papers. But some six months after paying £650,000 for the eighteenth-century Berkshire estate where Thames Television filmed most of the *Edward and Mrs Simpson* series, St George sold it at the end of 1980 for a reported £200,000 profit.

While success on the racetrack and deals such as Fort Belvedere reaped their rewards, life, like the racing game itself, was not always going to be so sweet. Indeed, events started to go wrong publicly for the St George family in 1981 as far as their Oakeley Vaughan company was concerned. It was in the September that James, who at 33 was the eldest son and a director of the company, was suspended by Lloyd's for two years with two fellow directors for breaking the Corporation's rules. Although St George called his son's activities a 'technical infringement', the Committee of Lloyd's said the three men had committed acts or defaults discreditable to them as underwriters or otherwise in connection with the business of insurance by failing to comply with established procedures in conducting insurance business at Lloyd's. All three were also barred from holding a directorship or partnership in any underwriting company or broking firm for five years.

When it ultimately became clear that all was not well with Oakeley Vaughan, it was reported that members of several of the syndicates were facing losses of perhaps up to £20 million and the controversy was threatening to become a major embarrassment for Lloyd's. It was some time later that individual members who had lost hundreds of thousands of pounds each began seeking legal advice. By 1985, three names had taken out writs against Oakeley Vaughan and Lloyd's themselves and, three years later, the list of those taking legal action was said to have grown to 47. Lester Piggott was a name in several of the Oakeley Vaughan syndicates but was not among the litigants. Other names included the former champion jockey Joe Mercer, Henry Cooper, and sports promoter Jarvis Astaire.

The writs claimed damages against Oakeley Vaughan for negligence and/or breach of duty for allegedly not supervising the members' affairs in the correct manner. They also claimed an alleged breach of fiduciary duty in failing to disclose the facts and conclusions of a Lloyd's enquiry into St George's suitability to continue as an executive director of Oakeley Vaughan, while a similar writ was taken out against Lloyd's and also one alleging breach of duty by the Corporation itself by failing to disclose the facts of the enquiry into Oakeley Vaughan in 1981. Although some settlements were made with a number of members, by the end of 1988 Oakeley Vaughan faced the threat of legal action by up to 34 names. Creditors at a liquidation hearing in November were also making claims of £2.5 million against the company.

On 23 July 1987, the Oakeley Vaughan company was not among the list of 234 underwriting agents registered with Lloyd's to fulfil a requirement of the new 1982 Lloyd's Act. The Act itself was a result of a lengthy and often critical report into self-regulation at the Corporation by a working party under the chairmanship of Sir Henry Fisher, hence known as the Fisher Report.

As 1988 saw Lloyd's celebrating its 300th anniversary, the institution was attempting to make plans to enter the twenty-first century with a more radical and outward-going review of its operations and attempting to put behind it the likes of the Oakeley Vaughan affair, along with others such as a scandal about an agency called PCW which resulted in 3,000 investors being left with £680 million of insurance losses and in which Lloyd's had to utilise its own market funds to help the stricken names.

Those problems aside, however, there was another force casting more than a casual eye over the establishment. This was the Inland Revenue itself which, armed with new powers under the 1987 Finance Act, was planning a major examination of certain accounting procedures it suspected were possibly being used for tax avoidance.

St George resigned as a director of Oakeley Vaughan's members' agency company on 28 July 1986, having resigned as a director of the broking side the previous June. He said publicly that he was sorry he ever went into the underwriting business. It seemed one of life's ironies that the man with the Midas touch at racing should end up a loser in a completely different sphere.

For Piggott, any losses were taken with the usual stoicism. He had lost money before, noticeably when a member of the syndicates 126 and 127, which were touched by scandal in what became known as the Howden affair. The scandal rocked Lloyd's and the City and prompted a five-year-long enquiry by Scotland Yard's Fraud Squad. But Piggott's personality allows for such occasions; it is a curious mix of independence and introversion. Like his favourite domestic animal, the cat, he prowls, private and totally alone, neither his actions nor demeanour betraying his thoughts. He speaks but there is little communication, no feel to the words that are delivered sparsely, almost shyly. Still, he is in his own world, suspicious, selfish, some might think uncaring. Secretive too; that impenetrable air of mystery spurning intrigue in those around him.

Maybe it was the mystique that led some people to believe Piggott was as good with money as he was with horses, his reputation growing each time a vague story was related with even more vagueness. That was not the case, however. His sorry losses with Lloyd's were not the only times when his monetary aim would prove to be off target.

10. A Fool and His Money

A peculiarity of Lester Piggott's character, perhaps one which provides the greatest paradox of this enigma, is his modesty. Mean, selfish, arrogant have all been labels stuck on the man from time to time, and often with a good deal of justification. While his judgement of such equine complexities as pace, distance, ability, motivation and response has, only rarely, been brought into question, the same cannot be said about his measure of humans. With amazing consistency Piggott has underestimated the effect he has had, not only on his fellow professionals and the racing public, but also on the millions of ordinary people to whom the man, Lester Piggott, has become a household name.

On racetracks throughout the world he has repeatedly been surprised, sometimes with an inward chuckle of delight, that thousands of people had turned up with the specific purpose of watching the great Lester Piggott in action. Whether it has been the élite tracks like California's Santa Anita, or the most basic surroundings of the cliff-top Les Landes in the Channel Island of Jersey, Piggott's reaction to the neck-straining crowds, the autograph-hunters and the well-wishers, has sometimes been one of incredulity: surely all these people haven't come to see me?

Yet this is, despite the constant media attention, one of the longest-running love–hate relationships of the turf, the glorification in print, often the hype, and much of it without his co-operation and to his subsequent embarrassment when reading about himself in superlatives that he considered must have applied to someone else.

Picture him in New York, staying at a Fifth Avenue hotel, one of those 'luxury' high-rise buildings where, inside, the smell of money from the gold jewellery, the Rolex watches and the hand-made Gucci shoes mingles in the air with wafts of expensive French cologne. This might be one of *the* places to stay in Manhattan but wealth does not mean Piggott has not got to queue for the lifts and cram inside like everyone else. It's the type of hotel where the cocktail waiter, resplendent in beautifully tailored morning suit, rushes after you because there is only a 10 per cent tip left on his plate instead of the 15 per cent going-rate.

Piggott is here to ride with the All Star Jockeys, Jimmy Lindley's team of top international jockeys, against a squad of home-based riders in a series of races at the Meadowlands track across the Hudson River and into New Jersey. It might be New York but Piggott's routine is the same wherever he goes. After a brunch-style press conference where Piggott casts anxious eyes on ways to escape from a posse of journalists, he returns to his hotel for an afternoon nap, a dish or two of his favourite ice-cream ordered from room service. There is a special dinner that night at the exclusive Tavern on the Green Restaurant in Central Park, one where Willie Carson, Greville Starkey and Joe Mercer join in the fun and have plenty of laughs with their generous hosts. But not Piggott. He has had enough of the palaver and is back in his hotel room, an early night on the cards.

Come race-night and the loner is still in his shell, a few muttered words when introductions are made to various officials, an almost coy smile for some of the American jocks; then he is alone once more, changing quietly in a corner of the jockeys' room, going through the same old routine, the elastic bands snapped tight around the cuffs of his silks, the thwack of his crop against skin-soft newly polished riding boots.

He is not happy with the mounts allotted him in a pre-race draw, but there is little he can do now except go out and do his best. Pressmen wander around the jockeys' room, chatting, taking notes, just as they also do in France but are forbidden to do in Britain. No one bothers Piggott. He is in his own world, quiet; the contemplative with only the purpose of winning on his mind. Out on the floodlit track Piggott canters his mount past the post as the public address system reveals to the expectant crowd that this is the man they call the maestro back in Britain. He is impervious to the cheers as, without a change in the set face, he guides his horse towards the starting gate accompanied by a pony outrider. Safely ensconced in the starting stalls – Piggott likes the roomier US version ever since that horrific accident at Epsom when Windsor Boy scraped underneath the stalls and broke out with him aboard – and with a handler for each horse leaning into the stall to prevent horses playing up, the field is sent on its way by the ringing bell synonymous with American tracks.

All is not well with Piggott's horse during the race, nor in two subsequent events. And the stinging dirt as his mount trails the field adds a painfully red-blotched face to the insult of not being placed in any of the races.

But it's all for the crack, a well paid trip away from the close season at home. Now maybe down to Mexico, the Caribbean, Florida, and on to Los Angeles and Australia, Hong Kong, a winter away in the sun getting paid for what he likes best. A working holiday is what Lester Piggott, the jockey, preferred to any other.

Throughout his career, Piggott managed to ride in no fewer than 32 different countries outside Britain, kicking home more than 800 winners from Argentina to Greece, Singapore to Trinidad.

And, wherever he went, always the cheering crowds, the attention and admiration, the back-slappers and the autograph-hunters all signalling to virtually everyone but himself that the name of Lester Piggott conjured its very own special type of magic.

Off the track Piggott's judgement of certain people could be said to have been anything but circumspect. One such man, with whom Piggott had an association lasting several years, was called Sam Bernard. It was another 'friendship' that was going to cost Piggott dear, not only in lost credibility but, more painfully to him, hard cash. The relationship with Bernard eventually led to another one of Piggott's loss-making business deals, one that also involved champion jockey Steve Cauthen in something that resembled a far-fetched film script. It was the day they lost a sum of money approaching £200,000 between them in a billion-dollar oil deal that never came off.

Bernard is an interesting character – at least to the police who know him quite well. A national newspaper once described the jockey-sized former stable lad as champagne-swilling Slippery Sam, an ex-bankrupt well known in racing circles as a punter who does not pay his gambling debts. They were not far wrong. The grey-haired punter, known to professionals as a heavy gambler, was warned off by Tattersalls' Committee. His daughter, Kitty, who also became embroiled in the oil deal fiasco, was fined £150 by the Jockey Club's disciplinary committee in June 1986 for acting as a nominee owner of a horse called Leodegrance – a breach of Rule 113.

The fact that Bernard had a reputation as a 'wheeler-dealer' and as a big punter on and off the track did not deter Piggott from maintaining his association with a man who had also been given an 18-month suspended prison sentence for trading while being an undischarged bankrupt.

Born in 1923 in Uxbridge, Middlesex, Bernard has had a chequered career since leaving school at the age of 14. There was a succession of jobs before war broke out; he worked for the family fur business for the first 18 months before trying spells in a solicitor's office and even as a stable lad in a racing stable. Acquaintances of Bernard were often taken by the talk of his long friendship with Piggott and how well he knew Steve Cauthen. Ensconced in his favourite haunt, London's Hilton Hotel in Park Lane, and expansive with the champagne, Bernard would fix his hawk-like eyes almost in a stare, his narrow features creasing into a smile and bringing a hint of colour to the pale cheeks as he talked of his past businesses, the property-developing, his knowledge of the fur trade, his entrepreneurial skill in the world of business.

He never talked about his early life, nor his war record, which is just as well. After being drafted into the Suffolk Regiment when he was 17 in the July of 1940, some ten months after the start of the Second World War, he was subsequently transferred to the Royal Armoured Corps to serve as a trooper. He did not much care for the life.

While the Allied troops were preparing for the invasion of Europe in the May of 1944, Bernard decided to get out while the going was good. He deserted. And for almost two years, while his Army pals were keeping their heads down on the battlefields of Europe, Bernard was lying low in various locations throughout Britain, hiding from the authorities and the Military Police. So successful was he that he was absent until giving himself up in the April of 1946, finally being discharged from the Army six months later.

Bernard, back in Civvy Street, then tried his hand at working for his brother Raphael before spells as a travelling furrier and as a commission agent in Scotland. He was back in trouble a year or two later, however, when he was sent to prison for two years on several charges ranging from theft, conspiracy to defraud and conspiracy to break and enter. By the time he was in his mid-30s he still had not mended his ways and was sentenced to another two-year jail stretch on several counts: obtaining two amounts of money and a motor car by false pretences.

Throughout the late Sixties and the early Seventies things took a turn for the better – at least enough to allow him more of a finer lifestyle and he became a director of several companies, some in the construction business. It was enough for him to live in a well furnished apartment in the fashionable district of Clifton in Bristol with his wife and daughter, Catherine, or Kitty to her friends. But by 1972 business took a turn for the worse and bankruptcy loomed. That same year Bernard was made an undischarged bankrupt with the usual proviso that he was not allowed to trade for ten years.

Such technicalities did not stop Bernard, however, and in 1979, having ignored the law of bankruptcy, he was up in court once more – this time Bristol Magistrates' Court – and was given an 18-month jail sentence, suspended, for being concerned with a company while an undischarged bankrupt. He was also ordered not to be involved in any capacity with any company for a further five years.

Throughout their association, Piggott and Bernard could some-times be seen having a drink together at the Hilton Hotel or at another one of Bernard's favourite places, Scotts, the well known seafood restaurant near Grosvenor Square in Mayfair and almost next door to the Adam's Row apartment where Piggott stayed when he was in London on business and from where he conducted some of his many deals. Piggott was not the only jockey with whom Bernard claimed a friendship. Steve Cauthen, the young man the American press labelled The Kid, and who took British racing by storm, becoming champion jockey five years after leaving the US at the age of 19, was soon latched on to by Bernard and they were also seen at Scotts shunning the company of other racing folk to dine together, deep in conversation. However impressionable the young Cauthen might have appeared in his early days in Britain, though, it must be said that he was a millionaire already and was practically an 'old hand' at the pitfalls of racing's hangers-on. He also arrived by Concorde first-class not, as the saying goes, on a banana boat. The fact is that Cauthen might have developed weight problems and other complications for a short time in his British career, but the American is basically only interested in one thing – riding winners, the job for which he is paid extremely well. Correspondingly, he was his usual courteous self when in Bernard's company as he is with most racing people.

Cauthen's trust in Bernard and his daughter was subsequently proved to have been misplaced, however, when he and Piggott became embroiled in the oil money-making deal that proved to be a costly flop. At least that was the way Cauthen viewed the situation. For, after losing close on £100,000, the American crossed the names of Kitty and her father off his Christmas card list. And if Cauthen ever has trouble sleeping at night in his Newmarket home (even after reading a little of his two bedside books, the Bible, and the sportsman's 'bible', *Eat to Win*) then it might be because he still grimaces at how he handed over all that money and has not seen a cent of it since.

It was not much more than a year after Bernard was given the 18-month suspended sentence for his trading-while-bankrupt offence that he became involved in the international oil deal. Using Piggott's name and his friendship with the top jockey, he acted as a 'salesman' for a company called Royal Incorporated. The plan was simple enough; the firm was going to buy 35 million barrels of crude oil from the tiny Gulf state of Abu Dhabi at a price of $25 a barrel, then sell the oil at a profit of a dollar a barrel. Bernard hawked the scheme around to various people on the racing circuit. Television racing commentator Jimmy Lindley was approached, but he had the foresight to ask the advice of a former oil man. Lindley was told to steer well clear of the deal.

For Piggott and many others, though, the scheme sucked them in and left them high and dry. Piggott was often entering into one deal or another, then seeking advice when it was too late. This was one of the weaknesses of Piggott the wheeler-dealer. His obstinacy was again going to take its toll.

Bernard and Kitty were introduced to a number of racing people and businessmen and women and persuaded some of them to put up varying amounts of money – paid to Bernard or his daughter in cash – in return for a stake in the deal. One businessman from Bristol who put around £200,000 into the scheme was told by the Bernards that he could expect a minimum profit of $1 million.

Lester Piggott put up £96,000 and Cauthen £100,000, it was subsequently said in court. Piggott was also a witness when one agreement for the deal, which went so far as to claim that a high-ranking member of the Saudi Royal family, Prince Bandar Bin Faisal Bin Saud, was involved, was signed at the Hilton Hotel. Some deals were transacted in various parts of Europe. In Hamburg, an international businesswoman, used to high-flying transactions and with a reputation as an astute negotiator, parted with £1 million.

Some of the money paid over to the Bernards was in the form of loans in the hope that the deal could be set up. A London solicitor sent out letters acknowledging receipt of the money for shares in the Royal Incorporated company. This was the solicitor who, a year earlier, had represented Sam Bernard in his Bristol Magistrates' Court hearing for trading while bankrupt when Bernard was banned from dealing in any capacity with any company for a further five years.

In one meeting with a prospective client, Bernard represented himself as a high-powered businessman, well connected in the City, and a very close friend of Lester Piggott. Another client who did put his money into the deal, was of the opinion that anything Piggott backed would be a winner – he had heard of the jockey's legendary prowess as a shrewd investor. Bernard looked the part too; smartly dressed in sober business suits, he chose the best places to meet his clients and drove to the venues in his newly acquired silver-grey Mercedes sports car.

Four South Africans are believed to have lost several million pounds after pouring their money into the get-rich scheme. The well-known and respected Yorkshire bookmaker and racehorse owner Colin Webster, a familiar sight as an on-course bookie and owner of a string of betting shops in the Leeds and Halifax areas, also heard of the deal. He became so interested that he parted with £200,000 and has not seen a penny of it since.

There is also evidence of similar fund-raising activities in Spain and Australia – all with the same results.

Punters in the scheme were shown official-looking documents. It all seemed too good to be true, but that, unfortunately for those investors, was how it turned out in the end. After more than two years when no oil and none of the investors' money was forthcoming, the painful truth dawned – the 'scheme' had collapsed. Most of those involved were glad by then to forget about it, to write it off as a bad experience. Most were wealthy people. Certainly, Piggott and Cauthen could afford to lose that much even if it did hurt. For Piggott, despite his experience with finance, the years of losses and gains on the Stock Exchange and as a member of Lloyd's, it was a salutory lesson that followed the old maxim: a fool and his money are soon parted.

After the whole deal folded, no one wanted to take any action. After all, who wanted to own up to being a fool? All except one man, however: the Bristol-based businessman. He was furious and so he decided to sue Kitty Bernard for the return of some of his money. It was the March of 1987 before the case came to court; the hearing was one of the most bizarre ever heard before Bristol High Court.

Before the case was heard, Kitty Bernard, who subsequently moved with her father from Kintbury, near Lambourn, into a luxury apartment in Redcliffe Mews, Earls Court, London, was ordered to pay the sum of £10,000 into the court – a usual practice. Up to that point and while all the briefings had been going on with solicitors and barristers, the work that was to form the basis of her defence, Kitty had been on Legal Aid. The prospect of having to pay £10,000 into court up-front upset her so much that she appealed against the amount and this was heard by the High Court judge Sir Neil Lawson in chambers at the Law Courts, London. He threw out her appeal and registered his disgust with the fact that, up to this point, Kitty had been receiving the Legal Aid – at the taxpayers' expense.

Sam Bernard was never asked to appear at the Bristol High Court hearing, nor did he offer to give evidence in support of his daughter who was being sued for the sum of £75,000. In a separate action against Bernard's solicitor, who was being sued for a similar amount, the case never reached the court because the solicitor made an out-of-court settlement of £50,000 plus costs. When the Bristol High Court hearing finally got under way, the solicitor, who was later the subject of a complaint to the Law Society, was out of the country.

During the case, which was to last over three weeks, and which was held before Mr Justice Henry, Kitty, said to be unemployed, and who told the court she was kept by her father, admitted that she played a secondary role to that of Sam Bernard. She was used as a 'front' for her father's activities, the court heard. It was because of this situation that Kitty was the person who was being sued for the return of the money, not her father who was, of course, still a bankrupt. Although Bernard's part in the scheme was not fully explained, the judge at one stage said that, by 1983, Bernard himself had misgivings that the deal between Royal Incorporated and an Arab businessman would actually go ahead.

However, it was Bernard who had sought the funds to sponsor the deal and, in return for several sums of cash paid in the form of loans, the Bristol businessman received from Bernard's solicitor two certificates which he was told were valuable documents and, for safety, would be better lodged with his bank. Each was a 'share' in Royal Incorporated, a company registered in Panama, which was said to represent a sum of $1 million.

The court was told that Piggott had become involved in the deal at an early stage. Piggott was a witness to the signing of one particular agreement at the Hilton Hotel in the April of 1980 while Cauthen parted with his cash two years later. Some of the negotiations also took place at Kempton Park Racecourse over a bottle of champagne in the members' bar. The Bristol businessman's counsel, Mr Nigel Hamilton, QC, also told the court that Cauthen had received a letter from the solicitor in the form of a receipt for his £100,000 and specifying that he now owned one share in Royal Incorporated. But at least one document relating to the oil contracts and issued to those seeking to buy the oil was a forgery.

Kitty Bernard herself told the judge that her father had made use of her own bank account ever since 1975, putting in money for her and for himself. She said that everyone involved in the oil deal seemed to be dreamers, and, to her, the whole scheme was just like fairyland – it was all wishful thinking, she said.

At one point in the proceedings, Mr Justice Henry threatened to imprison four bank managers for contempt of court. The incident arose after the trial had lasted a week and when the four managers had failed to appear in the courtroom. Two of the men, Bristol branch managers of the National Westminster Bank, were given half an hour to present themselves before the judge or face the threat of jail. Two other managers, from the same bank's London headquarters, were given until the following day to appear. All four men had failed to answer a subpoena to give the court details of Kitty's bank account. In the end the managers saved themselves the embarrassment of spending some time behind bars and duly made their appearances. One of the details that emerged about the unemployed Kitty's account was that, by 1983, she had an overdraft which had risen to almost £80,000.

The outcome to the trial was that the Bristol businessman was awarded the £75,000 against Kitty plus costs. The total bill facing Kitty Bernard was in the region of £102,000. After the case it was revealed that there was no evidence that the oil even existed. The Abu Dhabi National Oil Corporation had stated quite categorically that such a deal, even if rights to buy the oil had been in existence, would never have been allowed.

Other facts also came to light; Colin Webster, the Yorkshire-based bookmaker, was one of the men who hired a private investigator to keep a watch on Bernard after proof of the oil contracts had been requested. At one stage, Bernard had, under pressure from an investor, offered to make a trip to Geneva to obtain proof of the scheme. But the private detective reported that Bernard had driven his Mercedes to London where he spent the weekend, pretending that he had made the visit to Switzerland.

By the September of 1987, when the man who won the case against Kitty had still not received any of the damages awarded to him, it was revealed that Kitty had filed for her own bankruptcy – it looked highly unlikely he would receive anything. Some 18 months later, he and the other main creditor, NatWest Bank, had still not heard when Kitty's bankruptcy hearing would be heard. It was also discovered that the solicitor involved in the deal on Sam Bernard's behalf, had decided to retire from practising. He now lives abroad.

The whole shambles was a painful lesson to all. What was particularly mysterious and sinister about the episode, though, was the fact that no one had been able to discover just where all that money went. For Lester Piggott it was a punt with Sam Bernard that never came off. In racing parlance, it was another losing bet. And Piggott never liked to tell the world about things like that.

11. The Grudge Game

Despite Jockey Club rules to the contrary, some jockeys do have a bet on the horses. It is all a very secretive affair, of course, but there has been too much said by too many people who do know the score for it to be otherwise. Denials that it happens have never been issued by the racing authorities. Racing might be a somewhat insular sport, or business these days, but it would be totally unrealistic for anyone in authority to stand up and claim that horseracing is 100 per cent straight. Proving that some jockeys bet is not easy, however. If it were, there would have been far more cases than the odd ones that occasionally come to light; the claims of bribery, jockeys pulling horses, or receiving money for information. Like any institution comprising the human being, be it the police, the law or racing, there is bound to be corruption of one sort or another. This is not only a cliché, but a fact of life.

Racing's top detective, Peter Smiles, head of Racecourse Security Services, has admitted that up to 20 or so races a year are 'for the boys' or, in other words, fixed. Taking the top figure of 20, it represents a percentage of 0.35 of the total number of around 5,600 races run in Britain each year.

Those jockeys who bet usually do so through friends or relatives, making it virtually impossible for the authorities to prove, unless, as has happened in the past, a particular friendship is broken and someone wants to spill the beans. Friends of jockeys who bet for them and themselves are known in the business as that rider's 'punter'. Naturally, the shrewd jockey gamblers do not part with any of their own hard-earned cash. They prefer to steer the punter in the right direction and gain their remuneration by being on a percentage of the winnings, or 'odds' as it is known.

That certain jockeys have in the past, quite openly, associated or indeed made firm friendships with known heavy gamblers cannot be viewed as a healthy situation no matter how innocent the friendship or in whatever other direction it might lie. In a way it is akin to the policeman having a personal friendship with a known criminal – big punters who are known to be bad settlers or have perhaps been warned off the racecourse must surely at least create the suspicion that their association with a jockey is not reputable.

Of course, it could be argued that if such friendships or associations are known publicly – or at least to those in racing including the Racecourse Security Services – then that is a better situation than driving such an association 'underground'. A jockey often seen in the company of a punter known to have a bad betting 'record' or who has been warned off might be taken aside and given a quiet unofficial word by an RSS officer, but that would not stop the two people resorting to association in private – or by telephone.

However, in these days of sophisticated electronic bugging equipment, the easy access of telephone recording machines, talking on the telephone about anything to do with horses is a dangerous business for a jockey with a known punter. Even Lester Piggott, to his dismay, has been made aware of that.

Like other jockeys Piggott has found himself the subject of lurid allegations about betting rings. He has always vigorously denied these and no such charge has ever been proved against him. Not long after the start of Piggott's last season in the saddle, the May of 1985, came a Racecourse Security Services enquiry into allegations made in court proceedings to which Piggott was not a party, that Piggott was one of several jockeys in receipt of cash and cheques from a wealthy Indian industrialist in exchange for information regarding certain horses. The claims came to light at the South London Southwark Crown Court when a secretary to former Henry Cecil-owner Jagdish Prasad Goenka was acquitted of stealing cheques sent to her boss from British bookmakers. The secretary said she and the London office manager passed on to Goenka occasional recommendations and advice on various races. The office manager added that some of the horses won, and some lost. He claimed that the information was precise, specifying the name of the horse, the time and in what race it was running. Payments varying between £1,000 and £2,000 were said to have been made to various jockeys over a three-year period.

The Jockey Club's rules do not preclude jockeys accepting 'presents' from owners although there is a very thin line, a totally grey area, between a grateful owner, delighted at a jockey's skilful riding of his horse to win a race, and rewarding the jockey accordingly whether it be cash, cheque, a case of champagne or the latest colour teletext television set, and the owner who does similarly because that jockey has told him to back another horse in the race or, indeed, another horse in a different race.

In the latter case, it could be argued that, had the 'present' been made before the race, in other words as an inducement, then it could have affected the jockey's riding of the horse. Naturally, that would be a total transgression of the rules if such a situation could be proven. The trouble is that it cannot in the majority of cases.

After the Southwark Crown Court allegations, the matter was investigated by Racecourse Security Services' enquiry team over a period of several weeks. However, they had great difficulty in tracing the people who made the allegations – the secretary could not be found, and the office manager would allow contact only through his solicitor and no evidence was forthcoming. Piggott, when seen by RSS officers, denied the allegations vigorously.

On the whole question of jockeys gambling or passing on information, it puzzles me why anyone should want to ask, let alone pay, any rider of a racehorse for 'privileged' information. Jockeys are notoriously poor tipsters anyway and, as someone in regular contact with Piggott as the writer of his column for a national newspaper, I found that he was as bad as most if not worse – many of the horses he tipped to the newspaper's readers are 'still running'.

During the run-up to the Piggott trial at Ipswich Crown Court in the October of 1987, and as though Piggott did not have enough on his mind, it was announced that Peter Smiles and his Racecourse Security Services officers had launched a separate investigation into new allegations about Piggott as a punter.

Smiles and his team were in possession of a tape recording of conversations about betting, said to be between Piggott and a one-time gambler, the late Maurice Pitts. The tape had been handed over by the *Sunday People* following an exclusive by their top investigative reporter Brian Radford, the former assistant editor of the *Sporting Life* and the man who originally broke the Piggott–Cecil 'Cash Payments Plea' story.

To quote Daniel Defoe's *Robinson Crusoe*: 'In trouble to be troubled is to have your trouble doubled.' True to form, however, Piggott was showing no outward signs of being worried by the events around him. At the races and in true unflappable style he seemed his usual self whenever he had a runner to be saddled. There was still that intent walk, the shy smile of acknowledgement to acquaintances outside the weighing room, otherwise the face set just as it was through all those trying big-race preliminaries when the racing world could only guess at whatever emotion lurked behind the unflinching façade.

It was at this time, too, that another investigation featuring the name of Lester Piggott was in progress. The Stock Exchange, that hallowed institution through which Piggott had invested some of his money, were investigating the mysterious share-price plunge of the betting-to-hotels group Ladbroke which, in one day alone, wiped £130 million off the company's value.

The trouble started on Friday 1 May. Several rumours which had been circulating for some time in Fleet Street were finally picked up in the City. One stockbroker with links to some of the City's big institutional investors telephoned his racing contacts and decided he did not like what he heard. Even at this early stage the stories being bandied around were of a sensational, far-fetched (and unsubstantiated) nature. Correspondingly, the broker began advising clients to offload some of their holdings in Ladbroke shares which were then standing at the 448p mark. Now the stock market itself was going through a fairly volatile time. Much worse would come in the famous October crash, of course, but the market was still feeling the shockwaves from the Guinness affair while the General Election was on the horizon and there were conflicting views about Britain's ability to reduce unemployment and hold down inflation.

Against all this background, the stock market, which is prone to fluctuation on two of its investors' biggest motivations, fear and greed, did not need much urging to reflect a lack of confidence in any of a number of shares. By the close of business on the Friday night, Ladbroke share price had fallen to 441p, wiping approximately £25 million off the company's value.

With the weekend to fan the flames of suspicion over the rumours (and Monday's opening business failing to extinguish those fears), Tuesday saw the price slip dramatically to 404p, reducing the company by a further £130 million. By now, the Chinese whisper syndrome had taken over and many of the rumours, like Pinocchio's nose, had grown to absurd proportions.

By the Wednesday of 6 May, Ladbroke shares, now in a headlong tumble, fell to 386p, wiping another £70 million off the company. By the following midday the rumours abated and the shares staged a small rally which saw their price climb back to 403p. It was on the Friday that the Stock Exchange itself stepped in and announced they were going to hold an enquiry into the whole affair.

Dealing in Ladbroke shares had been running at about five times the normal rate. In four days almost 27 million shares had been traded, a most unusual level of activity prompted by a bizarre set of circumstances. While the Stock Exchange were announcing their own investigation – at the instigation of Ladbroke's financial advisers, Charterhouse Bank – Stein himself swung into action. Having taken counsel's advice, Stein and his board agreed to apply to the High Court for a writ against a business rival, the Extel Group, well known to punters as the company who send racecourse commentaries to betting shops throughout the country.

In a six-point writ, Ladbroke accused Extel of being the emanators of the rumours. Extel is a rival of a Ladbroke part-owned company, Satellite Information Services, which had been formed to beam by satellite live races to closed-circuit television sets in whichever of Britain's 10,000 betting shops wanted to pay for the service. In fact, the day of the Ladbroke share price's biggest fall coincided with SIS's first transmission from Chester Racecourse. Ladbroke's partners in SIS are the two other major bookmakers, Corals (part of Bass), and the William Hill/Mecca partnership (owned by Grand Metropolitan). Extel had been one of the companies vying for the contract to supply betting shops with satellite television before the racing authorities decided to award the rights to SIS.

Before the writ was heard, Extel completely denied the allegations that they had started the rumours. They stated their intention to strenuously defend any legal proceedings which Ladbroke might take against them. In the meantime, Ladbroke's financial advisers called on the Stock Exchange to hold an enquiry.

By the time Ladbroke's writ against Extel reached the court –
three weeks after the initial share-price plunge – the shares were
trading a little more steadily at 416p but still way down on their
initial 448p. The writ itself covered six rumours that Ladbroke
were seeking to restrain Extel from publishing or causing to be
published. The rumours were:

That Ladbroke were improperly using SIS to further their
own financial interests and have, in consequence, caused or
contributed to the investigation of SIS by the Office of Fair
Trading; that Ladbroke are culpably involved in a major tax
scandal; that Ladbroke have an improper and/or unlawful relationship with a major racing figure (Lester Piggott); that Ladbroke
have suffered a substantial loss by reason of a Scottish betting
coup; that Cyril Stein has resigned or is about to resign; and
that Ladbroke's merchant bankers have resigned or are about to
resign.

In the hearing in chambers before High Court judge Mr Justice
Leggatt, however, it was found that Ladbroke had failed to show that
there was any evidence capable of supporting the allegation that
Extel was the author of the rumours. Mr Justice Leggatt, therefore,
awarded costs to Extel and threw out Ladbroke's application for an
interim injunction. Both sides claimed moral victories after the
hearing. Ladbroke made a statement to the effect that the judge, in
dismissing the injunction, had made it clear that at no time in the
proceedings was there any suggestion that the rumours had any
foundation – subsequent events were to prove Ladbroke right. But
according to Extel's interpretation of the judgment, Mr Justice
Leggatt had said, in dismissing the application, that Ladbroke had
failed to show there was any evidence capable of supporting the
allegation that Extel were the authors of the rumours.

The judge's consideration, of course, was not really whether
the rumours had any foundation or not, but to rule on the claim
that it was Extel who had started them. On the Ladbroke claim
that Extel had suggested Ladbroke were using SIS to further their
own financial interests and had caused an Office of Fair Trading
investigation into SIS, Extel claimed the judge had said it was not
worth the paper it was written on.

The fact was that, by the autumn of 1987, the Office of Fair
Trading, who had considered it necessary to look into the role
of SIS over the question of restricted practices, concluded that it

was not necessary for the matter to be referred to the Restrictive Practices Court.

When Britain's 'Big Four' bookmakers got together to form Satellite Information Services, there was a scenario mentioned in racing circles where small bookmakers, unable to afford the direct satellite television service to their shops, might therefore suffer a lack of business from punters who preferred to patronise betting shops with the service. The scenario envisages those small shops perhaps then being run down to the extent that they are forced out of business, becoming easy prey to one of the SIS 'Big Four' who would step in and buy the shop much more cheaply than before.

Such a scenario is pure speculation, however. And, as the now three big bookmaking groups are themselves in direct competition with each other, it is difficult to envisage just how they would 'share' the vulnerable betting shops between them.

Ladbroke have come a long way since the firm was founded in 1902 and, until the Stein family took control in 1956, was known as Ladbroke of Mayfair, credit bookmakers to aristocrats and blue-bloods of Britain. It was Cyril Stein's Uncle Max, then an on-course bookmaker, who led the £200,000 buy-out of proprietor Arthur Bendir's original company. Cyril Stein's father, Jack, ran the London and Provincial Sporting News Agency, known to the betting trade as the 'blower', and for which Cyril worked until giving up on his father's ambition of him becoming an accountant and going to work on-course for Uncle Max. After the Ladbroke takeover, Cyril was brought in to look after the Mayfair shop. It was like something out of Dickens; a row of over a dozen private phone booths for the clerks to take their clients' confidential bets, more clerks perched on high-backed stools. All that seemed to be missing to this apparent antiquity were the quill pens for recording the bets.

Stein, who describes himself in his younger days as an 'impatient bastard' felt he had to centralise the business, expand its base and pitch it into the approaching Sixties on a firm footing. When betting shops and cash betting were legalised in 1960, Stein and his colleagues began to realise that the business of the common man being able to get his daily fix of excitement by walking into a 'turf accountant's' shop and depositing his few shillings was going to be very big indeed. Although at first he felt he still wanted to work within the parameters of the 'well-heeled' – 'we let Hill's take the 5s and 10s bets' – Ladbroke moved inch by inch down the social ladder until it emerged as a firm of bookmakers prepared to take bets of any size, big or small, from anyone, blue blooded – or merely red.

There were plenty of mistakes along the way. He blamed himself for not getting into cash betting two or three years earlier than they did. Ladbroke also ran into trouble with its fixed-odds betting on football matches in those early days. That side of the business boomed at first and, when the 1963–4 record profits of over £1 million were announced, the fixed-odds side had contributed £600,000 of that total. But when the government suddenly announced they were imposing a 25 per cent levy on all fixed-odds betting, the future did not look too bright. If there was one thing in his favour, the 'impatient bastard' Stein did not like messing about. It was a time to look and march forward. They dropped the football fixed-odds, concentrating instead on expanding their chain of betting shops and credit betting accounts, with horseracing as the chief earner.

Stein might not have made it as an accountant but when he took Ladbroke by the scruff of the neck and turned it into the beginnings of a profitable and expanding empire he was glad his impatience had got the better of him. He liked to consider the company as part of the entertainment or, as it is now called, the leisure business – early doubts about the moral responsibility of being in the betting industry were cast aside.

So what better partner with which to join forces but the hotel trade. He once said he would not be happy until he owned a 100-bedroomed hotel in the centre of London. Not only would his group do that, but they would, just months after their share-price plunge in 1987, pay a billion dollars for 91 hotels belonging to the Hilton International consortium.

Moving into the hotel and casino business as long ago as 1963 when Ladbroke took a stake in Malta's Dragonara Palace Hotel – with a casino concession already granted from the Maltese government – the company also took on board bingo halls, holidays, property investment and a chain of sportswear shops.

The rise to the top is never easy, though. Stein found that out when, in 1979, and with almost catastrophic results, Ladbroke lost their licences to operate three casinos which were then contributing something like £25 million a year to the group's profits. It was a traumatic time for Stein, his board, and the company's share-holders. At one time it seemed touch and go whether Stein would stay as Ladbroke's chairman – or be forced to resign.

But as if to show that the life of business can be every bit as much subject to the whim of fate and fortune as the racing game itself, Stein, who has admitted to friends that he has lost tens of thousands of pounds backing horses, steered Ladbroke into calmer seas, so much so that in the company's financial year ending in December 1987, pre-tax profits were up by 58 per cent to a record £160 million. With the threat of a Monopolies Commission probe into SIS lifted, and with Ladbroke looking to off-track betting ventures in the US, the future was indeed promising even better profits.

By the time those results were published in March 1988, no substance to any of the rumours had materialised. In the same month, the details of the Stock Exchange's confidential investiga-tion into the share-price collapse were handed over to Ladbroke. The enquiry had lasted almost ten months, partly because Stock Exchange investigators had met with a conspiracy of silence in trying to question members of the racing fraternity, but it concluded that an 'embittered' racing professional with a grudge against Piggott and Cyril Stein had been responsible for spreading the malicious and damaging allegations. That announcement was expected to surprise many City observers who had considered the rumours to have been mischievously generated from within the financial community itself. Ladbroke, it was said, were not told the name of the culprit by the Stock Exchange, merely that he was a *Porridge* character – referring to the popular television comedy series about life in prison.

What the report did not state, however, was that the numerous rumours emanated from the fact that Melvyn Walters was doing the rounds of Fleet Street once more with allegations involving Piggott. No one took up his offer.

When unsubstantiated rumours can knock £225 million off a leading company's shares in a week, it is no wonder that thousands of ordinary punters would rather put their money on the favourite in a novice chase running in the mud at Fontwell on a wet Wednesday afternoon.

With Ladbroke shrugging off any effects of the dreaded 'rumour

th his first winner already behind him, the 12-year-old Lester Piggott catches up on the form watched by
father, Keith, and mother, Iris.

◄ The first of Piggott's nine Derby winners – Never Say Die in 1954 – when he was 18 years old.

▼ Royal delight: Her Majesty the Queen leads in her 1957 Oaks winner Carrozza ridden by the 21-year-old Piggott.

ruary 22, 1960: Lester and Susan at their wedding.

Piggott with racing magnate Robert Sangster.

▲ The honour: Piggott receives a top jockey award from the Queen at Royal Ascot.

◄ Trainer Henry Cecil greets another Royal Ascot winner.

► Piggott arriving at Newmarket Magistrates Court for another hearing after his arrest in December, 1986.

◄ The humiliation as a handcuffed Pigg is led away to prison after his trial.

Piggott's long-time friend Charles St.
orge, with his family.

usan Piggott took over Lester's training
ce when he was sent to Highpoint.

Freed: Piggott with Susan's pony Pepe on the day of his release from Highpoint.

affair', it was announced at the end of March that the group had been named the most respected leisure company in the United Kingdom. An opinion poll of more than 1,000 industry and financial experts placed Ladbroke at the head of all UK leisure companies and seventeenth overall of all the United Kingdom's most respected companies.

12. The Raid on Eve Lodge

By January 1986, Customs investigators from the 'C' team were satisfied they had obtained enough information on the ostensible discrepancies in Lester Piggott's accounts, through his VAT returns and checks on the likely income he had received from riding fees, that they decided the time had come to take a more direct and harder line; the hit men would carry out a 'knock'. And so, on the dull, cold and rainy morning of Thursday 30 January, eight 'C' team officers were assigned to raid Piggott's Newmarket home.

A little while earlier, around 70 officers from several Customs investigation divisions had joined with the 'C' team in attending a London briefing by senior investigators. Inland Revenue officers who had been liaising with the Customs throughout the past twelve months were invited and they too heard details of the state of the enquiry so far, its aims, and how they would go about achieving them. Some of the officers present were old hands at the game; seasoned operators with many top VAT and drug busts under their belts. But even the most hardened had to allow for a flutter of excitement as the story unfolded before them. For it was not every day that someone as famous as Lester Piggott was their Number One target – nor for the others soon to be in the Customs net like Henry Cecil and a dozen other élite names in the world of racing.

Driving unmarked cars, the 'C' team officers met at Newmarket and made their way to Piggott's ranch-style bungalow on Hamilton Road. It was precisely 7.40 a.m. when they knocked on the door of the world's most famous sportsman, the man many of them had only ever read about. Susan Piggott answered the door; Piggott himself was out and would not be back until later that afternoon.

The officers were armed with an access order which had been granted by a magistrate the previous day enabling them to search the Piggott household from top to bottom. Consequently, they were invited in.

After being given tea by Susan the officers explained the situation and shortly afterwards began the task of searching the premises. Working quickly and efficiently with a precision born of past experience, the officers started with the most obvious files and documents, bank account statements and correspondence, then moved on to carefully collect and log every piece of paper relating to money or figures that they could find. In the meantime, Susan had contacted her husband and informed him of the situation. He advised her that he would be back at 2 p.m. – with his solicitor, Jeremy Richardson.

While the rest of the 'C' team officers returned to London with their plastic bags full of Piggott's papers, two men remained in Newmarket ready to grill Piggott; Dave Mussard and Frank Buckingham. It was 2.45 p.m. when the interview started. The early questions were asked with tact and centred around any income Piggott might receive from other sources such as television interviews. Piggott added that there were fees from appearances but that they were always put down and accounted for. Mussard and Buckingham worked well as a team of questioners, sometimes one asking a string of queries about Piggott's bloodstock involvement while the other sat back noting the replies and suddenly breaking in with a pertinent question of his own. Of course, both men held the upper hand anyway. For neither Piggott nor his solicitor were aware that the officers had with them that famous Cecil letter asking for cash payments and over-the-odds rates for a variety of Piggott's services.

After an hour, they all broke off for a half-hour spell. If Piggott thought the jousting was going in his favour then he was soon to be given a rude shock when the pace of the interview was stepped up when it resumed at 4.15. For, with his opening question, Mussard stepped in with the crunch: 'Have you ever entered into an agreement with Henry Cecil and his owners to receive extra retainers, percentage win money, and shares in colts retiring to stud?'

Piggott was slightly stunned but then replied: 'That's what it's all about, isn't it?'

The officers then produced a copy of the Cecil document which outlined all the extra payments; it was the point of no return. For another four hours the questions flowed thick and fast. The officers had to prompt Piggott, but he gradually began to make admissions to most of the points being raised. With each admission on a major point the officers noted almost a degree of relief in Piggott's demeanour; he seemed glad he was, at last, being given the chance to come clean.

The following day, Mussard and Buckingham spent a further three hours with more questions. Throughout all this time there was never a point when the officers felt Piggott did not understand his income tax and VAT responsibilities. Nor did he ever use the age-old excuse of having 'forgotten' to enter certain payments in his returns and thereby claiming it had all been an oversight. As far as Piggott's memory was concerned, the opposite was the case because both officers were amazed at the infinite detail regarding many of the horses Piggott had ridden during his career; he could tell them the date, the weather on the day, the state of the going, and the riding colours he wore.

While Piggott's home had been undergoing the raid by the 'C' team, squads of other Customs officers who had all attended the London briefing were systematically carrying out similar operations at the homes and stables of many other leading racing personalities. In all they would visit several top jockeys and trainers, more than a dozen owners and several major stud farms.

Now with their sackfuls of papers and files, the 'C' team hit men had returned to headquarters to begin more work on the case that was already twelve months old. If they were already half-way up the ladder to solving this major enquiry, then this new haul of information would see them on their way to the top. Over the next few months it would be compared and cross-checked with the work of three of the team – Jim Galloway, Chris Isaacs and co-ordinator Mervyn Mullins – who had combed the form books, the turf publications and newspapers in their efforts to assemble a picture of what Piggott's earnings should look like. The magistrate's access order had also allowed them to check Piggott's bank account at the National Westminster in Newmarket's High Street – the only one which he told them he possessed.

Throughout the following months, too, the Customs interest would spread to other top names in racing. Robert Sangster willingly visited the Customs and Excise offices in Manchester with the relevant documents and details of his arrangements with superstar jockeys like Steve Cauthen, Pat Eddery, Cash Asmussen and Brent Thomson. Sangster explained to them that his policy, within contracts with each rider, was to award them a fortieth-share in each Group One horse they rode to victory. It was, by now, common practice with all the Sangster jockeys in Britain, Ireland, the US, France and Australia. And, he told them, all such arrangements were registered with the Jockey Club of each respective country.

The outcome to all the raids and visits was that, apart from one or two minor problems with a particular jockey, no further action was taken. At least that was the official statement. It is believed, however, that Her Majesty's coffers were swelled somewhat considerably by out-of-court settlements along the way.

As far as Piggott was concerned, his problems were only just beginning. During the raid the officers requested access to the safe and any locked drawers in order to remove anything they thought would subsequently help them in their search for the missing millions. Their biggest surprise, however, had been when they were confronted by a locked cabinet. When it was unlocked it revealed three guns and over 400 rounds of ammunition. The cache was immediately confiscated and later handed over to the police at Newmarket; now there would be criminal charges to face.

It did not take long before Operation Centaur and its aims for a major crackdown on the world of racing became public knowledge. The effects on the industry as a whole were, as one prominent racing businessman observed, likely to prove of great benefit to the financial consultancy profession; leading lights in racing suddenly realised that some practices, particularly in the area of 'presents' to jockeys, to which a blind eye or deaf ear had been turned, were now going to have to be observed in a much tighter fashion. It was now no longer satisfactory for an owner to take the attitude that whatever was given to a jockey in the form of 'bonuses' or 'presents' was up to that jockey to declare to the taxmen. A lot of riders might be one-man businesses providing a 'service' as the VATmen say, but now extra vigilance was needed, for some owners did not want to be accused of having aided and abetted a jockey on the make.

No owner was too big or too small to fall under the Customs

microscope. Maktoum Al-Maktoum, eldest of the fabulously wealthy Maktoum brothers, was the subject of an official visit by members of the investigating team. They went to an address in London and, after checking on various aspects of the Maktoums' operation, satisfied themselves that everything was being run by the book.

Before the police would come knocking on Piggott's door to arrest him in the December of the same year, there were other repercussions of the 'C' team's raid on the Piggott household. The first of these came within weeks of the investigating team's return to their London base to begin piecing their newly acquired evidence together. Piggott had been set to receive a knighthood in the Queen's Birthday Honours List in the forthcoming June.

Having already been awarded the OBE in 1975 for his services to racing, the knighthood would have been the ultimate achievement and recognition for Piggott's 38 years as a jockey and there are few people in racing who would say the maestro did not deserve such an award. It would have put him on a public par with the late Sir Gordon Richards, the only other jockey ever to have been given a knighthood. For Piggott, too, the true Englishman, the title would have given him a personal pinnacle of which he would have been prouder than any one of his nine Derby successes.

Every Honours List nominee goes through a vetting process carried out by MI5, the intelligence service being the experts in the two types of vetting open to them, positive and negative. The latter process involves a fairly straightforward check with a nominee's local police collator in a bid to establish whether there is 'anything known'. Checks are also made with Special Branch and the likes of the Inland Revenue and Customs and Excise. In Piggott's case, of course, it was soon revealed that he was the subject of a serious enquiry into his tax affairs. He did not even receive the usual letter asking him if he would accept an honour if it were offered – the way that Buckingham Palace avoids any embarrassing risk of having an honour returned once the list becomes public.

Positive vetting is a more serious and painstaking process and is hardly ever used in the honours field. This is to investigate someone who will subsequently be in a position to handle classified material in whatever capacity. This is a costly business, too, estimated at around £5,000 in MI5 man-time and includes a thorough check on a person's domestic life, his political affiliation, interviews with colleagues, friends (including mistresses), checks on bank statements, club memberships and, finally, an exhaustive interview with the person being vetted.

As if by irony, following Piggott's realisation that that long-expected knighthood had now slipped totally from his grasp, the summer of 1986 heralded an achievement of a different kind, but still one that every racehorse handler dearly cherishes. This was to train a winner at Royal Ascot – in the presence of the Queen herself. Piggott's stable housed a two-year-old son of the top sprinter Sharpo called Cutting Blade who, early in his two-year-old days and before he had seen a racecourse, was thought to be capable of proving quite a useful animal. To have a two-year-old worthy of running at the famous June race meeting is a bonus in itself for most trainers; a horse must have that blend of precocity and toughness allied to a touch of class, one able to cope with the demands of a training schedule completely new to it in the first few months of this different life as a racehorse.

Cutting Blade coped well with the régime at Eve Lodge, pleasing his work-rider in the early-morning work and bolstering hopes that, come June, and providing there were no setbacks such as sore shins, pulled muscles, the almost ever-present virus, then Cutting Blade just might be good enough. The colt's first race was chosen – a six-furlong maiden event at Doncaster in the last week of May. The stable had already visited the winner's enclosure with several of its horses – always the sign sought by any trainer to tell him his string is in general good health. Starting at an unfancied price of 12–1, Cutting Blade equipped himself well on his debut, racing up with the pace and just outspeeded by two others in the closing stages to finish third, beaten one and a half lengths and a short head.

There were no doubts about him improving in his next event which came just over two weeks later at Leicester. Ridden by the same jockey, John Matthias, Cutting Blade was sent off the 13–8 favourite in a field of nine and was a comfortable winner by two and a half lengths.

The American Cash Asmussen was in the saddle when Cutting Blade lined up for the six-furlong Coventry Stakes, for two-year-olds, on the first day of the four-day Royal meeting. The tall Texan, Asmussen, then the first jockey to the Robert Sangster–Vincent O'Brien stable in Ireland after switching from France where he was champion jockey, has the class all top jockeys possess – the ability to win when the chips are down. Cutting Blade, at 11 – 1, appeared to be up against it in this 19-runner Group Three event, worth almost £25,000 to the winner. Favourite was the Irish top two-year-old filly Polonia (who was to win France's top sprint, the Prix de l'Abbaye the following season) and Cutting Blade's Doncaster conqueror, Polemos, trained by Thomas-Jones, was also in the field. The race provided one of those thrilling finishes, three horses in it as they raced almost together for the line. Asmussen summoned all the strength in his tall frame to wield the whip he still carries in the American vertical style and drive Cutting Blade to the post. The colt won by a short head from Polemos with another short head to the third, Amigo Sucio. There were great cheers as the colt was led back to the winner's enclosure and even Piggott allowed himself a rare smile.

He had proved he could make it as a trainer in the highest class. With his undoubted skill as a jockey and his powerful connections in racing, as long as people like Cutting Blade's owner Mahmoud Fustok continued to send him horses like this, then there would be no problem training winners.

There were soon to be further problems for Piggott off the track, however. In late August he was summonsed to answer to Newmarket magistrates on a charge arising from the 'C' team's discovery of the guns and ammunition during the raid at his home. The weapons were an Enfield revolver, loaded with six bullets and said by an expert later to be a particularly lethal handgun, a Colt automatic pistol, and an antique firearm. Represented by solicitor Jeremy Richardson, the man who would subsequently handle Piggott's problems arising from his arrest by police on the tax charges, Piggott himself did not appear in the courtroom. He had more pressing things to do – like buying yearlings at Deauville in France.

The court was told that Piggott had been given the guns ten years previously by a retired police officer. When asked by the police why he had them in his possession, he told them that he had always had an idle interest in weapons. Mr Richardson, offering a guilty plea to the charges of owning a gun without a firearms certificate and 463 rounds of ammunition without a licence, said Piggott had not realised at the time he was given the guns that he needed a certificate.

Magistrate Frank Christopher said it was a most disturbing case. Although it was acknowledged that the guns would not have been used for any criminal activity, Mr Christopher said it must always be a matter of concern for such weapons to be in the hands of someone not skilled in using them. The magistrates particularly expressed concern over the fact that the Enfield revolver was kept loaded. The bench fined Piggott a total of £1,000 – £750 on the guns charge and £250 for the ammunition – and ordered that the weapons and ammunition be destroyed with the exception of the antique revolver.

The magistrates were, therefore, content with Piggott's explanation of having had an 'idle interest' in guns as his reason for keeping a lethal handgun, fully loaded, with six rounds of live ammunition in his home. Although there is certainly no suggestion here that the reason was anything more than as given, it is a fact that Piggott was badly shaken by the news of the shooting of a friend. This was Ivan Allan, well-known racehorse owner and Singapore-based trainer, for whom Piggott rode that great horse Commanche Run to win the 1984 St Leger. The shooting had taken place several years earlier at his home, after which Mr Allan made a recovery. As we have already heard, Piggott had also received numerous death threats at various times throughout his career.

As Piggott's first season as a trainer drew to a close, it became time to take stock. In some ways the season had gone better than expected. Sure, there were problems as in any other yard, but Piggott had a good team around him, people he could work with, who understood what he wanted. Not that the man himself had envisaged he would be unable to overcome any of the dozens of difficulties facing the modern-day trainer. He had often joked, when asked just how long it would take him to set up as a trainer, that he would need about five minutes. The Piggott way of doing things involves slow and steady preparation so that when the time comes he can take things in his stride. That is his method – no rush, no panic, almost a laconic saunter into a new career. And by season-end, just three days after Piggott's fifty-first Bonfire Night birthday, the stable were looking at statistics that showed they had trained 30 British winners, a good first-term's work by any standards.

Of course, it was not long afterwards that Piggott suffered the shock of being arrested, culminating in that ignominious appearance at Newmarket Magistrates' Court once more, the spell in police cells, the undignified dash to raise £1 million bail, and the reliance on good friends Henry Cecil and Charles St George to step forward with their initial £125,000 sureties. And so, it was towards the rest of 1987 he looked, with a call on his personal qualities of courage, perseverance, and stoicism, and not without a certain amount of trepidation, in speculating how the events in this most important year of his life would finally evolve.

Soon after the initial court hearings in December 1986, with their inherent worldwide publicity and comment, Melvyn Walters, was making public noises about how he felt towards Piggott's situation. Although Walters was not named by the *Sunday People* (the newspaper which had originally run the 'Pay Piggott in Cash Plea' story) they quoted him as the 'owner who sparked the tax inquiry'. Walters said he felt sorry for Piggott. Other people should be up there with him but are not, he said. That Lester Piggott, the jockey who had ridden those big-race wins on the Walters partnership filly Bright Crocus, should bear the full weight of his revenge was a great source of frustration to the former Cecil owner.

On a purely personal note, the New Year of 1987 proved a sad one for Piggott and his family. His mother, Iris, had been in frail health for some time even to the point where Piggott was trying to keep worrying details of his arrest and subsequent trouble a secret from her. However, before January was half-way through, Iris died at the age of 81, in her home next door to Piggott's bungalow, the home he had had built specially for his parents.

Three weeks later, and with his passport having been returned by the police, Piggott flew off on holiday to Dubai at the invitation of Maktoum Al-Maktoum and joined up with Newmarket trainer Ben Hanbury and his jockey pals Pat Eddery and Willie Carson. Work was still going on at Eve Lodge, though, and when Piggott returned looking better than he had for months, he was soon organising the stable's pre-season raid on the southern French resort of Cagnes-sur-Mer.

The annual foray by several British trainers to the warmer climes of the South of France is an ideal opportunity for the stable wanting to have runners fit to win at the very start of the Flat season in late March at Doncaster – where it ends some seven and a half months later. Piggott duly made the trip worthwhile when the useful three-year-old colt Sunset Boulevard galloped away with the Prix de Besançon to win by an easy three and a half lengths to signal Piggott's first French training success.

If the short break in Dubai and the early racing victory in France gave Piggott a much-needed fillip, then it was no more than he was going to need for the months ahead. For just over a week after returning from across the Channel, the full extent of his problems was driven home when a VAT summons from Customs and Excise was served on his solicitors, Kingsley Napley, adding more charges to the original Inland Revenue holding charge which had been the subject of his arrest the previous December. The summons accused Piggott of intent to defraud between the dates of November 1979 and October 1985, and was to be heard at Newmarket Magistrates' Court in a fortnight's time when he was due to appear on the Inland Revenue charges.

And so, on 19 March, Piggott appeared before his home town's magistrates for the second time, facing a total of ten new charges now publicly made a little clearer. They related to an alleged total of £3,750,000 of undeclared income and were charges brought jointly by the Inland Revenue and Customs and Excise. Sitting impassively throughout the hour-long hearing and, once more, wearing his favourite camel overcoat and a smart suit, Piggott was remanded until 7 May. His bail, which in December had stood at £1 million and had been subsequently reduced on appeal to £500,000, was now reduced to £250,000. But the magistrates kept in force the surety of £125,000 from Charles St George and the one of the same amount from Henry Cecil.

Piggott has never been a man to worry too much about the past, about wrong decisions and unlucky breaks. It never paid him to be reflectively morose throughout his career in the saddle and, in spite of all the problems now facing him, he was prone to give the world a shrug of those slight shoulders and get on with his life and the job of training racehorses. The best thing he could do while waiting for that third appearance at Newmarket Magistrates' Court – the committal proceedings – was to keep himself busy.

And that was exactly what he did if only judging by the results of the stable in the seven weeks from the start of the season until the 7 May date with the Newmarket bench once more.

In the corresponding period of his first season training, Piggott had saddled two winners. This time, however, he and his horses were sharper, that little more experienced. He started the winning way with Geordie's Delight who was now becoming a firm favourite in the yard for his early-season ability. The same horse had given Piggott his first winner as a trainer when winning at Epsom in the April of the previous season. Now the four-year-old, under Pat Eddery, was opening the stable's account a month earlier, this time at Doncaster with the season only two days old. By Tuesday 5 May, Piggott had saddled a further 13 winners to reach a total almost half that of his first season's final tally.

For some of the time that Piggott realised he had a serious tax and VAT problem on his hands, he had employed the top people's international firm of accountants, Price Waterhouse, to help him sort out the mess. Three accountants from the company's City division had spent weeks examining the documents, files, correspondence and scraps of paper taken during the 'C' team's raid on Piggott's home.

Throughout this period, as complicated as the whole mess appeared, Piggott and his advisers had every reason to believe they were reaching a position where they could agree an out-of-court settlement with the Inland Revenue and Customs and Excise. But, incredibly, and even at this late and most serious stage of his problems, Piggott's overpowering greed, one of the only chinks in the characteristics that had made him such a great jockey, was to be revealed in dramatic fashion. And that, most sadly, was to prove his ultimate downfall.

13. Seventeen Secret Bank Accounts

Compromise deals between the Inland Revenue or Customs and Excise and someone owing tax to either agency are not an uncommon occurrence these days. Both Civil Service departments have powers granted under Acts of Parliament to bring their compounding rules into force. Each individual case is handled on a discretionary basis by the case officer concerned, although the more serious the situation, the higher on up the ladder it is referred until it reaches a senior management level. Customs and Excise have had the power to compound for over a century and the rules were enlarged under Section 38 (8) of the 1972 Finance Act to include Value Added Tax.

Anyone caught by Customs on VAT evasion does not have the choice whether to compound the issue or go to court, however. Those powers lie exclusively with Customs and Excise commissioners and a 'guilty' party has to wait until they are offered a compounding deal. As yet, there is not thought to be a case where the offer to compound has been refused, mainly due to the fact that there are few times when Customs do not feel they have all the evidence they need to prove a misdemeanour anyway.

The holidaymaker who returns from abroad with more cigarettes or alcohol than the permitted quantity and is stopped passing through the Customs green 'nothing to declare' channel is a situation where on-the-spot compounding takes place. Apart from confiscating the goods in question, a Customs officer is likely to hand out a fine commensurate with the offence.

In cases of VAT evasion, a compounding deal will include a penalty, paid on top of the outstanding amount of tax. Such penalties are also on a discretionary basis depending on the factors in each case. It could be as high as a 100 per cent penalty or as low as 5 per cent. In all but a few rare cases, compounding deals are accompanied by a 'no publicity' agreement. This is the area that makes it attractive to the apprehended party to prevent embarrassing details being made public. In serious cases of fraud, however, the Customs are likely to go ahead with a full-blown prosecution and trial. As a general rule, this is the way of most proceedings involving VAT amounts of £200,000 or more.

Latest statistics from the Inland Revenue indicate that, of 70,000 cases brought in the twelve months of the tax year 1984–5, only 332 ended in court proceedings, the rest being settled out of court with a three-part payment in settlement of the tax due, the interest, and a penalty. Naturally, in those cases that do end up in court, then that court's sentence is substituted for any penalty, though the offender still has to pay the tax plus the interest.

After raiding Lester Piggott's home and spending the ensuing months of 1986 matching and cross-checking the new evidence with all the information the Customs had secretly gathered in the previous year, the situation was rapidly approaching a possible compromise stage. The case officer in charge of the 'C' team had been in top-level talks with his superiors even to the degree where possible rates of penalty were being considered on Piggott's outstanding VAT. A similar situation was in hand, too, at the Inland Revenue.

Piggott, meanwhile, was anxiously awaiting the results of the months of work by the three Price Waterhouse accountants who had been granted access to the array of relevant documents by the 'C' team in order to provide the up-to-date position of where Piggott stood and exactly how much he owed, both to the Customs and Excise and the Inland Revenue. This was to be supplied in the form of a final Statement of Affairs, a multi-page document setting out in precise accountancy details the exact state of play. This file would then be vetted by both departments with the Inland Revenue then taking the major interest because the bulk of the substantial amounts in dispute was owed to them.

By the beginning of August 1986, Customs had studied Piggott's Statement of Affairs and, in discussions with his financial advisers, had come to a final compromise agreement. In other words, they were ready to offer Piggott a compounding deal. After all, it seemed, he had shown a willingness to fully co-operate with them, he wanted to make a clean breast of things. Now Piggott would simply settle the outstanding amount of income tax and VAT, pay the penalty that had been decided, and the matter would end there. There would be no further publicity, no court proceedings, and no more hassle all round. As far as the outside world was concerned, there could only be speculative guesses as to the extent of Piggott's transgressions; no one would know how much tax he had tried to evade, the whole affair would soon pass into history, and the man himself would continue his life as a trainer, his sights in his new career fixed firmly at the top.

But when the Inland Revenue began the task of studying that Statement of Affairs, they could hardly believe what they were being asked to accept. For, in the interim, they had discovered Piggott had 17 secret bank accounts, some in false names, with the Allied Irish Bank. And, in a final gesture of defiance, Piggott had tried to conceal these from the Inland Revenue by not declaring them in that Statement of Affairs. In fact he had not told his own accountants about them either.

Commissioners at the Inland Revenue were furious. They, too, had been willing to concur with Customs that a compounding deal was the most satisfactory conclusion to the whole episode, an enquiry that had cost them many hundreds of man-hours and which had now run for more than 18 months and at great expense to the taxpayer in general.

As we have seen, the Inland Revenue only prosecute in the most extreme cases. Those latest statistics show that only in 0.45 per cent of all cases was a prosecution the end-result – in other words, for every 199 cases settled privately with no further action, only one case ends in court. The Inland Revenue's official line on compounding states: 'To deter those who may be tempted to hide material facts from the Inland Revenue when they are challenged, it is the Revenue's policy to prosecute taxpayers who purport to make a full disclosure, but who have in fact deliberately concealed details of further income or assets – whether or not they have subsequently agreed to pay the outstanding tax.'

They decided there and then that Piggott's conduct deserved only one course of action. They would go ahead and prosecute. Consequently, in a joint co-operative move with the legal department of Customs and Excise, the Inland Revenue filed the charges which led to Piggott's arrest by police at the end of that year. Piggott, by his own folly, had therefore set the seal on his own fate. And that would now be decided by a court of law.

How did the Inland Revenue discover Piggott's Allied Irish bank accounts – worth a total of more than £2.1 million? There has been an allegation from a source close to the Piggott enquiry that Piggott's telephone was tapped at his Newmarket home. Although the Inland Revenue have experts experienced in similar investigations as this one, their powers do not include the use of telephone tapping, official permission for which has to come from the Home Office. However, those powers do exist for sections of the police, such as the Special Branch, as well as Customs and Excise and the secret services.

It is believed, though, that in that twelve-month period of secret investigations, and before Piggott himself knew of any probing of his affairs, special enquiry agents from the Inland Revenue and Customs kept close observation of Piggott and his movements between Britain, France and Ireland. Indeed, in January 1986 Piggott was grilled by Customs men at Heathrow Airport for several hours after he had just returned from a trip to the US.

Piggott, who likes to spend his winters somewhere warm in places like Hong Kong, Singapore, Australia or the West Coast of America, had just returned from riding in a jockey All Star's match at Bay Meadow racetrack in San Francisco when he was stopped while passing through Customs and asked to accompany officers to an interview room. There he was questioned for some hours about his movements before finally being allowed to go.

Some of the Allied Irish accounts were brought to light through circumstances even Piggott perhaps had not considered. For with terrorism in Ireland and in the North seemingly one of the boom businesses, checks on bank accounts are not an uncommon procedure by the Special Branch on both sides of the border. It was while investigating the suspected channelling of certain amounts of cash from illicit activities connected with the terrorists that Piggott's hidden accounts in the false names were discovered. Otherwise the accounts might have remained one of Piggott's financial secrets.

When Piggott made his third and final appearance before Newmarket magistrates in May 1987, the full impact of this most intricate investigation came to light. Piggott faced a total of twelve charges in the joint prosecution, eleven of them brought by the Inland Revenue.

*

In all, the total of undisclosed income amounted to £3.75 million of which the Inland Revenue were claiming £2 million tax plus £800,000 in interest. Added to the £184,000 of the VAT charge, it meant Piggott was about to say goodbye to almost £3 million.

At the hearing, Piggott displayed one of the characteristics those close to him found most annoying – his lack of punctuality. He arrived almost five minutes late, prompting one courtroom wag to remark that the only place Piggott ever arrived on time was the winning post.

The magistrates were in the middle of hearing licensing applications from local publicans when Piggott peered into the courtroom and, thinking his case had started, proceeded to the witness box completely unnoticed by his lawyers who were busy discussing last-minute details. Chairman of the bench, John Moore, saw Piggott in the dock and asked him to stand down and wait outside.

Dressed in grey trousers and his favourite dog-tooth light-grey tweed jacket, Piggott remained silent throughout the hearing which lasted just under an hour. His barrister, Julian Bevan, and counsel representing the Inland Revenue and Customs and Excise agreed, after the magistrates committed Piggott for trial, that the Old Bailey would be the most convenient court because the parties concerned and the papers were all in London. The bench agreed to the venue and also released Piggott's remaining bail of £250,000 on provision that it was paid over to the Inland Revenue immediately. Charles St George, who attended the court, had his surety reduced to £100,000 and signed the papers in court. Henry Cecil was at Chester races and Piggott had to spend 40 minutes at Newmarket police station after the case until it was confirmed that the champion trainer had visited Chester police station to sign his surety apers for the same amount.

With the trial date set for sometime in the autumn and the Old Bailey as the place where one of the most intriguing hearings of public interest would be staged, there was nothing Piggott could now do but wait for the dreaded day to come. It was some months later that the venue for the trial was changed; it would now be heard at Ipswich Crown Court. Then the date emerged as Friday 23 October – just 13 days before Piggott's fifty-second birthday. It was then, too, that the speculation started about the fate awaiting the man who had a place in the hearts of millions of people throughout the country.

The subject of the trial and its likely outcome became the favourite racecourse conversation. In fact there was so much gossip and innuendo that, had the subject not been so serious for post-war racing's most admired jockey, many bookmakers might have been tempted to start laying odds on the result. Initial 'jungle drums' suggested that Piggott was going to plead not guilty and that the case was likely to last a week, maybe ten days. It was soon learned, however, that Piggott would be offering a guilty plea. In fact, although it was not made public, several weeks before the trial started, Piggott had made the final settlements with the Inland Revenue and Customs and Excise, paying a total of £3.25 million to the former and £184,000 in VAT.

Informed sources at the Inland Revenue, meanwhile, were making their own forecasts as to Piggott's fate. The most 'popular' estimate was a three-year prison sentence while, over at Customs and Excise, officials reckoned he would get a suspended sentence.

The Jockey Club were monitoring the situation very closely, too. Not only were they awaiting the results of the Racecourse Security Services' investigation into the Piggott betting allegations (a subject many felt the Jockey Club were deliberately delaying until the Piggott trial verdict was digested), but they were conscious of the fact that they would have to study the implications of the trial very closely indeed. For, under Part 20 of the *Rules of Racing* entitled 'Prohibited Practices and Disqualification of Persons', Rule 201, sub-section vii states that 'Any person may be declared a disqualified person, or otherwise penalised by the Stewards of the Jockey Club in accordance with their powers under Rule 2 of these Rules who is convicted of any criminal offence in relation to racing in this or any other country.' And under the powers of that Rule 2, the stewards are entitled to withdraw or suspend a trainer's licence.

On the racecourse where Piggott was seen frequently throughout the summer months tending to his runners, there was at least the chance for him to get away from the accountants and solicitors and talk of the impending trial. There were still plenty of winners to come, although the flow of them had slowed down considerably compared to the early-season results. Those first seven weeks had produced 13 winners, but in the 23 weeks after the committal proceedings there were just three more than that total. Still, it was a good season even though his first season's tally of 30 was only just going to be beaten. It would be a foolish man who could say Piggott was not feeling the strain. And with more than 80 horses in the stable plus the autumn rounds of gruelling yearling sales, there was just no time for Piggott to take time off and relax or maybe contemplate the immediate future.

Things were not improved when, in the middle of September, an arson attack on the Eve lodge stables during the night resulted in a fierce blaze causing thousands of pounds' worth of damage. Neighbours of the Piggotts were woken at 2 a.m. by the commotion in the yard and saw what they thought at first was the whole stables ablaze. The fire, started deliberately, was confined to a £30,000 horse-transporter parked within the stable grounds and it took two fire crews over an hour to control the outbreak. Pressmen were quickly on the scene, too, which was the last thing the family wanted – though, naturally, the incident was news. Reporters trying for quotes from Piggott or his wife Susan the following morning were in for treatment that some of their predecessors had seen before.

Callers at the bungalow had the door slammed in their face, while Susan called the police to have the more persistent pressmen thrown off their land. The incident conjured up memories of an earlier occasion when a much younger Piggott scattered reporters from his garden by throwing stones at them, although not before first socking one of them squarely on the chin.

The year 1987 was not a good one for many of the people involved one way or another in Piggott's affairs (except for Henry Cecil who became champion trainer for the seventh time, breaking a 120-year record by saddling 180 winners). The Maurice Lidchi– Melvyn Walters UK company, Alchemy, was finally struck off the companies' register in February for failing to supply any company returns. In their last accounts, filed on 25 May 1984, and covering the year ending 28 February 1983, Alchemy showed a loss of over £25,000.

Alchemy's US operation with its stud and stallions at Lexington, Kentucky, was Lidchi's springboard to launch the UK company. Backed by considerable assets, the Alchemy Cecil deal seemed almost a natural progression to exploit business in Britain. But, following the short-lived association with Melvyn Walters, things for Lidchi went from bad to worse. By the middle of 1987, the

Frenchman was under severe financial pressure in many of his business interests, not only the Alchemy farm. It appeared to some of his financiers that he was falling into the trap of collecting too many assets and not generating enough cash.

Lidchi is an enigmatic character, hardly someone playing the part of the big businessman. When in London he drives an old Mercedes and, on his travels all over the world to manage his businesses, he stays in some of the cheapest hotels. A non-smoker and non-drinker, one of his interests is as the major shareholder in the world's largest mango estate in Puerto Rico. Many of his valuable carpets and art treasures are in bond in Vivey, near Lake Geneva.

In the summer that year Lidchi's Kentucky-based Alchemy faced six US lawsuits for nearly $1 million. These ranged from a $15,000 claim for commission by a bloodstock agent who sold a share in the stallion Lydian and had not been paid, to a claim for $275,000 for eleven horses bought on Alchemy's behalf at the 1987 Keeneland January sales. But the most interesting writ was for a sum of $286,000 from a London confirming house – a financial go-between. This particular company had been dealing with Maurice Lidchi for more than 25 years by way of financial services to the Frenchman's various businesses. The confirming house function is akin to a financial go-between operating with different parties in various parts of the world and providing payment and terms of credit between a customer and a client.

On 9 April 1984, the confirming house paid to Melvyn Walters's wife, Barbara, the sum of $285,941, and this was paid into her account with the National Westminster Bank. The payment was for a filly which had been sent to Alchemy in Kentucky and purchased by the Lidchi outfit – with the confirming house paying the money in the interim. That filly was called Bright Gemini, a two-year-old in training with Henry Cecil in the 1983 season but which, following several setbacks, never ran in a race. She did, however, win as a three-year-old at the small Ellis Park track in Kentucky – a race worth $5,175 to the owners, Alchemy.

Bright Gemini, probably named after the success Walters had with Bright Crocus the previous season (this filly was by Run Dusty Run out of Bye Doubles), was registered in the name of Barbara Walters who gave her address on the Weatherbys registration form as 144–6 New Bond Street – the same address as

Alchemy UK's office premises – rather than her home address. She did not work for Alchemy. All that became clear was that the confirming house had paid Barbara Walters a cheque for the $285,941, and, more than five years later, had not received a penny of that amount plus the confirming house's commission from Lidchi's company – hence the lawsuit, filed as a civil action at Kentucky's Woodford Circuit Court.

It looked unlikely they would ever recover the amount either, for in February 1989 it was revealed that Alchemy had filed for Chapter 11 – an interim stage in the US law of bankruptcy.

14. L. K. Piggott Limited

As long ago as 1959, Lester Piggott set up his own company to handle his affairs. He called it, simply enough, L. K. Piggott Limited and it was based at 255 Cranbrook Road, Ilford, the address of his accountants, Saunter and Chappell. The company's principal activities are those employing the services of Lester Piggott, and of property investment. Like any company it has a Memorandum of Association, a 'standard' certificate issued under the Companies Act of 1948 setting out the objects for which the company has been established. Such memoranda usually cover a host of activities related to the main function of the company. In the case of L. K. Piggott Limited, the Memorandum of Association states that the company is established to: 'Employ the services of and to promote and manage the professional activities of Lester Keith Piggott and in connection therewith to carry on business as jockeys, racehorse proprietors and managers, horse trainers, training stable proprietors and managers, farm owners, breeders of and dealers in thoroughbred horses,' etc. But L. K. Piggott Limited can also carry out business as turf commission agents and collectors and distributors of information relating to racing. Keeping in mind the *Rules of Racing*, this is a surprising inclusion, surely?

The establishment of any limited company, of course, is to benefit from the tax advantages available to it and to offer certain protections. A company is regarded in law as having an existence separate from that of its shareholders. If a company is sued or fined, the individual shareholders are not held responsible for the payment of such recriminations.

However, the immunity does not extend to that company's officers, its directors or managing director. And the fact that the directors might also be shareholders still does not mean the law allows them to escape prosecution. L. K. Piggott Limited's two directors are Piggott himself, and his wife Susan who is also the company secretary. The most obvious benefit a private limited company bestows is that its debts are its own responsibility and not that of the shareholders. In other words, a shareholder cannot be sued by a creditor and so that shareholder's personal wealth is never at risk – his or her liability is limited. The assets of the company, though, are available for paying any debts – providing the company has assets, of course.

In some areas of English company law (and also for that matter in the law of different countries) there is a thin line between tax avoidance – perfectly legal and respectable if perhaps in some extreme cases morally questionable – and tax evasion which, naturally, is illegal. Tax avoidance takes many forms and is the domain of accountants and financial advisers. One way of minimising tax is the area of offshore companies where, depending on which country is chosen, anonymity is usually a strong attraction, as are exemptions and concessions to home-based income tax.

L. K. Piggott Limited had two offshore subsidiaries, one in the Isle of Man, the other in the Cayman Islands. The Manx company was called Leadenhall Investments, formed in 1973 and with its registered office at Fernleigh, Palace Road, Douglas. Leadenhall was a £100 private company divided into 100 shares of £1 each. Piggott was a co-director, as was Susan, and held two of the shares. The other 98 were held by the Cayman Islands-registered Lambay Company Limited, a sub-subsidiary of L. K. Piggott Limited.

The Isle of Man has long been known as a financial centre, one of whose most obvious advantages is that income tax is levied at a rate of 20 per cent on its residents, the most famous of whom is Robert Sangster. Under the present government, however, committed to reducing taxes all round, Britain is narrowing the gap that made the small island such an attraction. In 1985, the Manx Parliament was so concerned with its dwindling number of resident millionaires that it launched a publicity drive to attract the wealthy and the entrepreneurial to its shores. At that date there were fewer than 20 millionaires on the island compared to the Channel Island of Jersey's 150.

The aim of the campaign was twofold: to bring in new wealth and to boost the population. Benefits mentioned in a report by Tynwald's Standing Committee on Population included the low rate of tax, no capital transfer or death duty, domestic rates at a level around one-tenth of those on the mainland, its environmental beauty, and stable community with little violence. The island was concentrating its efforts not on the multi-millionaires who would surround themselves with high walls and take no part in the community. Rather, they were looking for the entrepreneur who had built up a business in Britain, sold out and planned a semi-retirement, perhaps starting a new venture on the island after a short time to ward away the boredom.

The island also has big advantages for the non-resident. A non-resident company can be set up immediately for a cost of around £300 from the stocks of 'off-the-shelf' companies which have not traded and which are lying on the shelves of accountants and specialised firms all over Britain.

Such firms will provide a 'custom-made' method of incorporation to suit each individual customer's requirements. The service will include formation of the Memorandum of Association and all the other registration documents necessary for the new company's name to be added to the ever-growing list of non-resident companies. Nominee shareholders and directors can also be arranged along with a company secretary and registered office. While a private Manx company is required to hold an Annual General Meeting in every year but the first, lodging an annual return showing the names of the directors, shareholders and secretary, with the island's Registry Office, annual accounts are not required to be filed with the Registry as they are, by law, in Britain.

Piggott's Cayman Islands company, Lambay Limited, registered as a non-residential company at Georgetown, Cayman Islands, and run by Cayman Management Services, was struck off the register on 31 December 1986 for not filing company returns. The company's papers were subsequently transferred to a firm called Huntlow Corporative Services.

The last accounts available of Piggott's company, L. K. Piggott Limited, show that, for the year ending 5 April 1985, the jockey earned £194,148 in the previous twelve months, some £37,000 less than the previous year. Other income in 1985 amounted to nearly £27,000 but administrative expenses totalled £232,095 resulting in a loss for the year of £11,020. The company's tax bill for the year was £2,306. In 1984 the company made a £32,650 profit, paying tax of £9,150. In the company's report by directors (Piggott and his wife), it was stated that they were not satisfied with the development of the business during the preceding year and looked forward to an improvement in the future. As events would turn out, these were optimistic words indeed.

In the report of the company's auditors, Saunter and Chappell, it was stated that the Isle of Man subsidiary, Leadenhall Investments, had not revalued its investment properties as required by Standard Accounting Practice and, in the absence of such a valuation, the auditors were unable to quantify the effect of Leadenhall's non-compliance with the standard. It was also pointed out that there were no audited accounts for the Cayman Islands sub-subsidiary Lambay Company Limited. An ominous note was included making reference to L. K. Piggott Limited's investigation by the Inland Revenue and Customs and Excise, stating that the directors were unable to estimate the amount of any additional tax which may become payable and for which no provision had been made in the 1985 accounts.

It was with this in mind that the auditors said they were unable to form an opinion whether the accounts gave a true and fair view of the state of affairs of the company and of the group and of the loss of the group for the year ending 1985 or whether they indeed complied with the Companies Act of 1985.

The accounts also showed directors' remuneration of £52,500 and directors' pension of £94,445 with a further fee of £40,000 paid to the company chairman (Piggott) and a figure of between £10,000 and £15,000 paid to Susan Piggott as the other director. Two staff were paid a total of £8,781.

Sorting out Piggott's financial web of affairs was no easy task for the Inland Revenue and Customs and Excise or Piggott's own accountants. It took months of hard slogging, what the Revenue like to call dedication to the job. In preparation for his trial there was also a great amount of work to be done by his solicitor Jeremy Richardson and his counsel, John Mathew, QC, a man with one of the best legal brains in the country.

Morale at Piggott's two yards, Eve Lodge and Calder Park, had been quite bright at first, the stable staff were still exchanging jokes with each other, and more importantly with Piggott, despite the difficulties that lay ahead. Piggott, too, seemed his usual self – he might not have been found laughing too much in public but he always had the time to crack that grin, a somewhat private boyish smile which said he had not lost his sense of humour.

The yard was hit by a virus during midsummer, however, accounting for the drop in winners. But on a winner-to-runner ratio the stable staff were not unhappy – it is a fortunate trainer these days who goes the whole season without some sort of virus attacking the horses. Piggott's had all of the classic symptoms; they worked well on the Newmarket gallops, they seemed in general good health, but it was only once they got to the racecourse that the problems became manifest. Horses would run well for most of the race, sometimes taking up the running at the two-furlong pole, but then nothing, that extra effort just was not there. The odd one or two runners at first, then others, were running lifelessly, in some cases being tailed off. Then the 'runny nose' syndrome, the odd cough. The vet was called in, of course, blood samples taken. Subsequent analysis would prove the horses' blood counts were down, an imbalance of white corpuscles over red.

There was only one thing to do in such circumstances. Virtually shut up shop and let the horses get over the bug in their own time. The lucky yards get over it in six weeks and the horses come back bouncing. But a six-week setback can be multiplied by two to get horses back in full racing trim. There were those 'smart' observers of the Piggott stable, of course, who reasoned that with all his problems it was no wonder he was keeping a low profile on the racecourse, hardly surprising the stable were having so few runners. But Piggott and his wife, Susan, are true professionals. Their loyalty lay with the owners paying the bills. There was no question of letting personal problems interfere with the operation of a good yard.

Susan has her own bloodstock company, that occupies much of her time. But since the new life as a trainer's wife, her daily workload has doubled. Susan could well be called 'deputy' trainer at this time, with eldest daughter Maureen, her three-day eventing taking a back seat, the assistant, while Tracey was becoming more involved with Susan's bloodstock side of the business. Susan rides out, supervising three lots. She sits on the intricately decorated Western saddle atop her white dappled pony, watching the string work with the experienced eyes of someone who has been around horses all her life. Then there are owners to be seen or telephoned, visitors to the yard. And someone has to saddle up, too, when there are runners at more than one meeting.

As summer turned to autumn, the yearling sales season was getting under way. The Piggotts could not afford to miss the top sales for they had a healthy order book from the stable's patrons, Susan also had her clients of the Susan Piggott Bloodstock Agency to consider.

For the start of the 1987 season, Calder Park – where all the yearlings go to be broken and ridden away – housed almost 80 yearlings. By the end of the year Piggott was hoping to have as many new inmates if not more; some of the moderate older horses would go to the sales or be sold privately to make room so that, by the New Year, Eve Lodge and Calder Park could be looking at almost 100 horses.

The fading life of autumn is always a time for bracing oneself; the onslaught of cold dark days threatens. This year, though, the atmosphere was shaded differently. The burden of the forthcoming trial was taking its toll on everyone connected with the stable. Piggott's absence from the yard was now not just a one-off for whatever reason, it was becoming a more regular occurrence. There were trips to London, hours of meetings with his legal advisers, more meetings with accountants. And the staff all knew it. The laughter from Piggott gradually subsided. The tension was building up. That famous harrowed face looked pale, worry etched into those lines, the testament to a million missed calories. Now talk between lads was of the immediate future, sometimes their future. As the damp cloak of October wrapped itself tightly around the racing town of Newmarket, an impotence crept in, too, at Eve Lodge and Calder Park. For there was nothing anyone could do except wait.

15. The Trial Begins

The days leading up to Lester Piggott's Crown Court hearing on Friday, 23 October 1987, were notable for two major events in British history. The worst storms this century unmercifully lashed the south-east of England, killing 20 people, uprooting a million trees, and causing chaos and damage estimated at more than £50 million. Nature's vengeance also coincided with the man-made tempest that swept through the London Stock Exchange, wiping billions of pounds off equities and threatening the whole financial structure of the world stock markets. Piggott approached this most important period of his life with the same outward display of impassivity he had shown on all those big-race occasions when, to the racing world at least, it seemed everything was at stake.

Only now it was Piggott's freedom on the line, his reputation, and, perhaps, his future career in racing. Stoically, he said before the trial that he was hoping for the best. It was one of the bad things that happened in one's life. He just hoped everything would turn out okay.

As the 80-strong press corps moved in on the Suffolk town of Ipswich on the eve of the trial at the Crown Court, members of the Customs 'C' team, whose prolonged and determined detective work had led to this occasion, slipped quietly into the Post House Hotel two miles from the town centre and away from the main body of journalists. There, they had a quiet dinner and sat until the small hours discussing the likely outcome of the trial. Opinions were mixed. The general feeling, however, was that Piggott would receive a suspended sentence, a view that would be shared by many of the reporters covering the trial the following day.

What only a few people knew was that Piggott himself had been warned that he would most likely be sent down. Indeed, the

Inland Revenue had been privately forecasting a three-year sentence based on their experience of previous cases involving tax evasion. It seemed that those who were expecting Piggott to get off lightly had not, to quote racing parlance, studied form. Had they done so – and allowing for a consistency in sentencing that is not always apparent – then there was no way Piggott would escape a prison term. It was not realised at this stage, of course, that the facts which would emerge in this one-day trial would show Piggott's pathological obsession with money.

The crux of the case would be that twelve months into the two-year Operation Centaur investigation – in January 1986 – Piggott's home was raided. Following that raid, Piggott hired three top professional accountants to put his affairs in order. At a cost to Piggott of some £250,000 the accountants would, for the next six months, liaise with both Customs and the Inland Revenue combing the complexities of one man's financial mess with the aim of producing a final set of documents reflecting Piggott's true worth and the true amount on which he would settle out of court.

Even when given the chance to finally come clean, however, Piggott still kept secret from his own accountants some 17 bank accounts containing over £2 million. At this late stage Piggott was under the misapprehension that he could still pull the wool over the Inland Revenue's eyes. Had they not had evidence of the existence of these accounts, it would all have been a different matter. But the Revenue did know. And for them the court proceedings were the only option they could possibly take to combat Piggott's defiance and deceit.

The Ipswich Crown Court building is relatively modern; it was built in 1968 at a cost of £500,000 and houses three courtrooms. What had started as a bright sunny morning with a touch of overnight frost, now turned cloudy and grey with the hint of rain, as the first of the pressmen arrived at the court to be given cloakroom-numbered tickets reserving their places in the courtroom. Journalists drank coffee and chatted among themselves for the hour and a half wait until the trial got under way at 10.30 a.m. Outside, photographers and television cameramen positioned themselves at strategic points near the police-manned barrier at the rear of the building.

The black Rolls Royce of Piggott's counsel, John Mathew, QC, one of the country's finest barristers, arrived with little notice and parked in the court car park. Some half-hour later, a silver-grey Mercedes, driven by Piggott's solicitor, Jeremy Richardson, swept round the roundabout outside the court and made a left turn towards the same car park. The posse of photographers came to life. As the car drove swiftly past them, giving little opportunity for pictures, a group of the photographers ran towards the barrier where the rest of their colleagues had assembled, some on stepladders. One photographer had his foot run over by the car as it pulled sharply to a halt and was quickly waved through the raised barrier by a policeman. Stopping outside the rear door to the court, Piggott appeared just long enough for only the smartest of operators to snap the serious-faced figure in the camel overcoat as he walked the few paces to the open door.

High up on a stepped rampart leading to the town's outdoor market, shoppers peered down at the commotion; bemused bystanders whose normal Friday shopping was now touched by intrigue. On the roundabout, three gardeners raking up the last of summer's now-dead flowers, hardly raised their heads.

By 10.25 a.m. the courtroom was full; the pressmen seated in rows of wood-panelled benches, some facing the Royal crest on the plum-coloured wall behind the judge's seat, others at right-angles along the length of the room. The buzz of muffled conversation was momentarily brought to a hush each time a court usher appeared; idle chatter to fill the void of austerity only a courtroom exudes. Almost unnoticed by the majority of newsmen, Susan Piggott slipped quietly into a seat reserved for her at the opposite side of the room to the main body of journalists. Some of these reporters were racing men; they had seen Susan in happier times, on the racecourse after a famous victory by her husband, shared champagne at a celebratory dinner. Now, in a two-piece claret-coloured suit, she sat alone, her face set and her eyes occasionally glancing nervously around the courtroom.

A court usher's familiar command to 'all stand' signalled the entrance of the High Court judge, Mr Justice Farquharson, followed by his clerk and the High Sheriff of Suffolk and his adjutant. Bowing their heads in traditional respect to Mr Farquharson stood the prosecution and defence; Anthony Hidden, QC, leading his junior counsel Peter Rook for the Crown, and John Mathew, QC, leading Julian Bevan (brother of a racecourse clerk of the course, Hugo Bevan) for Piggott.

Moments later, Piggott was brought up from the court cells. And with a young prison warder towering over the grey-jacketed figure, he was escorted to the witness box near the judge's bench rather than the dock in order that he could hear the proceedings more clearly.

As he stood before the court, his head almost quizzically tilted to one side in the manner of someone with a hearing defect the charges, which had now been reduced from twelve to ten, were read out to him by the clerk of the court. To each one Piggott nodded, his reply barely audible. These were the charges, to which he pleaded guilty in each instance:

(1) *On 29 April 1983 he made a false declaration of complete disclosure relating to bank accounts contrary to common law.*

(2) *On 29 April 1983 he made a false declaration of complete disclosure relating to total income and assets contrary to common law.*

(3) *He omitted UK riding income of £211,677 from the accounts of L. K. Piggott Ltd for the years ended 5 April 1982, 1983 and 1984 contrary to common law.*

(4) *He omitted overseas riding income of £19,414 from the accounts of L. K. Piggott Ltd for the year ended 5 April 1984 contrary to common law.*

(5) *He omitted bloodstock operations income of £646,417 from the accounts of L. K. Piggott Ltd for the years ended 5 April 1983 and 1984 contrary to common law.*

(6) *He omitted additional UK riding income of £1,359,726 from the accounts of L. K. Piggott Ltd for the years ended 5 April 1973 to 1984 contrary to common law.*

(7) *He omitted overseas income of £28,629 from his returns of income for the years ended 5 April 1983 contrary to common law.*

(8) *He omitted Sch. D CIII interest of £330,155 from his returns of income for the years ended 5 April 1980 to 1984 contrary to common law.*

(9) *He omitted Sch. D CV (overseas) income of £522,127 from his returns of income for the years ended 5 April 1975 to 1984 contrary to common law.*

(10) *Between 1 November 1979 and 31 October 1985 he and L. K. Piggott Ltd did not pay, with intent to defraud, £140,000 in VAT relating to undeclared payments of retaining fees, extra prize money and bloodstock transactions in stallion shares and nominations.*

After the bespectacled Mr Justice Farquharson invited Piggott to sit down in the witness box, prosecuting counsel Anthony Hidden, QC, a large man alongside his colleagues, rose slowly to his feet. The trial of the greatest jockey in the world had now begun:

MR JUSTICE FARQUHARSON: Yes, Mr Hidden.

MR HIDDEN: My Lord, this defendant, Lester Keith Piggott, is a household name here in Britain and in many parts of the world. He has had a magnificent career in racing. A career that can only be marvelled at. It is inevitably sad that he should find himself where he does today, appearing in the Crown Court facing these charges. Unhappily, however, my Lord, it has to be said at the outset of this hearing that this case results not from the first investigation into the taxation affairs of Mr Piggott but from the third such investigation.

The first such investigation took place between 1970 and 1973 and the second ten years later and more recently between 1981 and 1983. I shall need to refer briefly to those two previous enquiries into Mr Piggott's taxation affairs in dealing with this, the current, investigation.

The case before your Lordship today involves a massive evasion of corporation tax and income tax over a period of more than ten years, as a result of a deliberate and persistent failure by the defendant to disclose to the Inland Revenue the true level of his personal income and the true level of profits of L. K. Piggott Limited, a company which he effectively controlled.

As to the amount of total income suppressed in that period, coupling together both the Company and the individual, my Lord, the total income which was not disclosed amounts to £3,118,788.

MR JUSTICE FARQUHARSON: Income undisclosed?

MR HIDDEN: Income undisclosed, my Lord. The tax on that income which was evaded totalled £1,730,290. That figure excludes any interest on tax evaded. My Lord, if I can split those figures down as between the Company and the individual, as to total income suppressed the figure for the Company was £2,237,234; that for the individual £881,554. Those together make the £3.1 million figure I have just put to your Lordship.

As to the tax split between the Company and the individual which was evaded, that for the Company, the figure for corporation tax, the figure would be £1,151,258, and personal taxation, £579,032, making the £1.7 million figure.

MR JUSTICE FARQUHARSON: I expect you are going to tell me all about the Company, but essentially it was a vehicle, was it, for his income?

MR HIDDEN: My Lord, yes, it was incorporated in 1959 and he took the income from riding. My Lord, leaving aside tax, Mr Piggott was also liable in relation to the Company to pay value added tax, and some of the income which the defendant failed to disclose to the Inland Revenue amounted to taxable supplies for VAT purposes: just as it was not disclosed to the Revenue, it was similarly not disclosed to the Customs in the VAT returns of L. K. Piggott Limited. By failing to disclose the true level of outputs in the VAT returns between 1980 and 1985, over £140,000 in VAT was evaded. My Lord, the actual sum was £140,836.

My Lord, Lester Piggott was, as everyone knows, a highly successful jockey. He was born on 5 November 1935, and he was champion apprentice by the age of 18. His life as a jockey spanned the years 1950 to 1985, when he retired and became a racehorse trainer. During his last years as a jockey he was retained as stable jockey by Henry Cecil, a very well-known trainer; that was for the years 1980 to 1984. As I have mentioned to your Lordship, it was in 1959 that the Company was formed, L. K. Piggott Limited, and by an agreement with Mr Piggott himself the Company became exclusively entitled to Mr Piggott's services as a jockey.

It followed from then, 1959 onwards, that whereas before, from 1950 to 1959, it was only the defendant personally who was liable to income tax in relation to his riding, from then on both the defendant and the defendant Company were liable to pay tax: income tax for the individual and corporation tax for the Company. My Lord, I had to say that this was not the first investigation conducted by the Inland Revenue into Mr Piggott's taxation affairs. Seventeen years ago in 1970 the enquiry branch in Bristol conducted such an enquiry which was concluded in 1973. The investigation established that there had been understatements of Mr Piggott's riding income totalling £83,000 for the 20 years to 5 April 1970; that is, 1950 to 1970.

Six years ago came the second investigation in 1981. It started then and the Inland Revenue Special Office investigated Mr Piggott's taxation affairs. The investigation culminated in a settlement in April of 1983. My Lord, I mention these matters because, of course, the settlement is a matter central to the first two counts in the indictment. That settlement was made upon the basis that Mr Piggott had made complete disclosure of all his affairs. Sadly, he had not. Subsequent disclosures in 1986 have revealed the settlement was made on a false basis and that Mr Piggott failed to reveal the true extent of his income and assets during the course of that investigation.

It has regrettably to be said that there is a theme running through the defendant's dealings with the Inland Revenue, and that is his persistent failure, even when claiming to do so, actually to make full disclosure of his assets and income to the Inland Revenue. On a number of occasions subsequent revelations have shown that the claims to be making full disclosure were very far from the truth; sizeable assets, sources and sums of income were still being concealed.

My Lord, may I deal briefly with the second investigation, having said all I need to say about the first one. The second investigation, running from 1981 to 1983, initially concentrated on Mr Piggott's involvement with various offshore companies, in particular there were two companies, Lambay and Zeus, and they were both Bahamian companies with offices in the Bahamas to which he had assigned rights to receive income both from overseas riding and non-riding activities. During the course of those two years, 1981 to 1983, there was a considerable amount of correspondence between Mr Piggott's accountants, Saunter Chappell, and a Mr Williams who was in charge of the Inland Revenue investigation. There were in addition a number of meetings between the accountants and the investigating officer.

The investigation established, and it was so accepted by Mr Piggott's accountants, that extra riding fees and prize percentages received from owners were being omitted from the accounts submitted both by the Company and the individual. The eventual settlement of that 1981–3 enquiry was at a total of £168,000 and it encompassed *inter alia* that United Kingdom riding income from 1971 to 1982 had been omitted and also overseas riding income. My Lord, that figure was calculated in the coming to the agreement of the settlement by reference to a mathematical calculation of what were the expected percentages of prize money worked out, in effect, from the published records of the races Mr Piggott had ridden.

In that investigation and in that settlement Mr Piggott's private bank accounts were not examined, even had they been examined in any event, as it now transpires, those accounts would not have revealed the true extent of Mr Piggott's income as many of his bank accounts were not revealed to the Inland Revenue during that 1981 to 1983 investigation. Indeed, in a moment or two we will be looking at the documents signed at that time on 29 April 1983 which are referred to in counts one and two which were said to be complete disclosure but which were not.

My Lord, as part of the 1983 settlement arrangements were made for dismantling the offshore companies, Lambay and Zeus, in which Mr Piggott was the beneficiary of a Cayman Islands settlement, and that settlement's only asset was a 100 per cent holding in the issued share capital of Lambay Limited, the holding company which I have already indicated. The only asset of Lambay Limited was 100 per cent of the share capital of an Isle of Man company, Leadenhall Investments

Limited, and it now transpires that substantial bloodstock interests had been built up by Mr Piggott and registered in the names of Lambay and Zeus.

My Lord, those bloodstock interests I shall come to at a later stage, but briefly they amounted to shares, nominations and annual breeding rights in relation to horses. My Lord, I shall not be dealing with a share; a share of a stallion was in fact a one-fortieth part and a share entitles the owner to a nomination per breeding season. I shall be referring to the nominations. A nomination is the right to nominate a mare to be covered by a stallion in one breeding season. My Lord, there is a third right too, which is basically of American origin I understand, an annual breeding right, that is a nomination in perpetuity, as it sounds, an annual breeding right, but no share in the stallion.

My Lord, the bloodstock interests of that sort, neither the interests themselves nor the income derived from them were disclosed to the Inland Revenue during the 1981–3 investigation. In that investigation Mr Piggott was not seen personally by the Inland Revenue despite some requests for a meeting. In response, however, to a request from Mr Williams, the investigating officer, Mr Piggott did provide a certified statement of assets and liabilities as at 29 April 1983. My Lord, that is the subject of count one of the indictment and it is exhibit one in the Revenue bundle. May I ask your Lordship to turn to it.

My Lord, the significance of what is omitted will immediately become apparent when one looks at the first page: 29 April 1983. The only bank accounts referred to are at National Westminster, Newmarket. They are said to be £70.72, a current account, £812.69, a deposit account, and a special deposit of £27,000. My Lord, they total £27,883.41p. Your Lordship sees on the third page of that exhibit above Mr Piggott's signature and the date, 29 April 1983: 'I certify that the statement above is a complete and accurate statement of my own, my wife's and my children's assets and liabilities as at the date stated.' Sadly, my Lord, that was not so. In fact, the statement excluded 17 different bank accounts with the Allied Irish Bank in various names. In particular, my Lord, Mr Piggott was operating two deposit accounts at the Bruton Street, London branch of the Allied Irish Bank, one in the name of K. and S. Day; another in the name of K. Armstrong, Armstrong being his wife's maiden name, and also an investment account with Allied Irish Finance Limited, Bruton Street, in the name of K. Armstrong.

My Lord, those accounts contained the monies the subject of count six, which your Lordship can see looking ahead is a count relating to additional United Kingdom riding income which by a much later stage had got to £1,359,726. That, by that later stage, was the total of monies that had been given to Mr Piggott by owners of horses that he was riding who had bet on his success and with the successful outcome of the race would pass on to him the winnings from that bet. That was clearly taxable money, and the accounts that I have mentioned, each of them had six-figure sums in them at the time the statement was signed. What they contained were the monies the subject of count six less, of course, £105,000 for the year 1983–4 that had not yet arrived, and the interest which had accumulated over the previous years as the sum built up. So something like £1.24 million was in those accounts.

My Lord, if your Lordship looks at count one your Lordship will see that the false statement, exhibit one, is what is charged. The document clearly sets out the only bank accounts held then at the National Westminster Bank, Newmarket. Quite apart from those undisclosed bank accounts in the Allied Irish Bank, if your Lordship would look at that particular volume, exhibit 34 of the Revenue bundle of exhibits at page 3, at serial 3, in a statement of bank and other accounts operated by Mr Piggott which was to come later from Price Waterhouse, your Lordship sees listed against the Allied Irish Bank the names of those accounts. Those are the accounts as at the date listed. They are, of course, not simply the 17 which were omitted in the statement of disclosure of 29 April 1983, because this is the list at 8 December 1986. So if your Lordship runs his eyes down the Allied Irish Bank your Lordship will see in London there were two Lambay accounts, a Keith Armstrong account and a K. Day account, in Dublin there were two Lambay Limited accounts, but, of course, as we move into the Jersey accounts none of those listed there were open as at 29 April 1983. The Jersey accounts were taken out after this disclosure. Taking out those in the left-hand column that have a date after 29 April 1983 and including the two Allied Irish Finances serial 4 at the top of the next page, those are the 17 accounts.

My Lord, in addition to those accounts omitted, the certificate, exhibit one, was false, the second certificate which is exhibit two was false because there were also interests in property. I will take your Lordship to count two in a moment, but the defendant owned Furzwick Farm, Wantage, and had done since early 1982, he had paid £140,000 for it. He also had a leasehold interest in a flat in West One which had been bought on 14 March 1980 for £95,000. There was one further bank account at the National Westminster at Newmarket, not in his own name but in the name of John Jackson.

My Lord, if your Lordship would now look at count two and at exhibit two, count two is in relation to the other document which the defendant signed on 29 April 1983. It is the certificate of complete disclosure. It is a one-page document saying over the signature of Mr Piggott and the date: 'I hereby certify I have made a complete disclosure to you of all banking accounts whether current or deposit, business or private, savings and loan accounts, deposit receipts, building society accounts, investments including saving certificates, premium bonds and loans whether interest-bearing or not, and other assets of whatsoever nature including cash and life assurance policies.' (B) is gifts, my Lord, and (C) is sources of income; as your Lordship sees, it is a joint one for husband and wife.

My Lord, in relation to that statement of assets Mr Piggott also failed to disclose funds held on his behalf in the Cayman Islands held by Mr J. Ashenheim of International Corporation Services which on 29 April 1983 amounted to approximately £1 million, part of those funds held by Mr Ashenheim related to Mr Piggott's bloodstock operations.

My Lord, so much then for counts one and two which relate to the failure to disclose assets at the conclusion and settlement in the second investigation in 1983. I move now to the current investigation. London Special Office began a project in 1984 in which the Inland Revenue investigated various aspects of the horseracing industry. Despite the certificate, which had been signed by Mr Piggott in April 1983, researches of the investigators indicated that it was likely Mr Piggott was still underdeclaring prize money and presents.

It appeared that Mr Piggott had received nominations and breeding rights and had not declared income therefrom. Furthermore there were disclosures in the press in early 1985 which indicated that Mr Piggott might have been receiving payments from owners over and above payments which were officially made. In the newspaper reports these extra payments were reported to be in accordance with an arrangement made with the trainer Mr Henry Cecil in respect of Mr Piggott's services as a stable jockey to Mr Cecil. They were said to be over and above the retainer which has to be declared at Weatherbys. The retainer which had been declared over preceding years had been a figure of £10,000 and these were said to be extra payments.

The officers of Customs and Excise were similarly engaged in an investigation and on 30 January 1986 Customs officers went to Mr Piggott's premises in Hamilton Road in Newmarket and that afternoon and evening two officers, Mr Mussard and Mr Buckingham, conducted an interview with Mr Piggott in the presence of his solicitor. During the course of the interview he admitted receiving riding fees and/or retainers which were not included in the company accounts. He also confirmed that he was aware that all riding income should be included in the accounts of L. K. Piggott Limited. Initially he sought to pretend that the only retainer he received was £10,000 paid by Henry Cecil through Weatherbys and denied receiving any other retainer through Henry Cecil or his owners.

My Lord, I will take your Lordship briefly to the interview which is Customs' exhibit Buckingham F, and it may well be in an orange folder. My Lord, the interview started at a quarter to three in the afternoon. I shall not take your Lordship through very much of it, but if your Lordship would go to page 4, Mr Piggott was asked: 'Do you receive any other income apart from Weatherbys, as for example TV interviews?' He said, 'Yes.' 'What other income?' 'Quite a few things, making appearances but I put them all down. They are all there. I will show them to you.' He was asked: 'Do you produce records of every part of your income as a jockey to Mr Chappell' – that is his accountant – 'for him to complete your VAT schedule?' 'Yes, as far as I am aware everything that is VATed. The VAT people have looked at my books a few times.' He was asked: 'Does the Weatherbys print-out contain a retainer fee for the times you were retained as a stable jockey?' and he agreed it did. Other questions were asked and he confirmed, in answer to a question, 'How much retainer were you receiving from Henry Cecil?' that the retainer was £10,000 from Weatherbys. The officer said: 'Did you receive any additional retainer?' He said: 'Yes, I received other bits and pieces in prize money.' The officer said: 'I am talking about retainers. Did you receive any other retainer payments from Henry Cecil or his owners?' And he said, 'No.'

The questioning continued until eventually just after he had been asked the question, 'Do you have any interest in any company which breeds racehorses?' and he answered it, 'Only as adviser,' and then been asked, 'As well as for value added tax do you understand any extra income over and above the Weatherbys income has to be declared to the Inland Revenue as well as Customs and Excise?' he said, 'Yes, it is,' there was a short break. My Lord, that break lasted something over half an hour and at just before a quarter past four when the interviewing started again there was a significant change. Mr Mussard said: 'Have you ever entered into an agreement with Henry Cecil and his owners to receive extra retainer, percentage win money and shares in colts retiring to stud?' Mr Piggott said: 'That's what it's all about, isn't it?'

My Lord, he was then shown a photocopy document and Mr Mussard said: 'I am producing a copy of a document headed "strictly private and confidential, Lester Piggott's 1982 retainer": Have you ever seen that document before?' His answer was: 'Yes. I don't know how many people have this.' If your Lordship would turn to exhibit 31 in the Revenue bundle your Lordship will see this was the document that was shown. It is headed 'Strictly private and confidential. Lester Piggott's 1982 retainer'. It reads in typing:

> Lester Piggott's retainer agreement for the 1982 season will be the same as registered with Weatherbys in 1981, i.e. £10,000. Terms of the additional private agreement made with Lester are as follows: (1) A cash payment over and above the amount specified in the retainer agreement to be increased from £25,000 to £45,000. (2) The additional 7½ per cent cash extra on first prize monies must be based on the penalty value of the race. (3) The additional 10 per cent on place monies to be based on penalty value. (4) Lester to be given a share in every Group One-winning colt ridden by him who retires to stud anywhere in the world to take up stallion duties. In the event of an owner wishing to sell any colt or horse outright he will then be paid the equivalent value of one share.

My Lord, the references to Group One races – they are of course the most valuable and prestigious races in the calendar, and the breeding value of any colt which wins any of those races is inevitably greatly enhanced; such races I am told as the 2,000 Guineas, Derby, St Leger, Coronation Cup and Ascot Gold Cup for instance.

My Lord, after those four terms were then the following words:

> The retainer will be collected as follows: First-half end of March, extra percentage up to 1 August will be collected end of August. Second-half retainer plus final extra percentages will be collected end of October.

The document went on:

> Lester has asked that for the cash element of the retainer and for the extra percentages he be given a cheque made out to cash.

It went on:

> It looks as if there will be 130 to 140 horses in training here next season so the cost of his retainer will work out at about £392 plus VAT per horse.

My Lord, that is dated 31 December 1981 and with it there was the preceding page on a typed heading of Mr Cecil's from Warren Place, Newmarket.

MR JUSTICE FARQUHARSON: The £392 plus VAT, payable through Cecil or directly to Piggott?

MR HIDDEN: My Lord, that would be to Cecil, I would think. It is collected from the owners individually by a bill sent out by Mr Cecil. That is 140 times £392.

MR JUSTICE FARQUHARSON: Your point is, I think, on count ten that this income was not declared?

MR HIDDEN: That is it.

MR JUSTICE FARQUHARSON: Where tax applied, they were chargeable with VAT?

MR HIDDEN: Yes, my Lord. My Lord, the letter with the document, 'Could you please return the authority to act and training agreement as soon as' – and the name has been blanked out by the time the Revenue had the document – 'has signed. I also enclose a copy of the informal agreement of Lester Piggott and Henry Cecil for the 1982 season. Perhaps it would be as well to destroy it as soon as you have read it.'

My Lord, that document of 31 December 1981 that the Revenue had was put to Mr Piggott, and having said, 'Yes, I don't know how many people have this,' he was asked when did he first see the document and he said: '1984. This man was trying to sell this document to the newspapers and that's how I came to see it. He was asking £50,000 and went to a lot of newspapers and then in February of last year it all came out. It took about nine months before it came out. That's the first time I saw it.' He was asked if he had ever discussed the agreement with Mr Cecil prior to 1984 and he said: 'Not really, no. It was not my doing anyway, it was his doing. From my point of view it was an amicable agreement.' He was asked: 'Did you ask Henry Cecil to draw up such an agreement on your behalf with his owners?' and he said, 'No.'

My Lord, further on after other questions at page 12 and having read Mr Cecil's statement in the middle of the page he said: 'What I would like to say really is not all the owners have this and not all of them agreed with it.' He was asked: 'Do you agree with Mr Cecil's statement that you approached him to put this arrangement to his owners?' and he said: 'No, not really, we went over that at the Jockey Club. No, I didn't say that in so many words.' 'Can you explain to me what was said?' 'I left it to him. I never pushed him for any money really.' He was asked: 'Was there a discussion between you regarding extra payments?' He said: 'There was probably a discussion but he was the one who had to decide. You have got to remember at that time I didn't have a job or anything, you know.' Mr Mussard said: 'Was this discussion between yourself and Henry Cecil after you were established as his stable jockey or before?' He said: 'I suppose it was September time before I started. There was a big change in jockeys. I left where I was and Henry Cecil's jockey was leaving him at the end of that season, so that's how it came about. He said, "Do you want to ride for me next season?" and I said I'd love to. It just went from there.' Mr

Mussard said: 'I put it to you that as probably the world's best-known jockey Henry Cecil stood to gain very good owners by having a partnership with you, and you in forming such a high-class partnership were able to name your own price which the owners would be more than happy to pay,' to which he said: 'I was an old man then.' Mr Mussard said: 'But you were still regarded as the finest jockey in the world,' and he said: 'I wasn't champion and hadn't been for ten years.'

Unless there is anything further my friend would like me to read, my Lord, that is all I propose to take from that interview. I would seek to make one particular point at this stage in the defendant's favour, my Lord. It is no part of the Crown's case that Mr Piggott devised these arrangements for receiving retainer fees from owners over and above those disclosed to Weatherbys, or indeed that he was the only jockey to benefit from them.

My Lord, in relation to those extra payments the Customs officers that day saw Mr Cecil and indeed the day after they saw Miss Ann Scriven on 31 January. Your Lordship will find her statement at page 3 of the Customs' statements immediately after Mr Cecil's. She had been Mr Cecil's secretary since 1969 and as secretary she had to type correspondence, deal with telephone enquiries, prepare accounts, and general assistance. She knew of the additional arrangement and in fact said in the spring of 1981 she became aware of an additional arrangement between Lester Piggott and Henry Cecil: '. . . which I was instructed to prepare in type form for distribution to a number of racehorse owners. I understood this additional arrangement called for a cash payment of £25,000 over and above the amount specified for in the retainer agreement registered at Weatherbys. Extra monies based on riding, win and placed horses and also shares for riding and winning colts retiring to stud.

'I understood Mr Cecil advised the major racehorse owners himself of the terms of the additional arrangements with Lester Piggott, leaving the remaining owners to be contacted by post. I can confirm that I prepared a similar typed document on Lester Piggott's behalf for the following three seasons he was retained as stable jockey. To the best of my recollection approximately 15 to 20 owners were contacted in this way each season. In addition to sending a copy arrangement document to the owners, I also prepared a covering letter on Henry Cecil-headed paper.' She was then shown Revenue exhibit 31 which I just referred your Lordship to, and she said: 'I have examined them and they appear to be true and accurate copies of the correspondence referred to above as being sent to racehorse owners on behalf of Lester Piggott.'

She said: 'Each agreement contained a request that payment be made by cheque made out to cash. This was done at the specific

request of Lester Piggott.' If your Lordship would look at the Customs'
bundle of exhibits at page 82 there is what seems to be a common form
request for payment in relation to the first half of the 1982 retainer. As
your Lordship sees in the second paragraph: 'Can you please send
Warren Place a cheque made out to cash.' My Lord, at 94 there is a
similar request in a different type of document; a letter from Mr Cecil
to an owner which in the second paragraph says: 'Lester has asked if it
would be possible for him to have a cheque for that amount made out
to cash. If this can be done I know he would greatly appreciate it.'
Page 29 is a similar document that I need not read out, again a request
for cash.

My Lord, there are examples, one of them is at page 76 of that
bundle, that when a cheque was not made out to cash a request was
made to alter it. My Lord, that is a document dated 16 September
1981 at page 76 to an owner from Miss Scriven and it says: 'Lester
Piggott has asked if this cheque could be made out to cash and the
crossing opened. I am so sorry to have to trouble you over this.'

My Lord, finally Miss Scriven's statement says: 'All cheques
received at her office for Mr Piggott in relation to the additional
agreement were held by me and either passed directly to Lester Piggott
or were delivered to his home address. On a number of occasions I was
approached by Lester Piggott who instructed me to remind late payers
of the amounts still outstanding in the agreement. On these occasions I
would either telephone or make a further written request to the owners
for the amounts.'

My Lord, that of course was not something known to the Inland
Revenue in detail until their investigations in January of 1986 on the
30th when they saw Mr Piggott and saw Mr Cecil, and on 31 January
when they saw Miss Scriven. Ten days or so later on 10 February 1986
Mr Richardson, Mr Piggott's solicitor, wrote a letter setting out Mr
Piggott's then general disclosure of irregularities. My Lord, that is at
exhibit 29, page 1, of the Revenue documents. Your Lordship, I know,
will have read it. Therefore I do not propose to rehearse it at length. It
is headed 'Without Prejudice, L. K. Piggott Limited,' and mentions
the extensive activities of the Customs officers on the morning of 30
January and including the raid on Florizel [Piggotts's home]. I need
not read the next paragraph. It was clearly accepted as a genuine
attempt to avoid prosecution and it has set out a promise in the fourth
paragraph that in addition he will make full disclosure of all transactions, income, etc. during this period and provide full documentation in satisfaction of his affairs.

To this letter of instruction was added an appendix (A) on the next
page in relation to disclosure which was said to be going to be

complete. Just before the set of appendices was listed, as is so often the case with such complex matters: 'Disclosure at this stage is limited to everything Lester or his Company now own as of 10 February 1986 so the following appendices are attached.'

My Lord, amongst them, apart from matters of annual breeding rights, brood mares and horses not in training, there was real property, at (E) and at (F) a list of companies both English and foreign-based in which Lester Piggott or his Company had an interest. My Lord, we will look at what was said at appendix (F) in a moment. Appendix (G) was a list of bank accounts but that was still only the National Westminster at Newmarket. Appendix (F) is mentioned at page 295 and it revealed a new name. The existence of these companies is known to the Inland Revenue except for Western Agency Incorporated. This, unlike Lambay and Zeus, had been brought onshore and it had been Bahamian. This was set up by Lester Piggott in 1983 and this name was used for his bloodstock interests: 'I have obtained such details as I can and will be handing them to Price Waterhouse who will be given such assistance as is necessary.'

My Lord, that was the disclosure on 10 February 1986 with significant omissions of the Allied Irish Bank bank accounts and indeed of Western Agency Incorporated. There followed an investigation by Price Waterhouse and on 27 August of 1986 their report purporting to show all irregularities was sent off to the Inland Revenue. A similar report a month earlier had gone to the Customs, similar in ground, which covered the fact of evasion of VAT matters. Price Waterhouse had access to all the material held by the Customs, that is, exhibit 30. Your Lordship can see the format of the covering letter. It is to the Inland Revenue Special Office: 'At the request of our client we now submit a report – three copies are enclosed – which sets out the total income derived by his Company from various sources over the period from 6 April 1968 to 5 April 1984 and list the accounts remitted to be taxed again and accounts for each year. This report has been stamped "draft". We look forward to an early meeting with your department to discuss the report which we suggest should form the basis of a negotiated settlement.' What was being looked for was a negotiated settlement and in the letter of instruction, the next document, from Price Waterhouse to Mr Piggott there appears in the top paragraph: 'Dear Sir, L. K. Piggott Limited, in accordance with the request contained in your letter of 5 April 1986 we have launched an investigation into the affairs of your Company to enable you to make voluntary disclosure of omissions.' Then they deal with what they have produced.

At the bottom paragraph the significant words: 'The reports

attached appear to have been considered by you. In the course of their preparation you confirmed to us that to the best of your knowledge and belief the information contained in these reports is accurate and complete and no further matters were required to be brought to our attention. Due to the passing of time it has not been possible to process the two individual incomes. This has been noted in the relevant appendices. You have, however, confirmed that the differences involved, if any, would not be significant in the overall context of our investigation.'

My Lord, the report disclosed a number of irregularities. The first of them was United Kingdom riding income. Would your Lordship look for this purpose to the seventh section of the bundle and to page 118, a Price Waterhouse document, the last page; it would be headed 'United Kingdom riding income for 16 years ended 5 April 1984'. Looking at the last entry for the last three years, for 1982 taxable but not paid £45,743 extra riding income for the United Kingdom, 1983 £102,820 and 1984 £63,114. My Lord, the total figure of those three years, 1982, 1983 and 1984 is £211,677. That is count three. It alleges the omission of United Kingdom riding income of £211,677 for the three years ended 5 April 1982, 1983 and 1984. That, of course, was the additional riding income in relation to the additional agreement with Henry Cecil for the retainer and for the price percentages.

My Lord, there was included in that overall figure of £211,677 in addition to the Henry Cecil monies, as it were, a sum of £10,000 which had been received in 1982 from Mr Huffer's stable as a retainer for riding Prince Yazid's horses. The terms of Piggott's contract did not confine him to riding only for Mr Cecil. If there was not a Henry Cecil mount he was free to ride others.

May we turn from United Kingdom riding income to overseas riding income, this is the subject of count four and count seven. Again, this was a disclosure in the Price Waterhouse report: understated income in respect of overseas income. In one case it is in relation to the individual and in another it is in relation to the Company. The reason for that is that at the end of 1983 there had been an agreement that Mr Piggott's overseas income for riding and commercial activities was to be assessable under him for the year up to 1982, but from 1982 onwards it was to be a limited company return.

For those two years, therefore, count seven relates to the year ending April 1983. The overseas understatement was to the extent of £28,629 for that year. Count four, out of order, was the following year overseas riding income of £19,414. Your Lordship should have, I hope, a notice of additional evidence of Mrs Chaloner. I was just going to show your Lordship where the figures come from on the schedule. The earlier year is schedule 2 and it is the top figure from Mr Piggott: Details of assessable income omitted from tax returns, overseas income, column four 1982–3 and of course the total column £28,629. Your Lordship might want to put count seven against that, and though I have not come to them yet the next two right-hand entries will be count eight and count nine, that is the £330,156 which is schedule (D) case three, that is the interest on the United Kingdom income. The next figure, £522,769 schedule (D) case five, that is interest on overseas income and that is count nine. That is the overseas income for the earlier year, 1982–3, for the individual.

If your Lordship would turn back to schedule one, the second entry down, overseas riding income, this of course being the Company by now, that figure of £19,414 which is count four. My Lord, if it assists at this stage your Lordship could put count three against the top entry which we have come to already, the understated United Kingdom riding income, and count five against the third entry, net income from bloodstock operations £646,417. Equally the last entry, additional understated riding income disclosed 8 December 1986, is count six.

My Lord, that is a convenient point to move to the income from bloodstock operations. In the 1981–3 investigations, your Lordship remembers, there had been no disclosure by Mr Piggott of income from his bloodstock operations, but the Price Waterhouse report when it came through in August 1986 disclosed that Mr Piggott had undertaken bloodstock breeding activities since 1968. My Lord, if your Lordship would look at that report, exhibit 30, page 4, paragraph 9, that is a paragraph headed 'Income from bloodstock operations', and it says: 'Bloodstock breeding activities have been undertaken since 1968. Mr Piggott has owned shares, nominations and annual breeding rights in stallions, and has owned mares either wholly or in part. Based on information supplied by Mr Piggott we have constructed a history of these activities which is set out in appendix three. This details acquisitions, disposals and transactions relating to progeny. We have substantiated the information where possible by reference to the return of mares and this has also been confirmed by Mr J. Ashenheim who handles some of the financial aspects of these matters for Mr Piggott. He is the director of International Corporation Services Limited, ICS, a company based in Grand Cayman. A copy of a letter to this company is included in appendix six. These activities have not previously been disclosed to the Inland Revenue.'

My Lord, at page 21 further on in the report, paragraph 10, under 'matters arising', there is a reference to the previous companies which had been dismantled and brought onshore, Zeus and Lambay and also Western Agency Incorporated. I shall only be taking your Lordship to a very few entries where they have significance, and this is one of them in that Price Waterhouse were saying in the previous entry that the activities had not previously been disclosed to the Inland Revenue. Now under 21 at 10, 'matters arising', it says: 'L. K. Piggott informed us of the company names under which his bloodstock interests were operated. These were Zeus and Lambay, which came onshore after the last Inland Revenue investigation, and Western Agency Inc. These names enable the bloodstock interest to be confirmed.' Your Lordship will remember that Western Agency Inc. was formed in 1983.

My Lord, Mr Ashenheim had provided lists of various bloodstock interests and further into the report there are the names of a number of stallions and mares. It is quite clear, my Lord, that Western Agency was used specifically for the registration of these bloodstock interests if one looks, for instance, at page 45, your Lordship will see the ownership of stallions, Adonijah ownership Western Agency, transactions, nominations and foal-sharing. Ardross at 47 – I am merely showing your Lordship the names of some of these stallions in the name of Western Agency – 54 Commanche Run, and there are others, Roberto at 73 which perhaps we should look at for the link between the two companies. Ownership Zeus, Lambay and Western Agency, and transactions with the nominations sold each year from 1975 to 1985. A very successful horse which I think was a Derby-winner but I stand to be corrected.

My Lord, mares, there are examples on page 86 onwards, 88 a mare, Bentink Hotel, and your Lordship sees the ownership Zeus and Western Agency. If your Lordship would move to 105, I merely show that as an example, that is the letter from Mr Ashenheim of International Corporation Services Limited to Price Waterhouse, saying: 'Western Agency Inc., Zeus Company Limited and Lambay Company Limited, we enclose herewith schedules showing the receipts and payments, cash summary and asset summary of above in so far as the transactions of the company have been advised to us and receipts and payments have passed through our office for the calendar years 1979 to 1985 inclusive. As far as we can determine from our records, advices we have received and information given by Mr L. K. Piggott, the schedules of receipts and payments and summaries attached represent a true record of the Company's activities for those years.' Your Lordship will see the names of horses set out under the various years.

My Lord, the next undisclosed income from bloodstock operations can be seen at pages 109 and 110, though it can be seen in dollars only and translated into sterling for the relevant years, it is count five. My Lord, 109 the total figure in US dollars, the Irish pound and sterling, I am sorry, it is there as well. Your Lordship sees the middle column

1983 215, 4. If your Lordship would go now to the indictment, in relation to the figure your Lordship will see that the net income from bloodstock operations for the year 5 April 1983 to 5 April 1984 was £646,417.

If we turn to count six now which is the count in relation to owners' bets covering the years from 5 April 1973 to 5 April 1984, your Lordship will see that that figure is £1,359,726. My Lord, a close examination of the Price Waterhouse report revealed that the accountants had concentrated on calculating the expected level of additional income from the records of races. Therefore it was a calculation on the expected level of additional income, and it did not in fact trace where the actual money had gone to despite the fact that it clearly had not been paid into Mr Piggott's private current account with the National Westminster Bank. It would appear that Mr Piggott had informed them that the money was retained in cash until spent. The accountants had calculated omitted income by reference to published data about Mr Piggott's races, the terms of the retainer agreement with Cecil and the papers held by the Customs. The Inland Revenue suspected that the report did not represent a full disclosure of all irregularities even at that time, that is to say the report of the summer of 1986. It was considered possible that the undeclared income had been invested in other income-producing assets.

In fact, of course, as it was later to be discovered after the original Price Waterhouse report, the Price Waterhouse report had failed to disclose – I do not say that in criticism of them because they did not know and could not know – all the accounts at the Allied Irish Bank, five of them being in false names, the further United Kingdom riding income of over £1.3 million derived from gifts by owners of their successful bets on Mr Piggott's riding, count six, nor the interest from United Kingdom banks, count eight, nor the interest from overseas banks, count nine. These were to be discovered at a later stage not in the original Price Waterhouse report, but the way in which they were discovered was as a result of a letter written to Price Waterhouse on 10 November 1986, we are moving still further through 1986 at this stage.

My Lord, it was to explore the possibility that that Price Waterhouse report was not a total disclosure, exhibit 30, that the Inland Revenue Enquiry Branch wrote the letter your Lordship finds at exhibit 33 of the Revenue documents.

We are now into November and Mrs Chaloner, the investigating officer, on 10 November wrote a letter in these terms in view of the suspicions that were then held, addressed to Price Waterhouse: 'Dear Sirs, Lester Piggott, L. K. Piggott Limited, further to our meeting I should be glad if you would arrange for me to have the following: (1) a certified statement of bank and other accounts operated by Mr Piggott in the period from 6 April 1971 to 5 April 1984. This should include all accounts which Mr Piggott and/or his wife had the power to operate whether in his name or in any other and including accounts both in the United Kingdom and abroad.' Certain other banks were mentioned, as well as Swiss banks, accounts in Grand Cayman and a bank in Singapore.

My Lord, that letter and that investigation did have fruit, but only as a result of that letter because, my Lord, it was at this stage and this stage only that an indication came from a partner in Price Waterhouse that a further disclosure was to be made. Mr Piggott's accountants and his solicitor attended a meeting with enquiry branch officers in London on 21 November 1986. It was then indicated that, faced with the Revenue request for details of all bank accounts in that letter dated 10 November 1986, Mr Piggott had admitted that the disclosure so far was very, very far from being the full story. There were the 17 at least by then, more in fact by now, different accounts held with the Allied Irish Bank, and those bank accounts were at branches in London, Dublin, Jersey and the Isle of Man.

My Lord, interest arising on the various bank accounts totalled about £850,000. It was admitted that the accounts also contained additional United Kingdom riding income which by 15 July amounted to £1,359,726.

MR JUSTICE FARQUHARSON: You are saying that had not previously been disclosed?

MR HIDDEN: My Lord, that figure had not been disclosed until this stage. This income was said to derive from owner bets on horses ridden by Mr Piggott, and if the horse won Mr Piggott would be given the winnings. Since the income arose from his profession as a jockey it was accordingly properly assessable to the Company because of the agreement between Mr Piggott and the Company. Full details of those matters, all bank statements and a reply to the letter of 10 November were promised within a week. In December of 1986 Mrs Chaloner, the officer in charge of the investigation, received an affidavit from Mr Piggott dated 8 December 1986 and your Lordship will find that at exhibit 35.

The affidavit itself is at page one of exhibit 35 and in it Mr Piggott attaches a statement of all assets 'owned by me as at the first day of December 1986, save for personal borrowings neither I nor any of my companies owns any other assets either in this country or abroad'. Your Lordship then sees on the next page, property investments, bloodstock and bank balances. The property investments set out at

35.3, the interest and bloodstock at 35.4, statement of bank accounts operated set out at 35.5, dealing with the position as at 4 December 1986.

My Lord, if your Lordship would now turn back to the letter of 8 December 1986, exhibit 34, your Lordship will see the letter written on 8 December from Price Waterhouse to Mr Hugo of the enquiry branch. Your Lordship sees on that document at page 34.3 the statement of bank and other accounts operated by L. K. Piggott Esq. and or his wife in the period 5 April to date, the National Westminster Bank being the top one. No disclosure in fact at that stage of the John Jackson account. The John Jackson account was only discovered by the Revenue in September of this year. My Lord, the Allied Irish Bank includes the 17 that were extant on 29 April 1983, but your Lordship will see other names as well.

MR JUSTICE FARQUHARSON: What was the extent of the usage of the John Jackson account?

MR HIDDEN: My Lord, it was an account which was opened for three and a half years. It was an account which in fact had pass through it something like a few pounds under £300,000 over the whole period, but in relation to it nearly all of that money did in fact find its way through the Allied Irish Bank accounts in Jersey and so it does not fall to be doubly considered.

My Lord, the effect of this further disclosure in December 1986, not disclosed in the Price Waterhouse report in the summer of 1986 because they had not got the information, really reacts, of course, on counts one and two as showing what the falsity of disclosure was as at 29 April 1983, but it also indicates that very large sums were still being suppressed until, sadly, December 1986. The effect was that substantial amounts of income had been concealed and had continued to be concealed in the current accounts for the years ending April 1983 and April 1984.

My Lord, there were three elements which only got disclosed now. First of all, count six, the additional United Kingdom riding income of £1,359,726, then count eight, the interest from United Kingdom banks, schedule (D) case three, 1980 to 1984, for those five years, £330,156, and thirdly count nine, the interest from overseas banks, schedule (D), 1975 to 1984, ten years, £522,127.

If your Lordship therefore looks at the schedule again – Mrs Chaloner's schedule – your Lordship sees that so far as the Company is concerned, this December 1986 disclosure is the bottom entry and by far the largest, the £1.3 million. All that was being disclosed before that time were the top three, counts three, four and five. So far as the individual is concerned, on schedule two it is the bottom two matters that are now being disclosed: £330,156 which is count eight and £522,769 which is count nine. So putting those three items together, counts six, eight and nine, the total disclosed in December 1986 which had not been disclosed before is £2.2 million – in exact figures, £2,212,009.

If your Lordship would look now at exhibit 34, 19, and we are nearly at the end of the road – I do not take your Lordship through any of the figures and in fact your Lordship does not need to look at the document, it is clear from other documents that initially Mr Piggott had bank accounts in the Republic of Ireland, for instance the Lambay external deposit accounts at Allied Irish Finance, but in 1979 he seems to have become concerned at the falling value of the Irish pound and paid substantial amounts into accounts in London: the K. Armstrong deposit account at the Allied Irish Bank at Bruton Street and also the Isle of Man. My Lord, he equally operated deposit accounts in the name of K. Armstrong in the Bruton Street branch.

Your Lordship will have a notice of additional evidence which has Mrs Chaloner's evidence and with it the schedules; if your Lordship would turn to that, your Lordship will also find the additional evidence of Mr McHale. I digress to your Lordship, that money was moved from Ireland to the Allied Irish Bank at Bruton Street and also in the Isle of Man. Mr McHale, the manager of the Bruton Street, West One, branch of the Allied Irish Bank, produced a memorandum which your Lordship sees attached at TJM 1, 1979, which is support for the matter I put to your Lordship earlier about the concern by Mr Piggott as to the falling value of the Irish pound.

My Lord, the letter reads, dated 3 April 1979 to Tim Godfrey: 'Our mutual friend, Lester Piggott, controls this Company' – the heading above is Lambay Company Limited – 'but is not a director. He wishes to open an account with you and will be calling on you next week for this purpose. In the meantime we are enclosing all the necessary documentation to enable you to open the account. I would mention that I had Lester with me today for over two and a half hours and he was very concerned at the falling value of the Irish pound. As you are aware he has a very considerable sum of money in this country. However, the rules and regulations were set by the Central Bank, nothing much I can do about it. It is well for you to know this.'

My Lord, the other documents TJM 4 and 5, certificates under the Finance Act 1952 and tax measure 1970. As your Lordship can see from those documents, they are documents that have to be signed to open an account at the Allied Irish Bank in London and one of them is in relation to an account in the name of K. Day and S. Day. What it is is a declaration that: 'The person who was beneficially entitled to the interest shall be paid or credited in respect of money received or retained in the above stated account, if not ordinarily resident in the United Kingdom at the date of this notice.' Your Lordship sees that it is addressed to the Allied Irish Bank at Bruton Street.

MR JUSTICE FARQUHARSON: It has an overseas address.

MR HIDDEN: My Lord, yes, but the overseas address, 1 Lower Road, Collins Street, Dublin, is the Dublin branch of the Allied Irish Bank. The effect of those declarations, of course, ensured that the Inland Revenue were not informed of the interest which was arising.

My Lord, the effect finally, therefore, I hope pulling all the threads together, of that disclosure revealed that false accounts for the Company, L. K. Piggott Limited, had been submitted to the Inland Revenue for each of the years 5 April 1973 to 5 April 1984, twelve years, and false tax returns by Mr Piggott himself for each of the years 5 April 1975 to 5 April 1984.

My Lord, there is one further schedule to refer your Lordship to which will show the difference so far as the Company is concerned between that which was declared and that which was not. Would your Lordship go to the last schedule, schedule nine. Schedule nine is a comparison of the Company profits disclosed with the actual profits. It runs from 1973 to 1984 tax years. The first and third columns are disclosed columns, and the second and fourth are reality. Profits chargeable to corporation tax as originally disclosed over those years were declared as £127,104. The actual profits were £2,364,367. The consequence of the actual tax paid on the profits returned had been £49,077, the correct corporation tax payable is £1.2 million. Exactly, £1,200,335.20.

My Lord, finally may I turn to the question of VAT and count ten and deal equally and specifically with the question of what the position was as to the retainer. My Lord, as to value added tax, certain cases where income was not disclosed for Inland Revenue purposes, undisclosed income, represented taxable supplies for VAT purposes. L. K. Piggott Limited was VAT-registered, but Mr Piggott failed to disclose to his accountants, Saunter Chappell, who prepared the VAT returns, substantial amounts of income and upon which VAT was truly payable. After the visit by Customs and Excise officials in January 1986 on the 30th to Mr Piggott's home, Mr Piggott employed Price Waterhouse to analyse the records of L. K. Piggott Limited and to calculate the exact amount of VAT evaded.

My Lord, the figure for which he failed to account in total is £840,836 over the period 1 November 1979 to 31 October 1985. A calculation was made by Price Waterhouse on a VAT-inclusive basis. Although it appears that owners were charged for additional L. K. Piggott retainers, they were not charged a specific amount of VAT. There was not a 15 per cent added to the extra amounts. It was a global extra amount, of course, would have included, as it were, a VAT element, but there was not a surcharge collected and kept. I say that as a point in favour of this defendant.

The way in which the money broke down was this. The main category was bloodstock operations and that amounted to undeclared income of £78,721. Two other categories were additional prize percentages, £21,915.53, and finally, the matter I have just mentioned, the retainers, retainers not registered with Weatherbys amounted to £24,521 in relation to VAT.

My Lord, a letter had been sent to the Company by the Bury St Edmunds office which made it clear that VAT was due on extra retainers whether or not registered with Weatherby's, and, my Lord, of course in the answers given to the Customs officers on 30 January Mr Piggott accepted that.

My Lord, unless I can assist you further, that is the explanation for the ten counts.

MR JUSTICE FARQUHARSON: There are just one or two things I would like your help on. With regard to the Company, which of course is liable to fines, do you have any information or instructions as to its assets or capital, or indeed the value of its overall assets?

MR HIDDEN: My Lord, I have not, but I anticipate my learned friend will be able to assist your Lordship.

MR JUSTICE FARQUHARSON: Repayments of tax?

MR HIDDEN: My Lord, there have been payments. The figures I can put before your Lordship are these. A total of £3,091,653 paid on account between the period 5 March 1986 to 15 October 1987. My Lord, there were two payments of £200,000 in March 1986, one of £100,000 in June bringing it up to £500,000, and there was a payment of £1,849,710 in February of this year, one in March of £215,338, £250,000 in June and the final payment of £276,605 on 15 October.

MR JUSTICE FARQUHARSON: This is repayment of tax underpaid, is it?

MR HIDDEN: My Lord, it is, yes.

MR MATHEW: I am so sorry to interrupt, but that figure of £3 million is tax underpaid, £2.86 million tax and interest. It is those three figures. The tax underpaid and interest in relation to the matters in the indictment are about £2.8 million. So it is just £200,000-odd more than his liabilities in respect of these matters.

MR HIDDEN: My Lord, I will have that checked and will be able to confirm it to your Lordship, but I am sure my friend would not say it unless it were right.

MR JUSTICE FARQUHARSON: It is of considerable importance as sometimes it is reflected in any sentence. So if he has substantially repaid there is no need for me to consider that aspect, but presumably the Revenue have their own remedies about any balance.

MR MATHEW: I shall be explaining that in detail to your Lordship.

MR HIDDEN: My Lord, by virtue of the fact that the sums involved in the indictment amount to £1.73 million the clear inference is that that tax is paid back and more. I will certainly have full details for your Lordship.

MR JUSTICE FARQUHARSON: The last one is a fairly technical point. I see your VAT count – count ten – is in a form I have not come across before in relation to VAT matters. It is common law, cheating of the Revenue?

MR HIDDEN: My Lord, yes. The reason for that is a simple and statutory one, that two years is the maximum time-limit in relation to the substantive offence. My Lord, there is an officer for the antecedents but I anticipate your Lordship will not want one.

MR JUSTICE FARQUHARSON: Unless Mr Mathew requires him?

MR MATHEW: No, my Lord, I do not.

MR HIDDEN: My Lord, I am instructed to ask for costs and to tell your Lordship that the figure as an aggregate both to Customs and the Revenue is £34,000.

MR JUSTICE FARQUHARSON: Thank you.

After almost an hour and a half on his feet, Mr Hidden sat down. He had outlined the case precisely, causing the most hardened of observers to shake their heads in disbelief as the facts emerged. Throughout the prosecution evidence, Piggott had sat impassively, his eyes on Mr Hidden, except for when he occasionally glanced up towards the packed public gallery.

When Mr Justice Farquharson announced an adjournment for lunch, it gave Piggott's solicitor, Jeremy Richardson, a brief moment to talk to his client. His half-moon spectacles perched on the end of his nose, Mr Richardson was joined by Susan Piggott and the three of them spoke together for a minute or so before Piggott was led away.

Outside the courtroom, a small crowd had gathered as word of the case spread through the town. The local newspaper, the *East*

Anglian Evening News, was already on the streets, a picture of Piggott arriving at the court emblazoned across the front page.

Just over an hour later, it was time for Mr John Mathew, QC, to continue his plea in mitigation. But after what the court had heard already, the feeling was that it was going to need a miracle to keep Piggott from going to prison.

16. A Reputation in Ruins

The services of Mr John Mathew, QC, do not come cheap. Renowned for his sharp legal brain and as one of Britain's finest criminal defence advocates, the 61-year-old barrister was up against it as he tried to explain away Piggott's actions. Before he made his opening address, Mr Mathew explained to Mr Justice Farquharson that, of the £3,091,653 paid in tax, £1.7 million was the total amount of the tax evaded. Starting his submission some 45 minutes before the lunch adjournment, Mr Mathew had passed to the judge a small folder containing a medical report from a Professor Russell to which he would be referring during his address.

So it was with the packed courtroom hanging on his every word that Mr Mathew continued his plea to hopefully keep his client a free man.

MR MATHEW: May it please your Lordship. My Lord, every so often courts are faced with what can only be described as an overwhelming personal tragedy for which, on the face of it, there does not appear to be any reasonable explanation – and this is one of those occasions. How is it conceivable that someone who has – and one genuinely so – become a legend in his own lifetime, one of the world's greatest sports personalities probably in all history, a man who has given so much pleasure to so many and a man who, I was going to say, commanded, but it would be right to say commands, so much adulation and respect: how is it conceivable that he finds himself in your Lordship's court having pleaded guilty to tax offences involving such very large sums of money and of course that castle of his achievement and reputation in ruins at his feet?

As well known as he is perhaps in actuality, as I will be attempting to explain, a few if any know him well enough or are capable of understanding his complex character. To answer that question with any degree of certainty it is my task now to try and persuade your Lordship, as I hope to do, that, despite the very serious circumstances disclosed by these offences, there are in fact mitigating factors here which could properly persuade your Lordship to show a degree of leniency, which might not otherwise have seemed possible.

My Lord, may I start with the personality, the defendant himself, because in our submission it is so important to try and understand his personality in order to judge how intentional and dishonest was this course of conduct. He is a man whose whole life from childhood to his present age of 52 has been racing. Horses were his father's job, his mother's interest, and the family tradition. Racing became for him physically and mentally a total and obsessive occupation to which his dedication was supreme for most of the 24 hours of the seven days of the week in which he applied himself to it. When he was not actually racing, as I will be explaining in a few moments in a little more detail, he was visiting trainers, riding, working in the early hours of the morning, travelling endlessly from racecourse to racecourse and, indeed, from country to country; at times suffering, I underline that word, *suffering* from the agonies and constant struggle of making the weight of eight stone three.

In trying to give your Lordship a picture of this man's character which I have already described as complex, perhaps it is unnecessary for me to detail the incredibly successful career which began at an abnormally early age, but I intend to do so only in a few sentences. As I have said he comes from a racing family. Indeed his wife is also the daughter of a well-known trainer. His father was a trainer. He was, as is probably well-known, deaf from birth and has suffered from the additional handicap of speaking indistinctly almost as if he had an impediment, which in fact he has not got.

At the age of four years he was first consciously put on a horse. At the age of 12 years, it would not be allowed now, he won his first race. From then his career as a jockey spanned the next 37 years until two years ago, almost exactly two years ago. At the age of 14 he was champion apprentice jockey for a year. He left school again as one could in those days with having taken no exams and really, no academic interests at all even at that stage in his life. At the age of 18 he rode his first Derby-winner and from that time was really coming out in the public eye, riding 29 Classic-winners over the next 36 years in England and abroad. He has, as I said, over that period married Mr Armstrong's daughter and he has two daughters of his own, now grown-up.

During the 1970s – I mention these facts because they will be relevant to the story which I hope to be able to unfold – he had an arrangement not exclusively to ride for a very well-known Irish trainer, Mr Vincent O'Brien. He stopped that arrangement and, as from the 1981 season, as your Lordship has already heard, he became stable jockey for Mr Henry Cecil at Newmarket, retiring at the end of the 1985 season. For the last two years he has turned to training at an establishment in Newmarket which he had purchased and slowly put together gradually over the previous years in preparation for the retirement which he dreaded.

My Lord, therefore, as a jockey he had really dominated his profession for 30 years and had done so not only by his skill but also, and this is accepted on all hands as I understand it, his unlimited courage and tremendous determination about which those who know him really speak with awe – I have spoken to some of them; an incomparable genius on the back of the horse, but while he can thrill the crowds in that way he was by no means a charismatic person himself. I think some have alleged him to be shrewd and clever, based no doubt upon his superb judgement and dedication as a rider. The fact is, as your Lordship will have seen in Professor Russell's report, that generally speaking, in life away from horses, I stress those words 'in life away from horses,' he is in fact a man of limited intellectual capacity, in the low/average range of intelligence which, as Professor Russell suggests, will have been lowered more in the recent years by a degree of brain damage resulting from head injuries which had been caused over the period by a number of substantial falls.

No doubt – there does not seem to be any doubt about it – because of his defects and resulting speech disability he has never been an easy person with whom to communicate. I can speak for that myself. Therefore he has few real friends and even those few do not feel that they really know him and speak at times of finding it impossible to understand his thinking, reactions and behaviour. Basically he is accepted as being a loner and a very secret man by nature. Secretiveness which has built up because by the very nature of his profession he has to be secret. He cannot talk about what he knows. He cannot make suggestions to all those persons who pursue him both from the press and those interested in the racing world. Those who have grown up with horses and are involved in the world of racing tend to have few if any other interests, and they have little contact with people in other walks of life. This, so I am instructed, is particularly so with jockeys who do tend to be a somewhat small and insular crowd and certainly isolated from the business world and the distances which go with it.

If I be right about that and if those employed in the racing world tend to be isolated people, then Lester Piggott was totally so. For him the real battle of deafness kept away the rest of the world, the rest of the world who if not connected with racing were of no interest to him in any event. It was not only his difficulty in hearing which turned him inwards upon himself, but his upbringing: the fact that he was an only child, the very nature of his jockey's life, so much so that even his wife, who hears what I say, has herself sometimes wondered whether she really knows him and understands on occasions really what makes him tick.

My Lord, I have suggested that his way of life has contributed to the development of his personal characteristics. It was a very tough – I say 'was' because he is now a trainer rather than a jockey – it was a very tough and vigorous life during the eight-month season's racing, as was each and every day's occurrences and frequently seven days a week because on Sundays he rode on the Continent, particularly in France and Italy. Just as an example of the life he lived, in 1981 he had 703 races in England, that is about 20 races a week, at different racecourses, winning 25 per cent of them, perhaps one should add this in parentheses, being placed in 50 per cent of them. Also, unlike other sports, that entailed many thousands of miles to racecourses up and down the country. His whole life was either being on horses, in motor cars or in aeroplanes.

One does not associate Flat racing as distinct from steeplechasing with accidents and injuries, but one knows that thoroughbreds are temperamental beasts and racing is intrinsically dangerous. Lester Piggott has had more accidents than he can remember. He has broken practically every bone in his body and still suffers from the after-effects of a fractured skull in 1964. I quote this from Professor Russell's report: 'head injuries of minor or moderate severity caused by repeated falls'. Indeed, as my Lord will see Professor Russell seems to have little doubt that some degree of brain damage has resulted and that has impaired his capacity to learn new material, to retain it and even suspects that it may well have affected his judgement.

My Lord, the fact is that his dedication to that hectic sort of life really left him no time for other interests, nor to develop relations and friendships with anyone outside racing. Possibly more importantly in the context of this case he had not time – I will come to the inclinations in a moment – to spend his hard-earned money even if he wanted to. The fact is he had no tastes which meant he bought nothing, he collected nothing, he had no hobbies, he virtually has no possessions except what is in his house which are largely trophies. He just never spent any money at all on himself or in fact on others.

The fact that he had no time to spend is probably only part-explanation for being so frugal in his ways, because, as anyone who has had dealings with him will confirm, he was a thrifty person by nature and upbringing. He just did not like or want to spend money and would never volunteer payment for anything unless he had to. He therefore has a reputation, maybe this is merited, of meanness and for keeping his hands in his pockets. He was asked about this by Professor Russell and he attributed this to a life-long habit from a very early age when his parents drummed into him that every penny had to be looked after.

Of course, proof of this is to be found in the fact that he never spent any or virtually none of this money, the subject of this indictment, which should have been paid in tax. It was all there at the end. It was sitting in these bank accounts, disclosed and undisclosed – I will come to that in a moment – unused and apparently unwanted rolling up with interest year after year to absurdly high proportions, but he was a hoarder and not a spender. None of that money was used for his own gratification. The fact of the matter is that he then in reality really did not need it, and for that reason he now finds his conduct in respect of these matters over the years really impossible to explain. Again your Lordship will have seen, when asked about this by Professor Russell, he found himself in that situation of only being able to say that he really did not know and that of course it was quite ridiculous.

My Lord, there may be yet a further explanation for this – I suppose 'hoarding syndrome' could be a phrase for it. For 30 years he controlled his weight at nearly two stones below his normal weight by self-imposed food deprivation. In other words he systematically starved himself. One of his friends and contemporaries described it as him waging a war on his body. Everything in his life turned to his obsession for success no matter what the sacrifices. Indeed his wife has told me that frequently, when being driven by her travelling to racecourses late in a car, wrapped in jersies in a plastic suit, he had the windows closed and the heater full on in order to lose two or three pounds by the time he got to a Midlands racecourse where he was racing that day. I have told your Lordship that because that does describe the sorts of pressures and strains under which he literally drove himself day after day, month after month and year after year.

So nobody probably really knows the effect of that type of physical self-denial upon the mind and character. It obviously would vary as between individuals, but hoarding is a well-known symptom in those who deprive themselves of food. An anorexic tends to behave in that sort of way or even to steal. No doubt for that reason Professor Russell – I do not put this too highly because your Lordship sees what he said – does think it is possible at least that this habit of undernutrition may have become more generalised into a pattern of extreme thrift and hoarding and he feels could well have impaired his good judgement in other respects. So, for whatever reason, certainly through no fault of his own.

Perhaps the nature of this man could be summarised in this way: a genius as a jockey by ruthless determination, dedication and self-denial, but an introverted and isolated person with an inability to communicate; a person of extreme thrift and a hoarder of money; a man with no interests, no relations or indeed any knowledge of anything outside racing; brilliant within his own little tiny sphere, but really uneducated in all other aspects of life about which he was uninterested, uncaring and probably without the mental or physical energy left even to try to cope.

As I indicated, his wife is here. She could confirm what I have been saying to your Lordship, but, my Lord, it is not my intention to call her unless your Lordship felt it would be of any assistance to the court.

MR JUSTICE FARQUHARSON: No, it has come from you in this way and I would not want to put her through the experience of having to give evidence. I accept what you say.

MR MATHEW: She would be only too happy to do so if necessary. May I, hopefully having given a short and accurate sketch of the man, now turn to the matters the subject of this indictment. I would like to take it chronologically in the same way as my learned friend. May I therefore start by saying just a little, not very much, about the 1970 investigation because it is part of the story. There was one very relevant factor in 1970 which one can say affected what happened at a very much later period. My Lord, that investigation which took two or three years to finalise resulted in what we call the 1973 settlement. His accountant up to that time had been a Mr Ray from a small firm of accountants. I make no criticism about Mr Ray, far from it, but it was quite a small firm of accountants in Oxford.

If we are dealing with the period, as we are, for 20 years up to 1970, Lester Piggott's earnings were minimal in the past compared with what they became certainly in the 1980s. Up to 1970, jockeys received only riding fees. A percentage of the prize monies was payable subsequently, shortly after 1970, the following year I believe . . . it was introduced at about that time and, because there was only a taxed riding fee, cash presents, to use a neutral term. Cash presents from winning owners had become commonplace to the jockey that rode their winning horses. It appears that nobody in the racing world had been declaring them for tax at that time, and it was to that aspect that the enquiry was directed, taking over a period of 20 years.

As your Lordship can appreciate there was a demand for tax. It was assessed at £50,000 or thereabouts over that whole period of 20 years which again he had to pay, but there was a matter of some relevance to the subsequent disclosures or non-disclosures which took place in 1986. There was a matter during the course of that enquiry fairly early on in the investigations Lester Piggott voluntarily disclosed, in fact he did so in writing through his accountant, that he had received some cash payments from owners who had placed a bet on his behalf. I do not think it is necessary for me to show a copy of this document to your Lordship, but it is in the 1973 investigation file. What he said was: 'The few occasions on which owners have voluntarily placed bets on my behalf have not been included as earned income. I have regarded them as personal and untaxable.'

Two years later he was asked to comment further on that statement. We know that because it is in the correspondence. He was asked to comment not only on that but on a number of other matters. I think he made no further comment on that and the matter was never pursued by the Inland Revenue either in correspondence or in the meetings which they had with Mr Ray, Mr Piggott's accountant. This did have some relevance of course, but it was only literally two or three months in August of this year that it was appreciated it might be relevant to this case. Mr Ray was asked about this not only by those instructing me but also by those who instruct Mr Hidden. Statements were taken from him by both parties.

What Mr Ray had to say was this, harkening back to 1970, that if that matter had been pursued his argument would have been that in so far as a bet voluntarily and freely put on by an owner for the benefit of the jockey, if that had been pursued, it would have been argued that the winnings as distinct from the stake would not be taxable, that the stake would be considered a per cent and the bet would be put on, but the winnings would be treated as any other winnings. That would have been the argument. I think neither he nor Lester Piggott has any direct recollection of this because it is 1970. Mr Ray feels quite satisfied that he must have advised Lester Piggott in that way.

MR JUSTICE FARQUHARSON: You did say the investigation was relevant directly to this particular part of the income. Did anything come of that?

MR MATHEW: What happened was this. This dragged on for two and a half years, not at any great pace or with any sense of urgency, as I understand it, but a settlement in the end was arranged on a shortfall basis. What happened was in the end it was estimated what was the difference between – I think they took one year for this purpose – his living expenses in that year or years and the assets produced, and they then compared that with the disclosed income. They bore in mind the basis on which he had been receiving cash presents approximating to 10 per cent of the winning prize money on the horse he rode, and upon that basis this figure of £50,000 was arrived at. It was done for one or two years and then spread over the period, but it was a total estimate.

MR JUSTICE FARQUHARSON: Underestimating the subject of the 1970 enquiry was in relation to these cash presents?

MR MATHEW: Entirely, I think I am right in saying because it has been on cash presents in one form or another and this kind of betting freely and voluntarily by Lester Piggott had not been declared and was not being declared to the racing industry at that time. That was the basis of that enquiry. So duty on what part of the owner's bet if any part was liable to tax was not directly received.

May I turn to the 1983 agreement and I can probably deal with this in a few sentences before your Lordship adjourns. My Lord, as to the 1983 settlement, as we know, but it is important to bear this date with respect in mind, this enquiry started in September 1981, that was towards the end of the 1981 racing season, the Flat racing season which ran from March through to early November. By now the accountants had changed. The accountants had changed at the end of or at the time of the 1972/3 settlement first to senior Mr Chappell and then I think his son took over in the mid-1970s.

As Mr Hidden has told your Lordship, the principal issue again there was the inadequacy of the disclosure of cash presents since 1973. The settlement was again based on estimates, as I explained to your Lordship just a moment or two ago, in 1973. It had been conceded that cash payments of approximately 10 per cent had been made at that time and 10 per cent that is of prize money in winning races. What the Revenue were basically complaining about was that it now appeared that, subsequent to 1981, although some cash presents had been declared they did not amount to 10 per cent. It was nearer to 8 per cent and therefore ultimately in respect of both the United Kingdom and overseas riding the figure which has been broken down by Mr Hidden was £58,000 estimated in respect of United Kingdom riding and £27,000 in respect of overseas riding. Then there was a further figure of capital gains which had nothing whatsoever to do with riding at all, but that was the position in the 1983 settlement.

I had indicated to your Lordship with respect to note that that enquiry had started in September of 1981. That was towards the end of Lester Piggott's first season with Henry Cecil. A year before, or approximately a year before, during the autumn of 1980 leading up to the 1981 season, towards the end of which this enquiry started, in the autumn of 1980 the first arrangements – when I say 'arrangements' the first owners-paying-cash arrangements about which you have heard and seen the documents – had been entered into for the purpose of the 1981 season. Although your Lordship has seen the documents dated the end of 1981 relating to the 1982 season, in fact this happened first in the previous season, his first season riding for that stable.

MR JUSTICE FARQUHARSON: Yes, Mr Mathew.

MR MATHEW: My Lord, I was going to come straightaway to what I have termed the Henry Cecil arrangement, that is count three and exhibit 31 to which Mr Hidden referred your Lordship which is the letter which was circulated to the owners. Your Lordship will remember it was the letter dated December 1981 with the attached 'strictly private and confidential' note. My Lord, perhaps it is this document which gives an insight into the thinking or lack of it, possibly, and the total failure not only by Lester Piggott but many others to appreciate the seriousness and dangers and indeed dishonesty involved in entering into an agreement such as this, because it was done in such a blatantly open way.

My Lord, could I just in a few sentences without making any comment at all, I will though in a moment, just remind your Lordship of the history of this matter. In November 1980 at the end of the 1980 season during which Lester Piggott had been riding for Vincent O'Brien, he agreed then – there was a change around of jockeys in fact at the end of that season with the various trainers – to ride with the Henry Cecil stable as stable jockey. Before he started, as your Lordship is aware, a written agreement, it is not a document which is now available and therefore has not been exhibited, was entered into as between Lester Piggott and Cecil. Your Lordship will see reference to that made in the very first statement in the prosecution bundle, that is, Mr Cecil's statement. Your Lordship will see that Mr Cecil's company solicitor was a party to that agreement.

My Lord, subsequently nearly all the owners, there were 60-odd owners, I think, at that time, were informed by the letter exhibit 31 as to what that arrangement was. The agreement upon which the letter was based as between Piggott and Cecil was of course well known to Mr Piggott, but the letter itself which was circulated by Mr Cecil's secretary to the owners was not in fact ever seen, certainly Mr Piggott cannot remember seeing it, until it came to be published as it was in a Sunday newspaper in February of 1985 having to Piggott's knowledge at the time been touted around Fleet Street for nine months, the person concerned seeking to obtain a payment of £50,000. Needless to say, when it was eventually published in February 1985 that publication alerted the Inland Revenue and led to this enquiry and ultimately this prosecution.

Now, my Lord, those are the facts, the bare facts. Having told your Lordship what they are, and I do not think there can be any dispute about them, I now do have some comment to make. First of all on Mr Piggott's behalf I want it to be clearly understood that if it be said, as it certainly is in that statement to which I have referred your Lordship, that this arrangement was the brainchild of Lester Piggott, then it is categorically refuted. Indeed, that now seems to be, if I may say so, very properly and fairly conceded by the Crown.

MR JUSTICE FARQUHARSON: Yes, it was said this morning.

MR MATHEW: Because the fact is that this was by no means the first cash arrangement which had been entered into by a training establishment with a jockey. Unhappily up to the time these matters surfaced and matters relating to other jockeys at about the same time, cash payments by owners were not unusual and everyone knew they were being made, everyone connected with racing. It was an open secret.

My Lord, racing has always tended to be a cash business and payments of cash which went straight into the pocket had unfortunately, and I say this quite frankly, become an accepted way of life. So much so that, unbelievably, there was nothing secret or underhand about it, as demonstrated by the way that letter, exhibit 31, to the owners was produced and distributed. The original arrangement as between the jockey and the trainer drafted by the trainer's solicitor, entered into by the trainer, the terms circulated as I have already indicated openly to owners of standing in the racing world, including members and at least one steward of the Jockey Club, most of whom – I say 'most' because it was not compulsory – made cash payments in this way.

My Lord, the sins of others are certainly vested on this man's shoulders. Did anyone, anyone, advise him against it, professional advisers, lay advisers, trainer, friends, owners, members, stewards? No. Did anyone take any sort of step to prevent it? No. Of course the fact that others may have known and been a party is in one sense irrelevant to the degree of this man's culpability. May I say at once he makes no complaint that others who took part and must in some degree share the blame remain unaccused, but am I not entitled to say, because I am going to on his behalf, that on those facts inevitably it was bound to come to light. He could not, as he did not, so I am firmly instructed, have appreciated the extent of the wrongdoing in which he had been brought up and become enmeshed. This is so amply demonstrated, is it not, by his conduct when he discovered, as he did nine months before the event, that a copy of that letter, efforts were being made to sell it to the press. What did he do? Absolutely nothing. He made no effort to stop what he was doing. He made no effort to cover up what he had been doing. He just carried on as before and no advice or suggestion came from anyone, let alone his professional advisers.

MR JUSTICE FARQUHARSON: There was one statement amongst these where somebody rather admirably took a line, is there not?

MR MATHEW: There is one statement, if it is the statement to which I think your Lordship is referring, where somebody took a line, made it known to the necessary authorities, spoke to the persons concerned but not to Mr Piggott and then paid the cash himself. My Lord, that is the situation.

MR JUSTICE FARQUHARSON: Well, I think the payment was made on the basis of what he understood was registered at Weatherbys.

MR MATHEW: My Lord, with respect, no. There is no way that that could have been the suggestion because payments were made through Weatherbys in addition to that payment about which your Lordship has seen in that statement. Payments were properly made by that owner to Weatherbys and then in addition a cash cheque to Mr Piggott in that amount of £649, whatever it was, in accordance with what he must have appreciated could only have arisen under this particular arrangement about which he had taken some steps but which were not followed up and the persons whom he had approached took no action themselves.

MR JUSTICE FARQUHARSON: Whether he did or not, the point you make that this was a widespread habit no doubt would provide some protection to accusations made against your client, but really the *gravamen* of the offence so far as that count is concerned is that when he was asked to reveal what had taken place more than once he neglected, refused or omitted to do so. If it was merely one of an understatement or a non-payment that was endemic throughout the trade or profession, whatever, vocation, if you like, that would be rather a different matter, but it is the subsequent events that influence me to some degree.

MR MATHEW: Of course, my Lord, but in relation to this particular matter there was at this time such payments being made to others on a very widespread and well-known basis. It is those sums of money which are the subject of count three about which no disclosure was made in 1982 at the time of that enquiry, I accept that, but it was at a time when it was being carried out by everyone throughout, really, the whole of this particular industry.

My Lord, let me then, if I may, come chronologically to 1986. As I was saying just a moment or two ago, that document was published in the press in February 1985. It was inevitable, as anyone in their right mind must have realised, that another Inland Revenue enquiry was instituted resulting in the action which was taken in January 1986 when Piggott was approached and documents and so on were seized. Eleven months, that was, after the publication of that letter. As your Lordship has been told, he immediately agreed to co-operate and appointed accountants at his own expense to investigate and report. That he did at a cost to him of £250,000 or thereabouts. The enquiries were voluminous and your Lordship has seen the sort of report which was the final result of that widespread investigation by those highly reputable accountants.

Again, as your Lordship has been told, in addition to the cash benefits which were described in the article which I have just dealt with in count three, the matters which came to light were really threefold: the overseas income, that is counts four and seven, totally just under £50,000 of omissions and therefore – I have not got the exact figure in front of me – approximately half that as a tax evasion, mostly riding and professional fees abroad, and, I think I am entitled to say this, a comparatively insignificant sum in the overall context of this case. More importantly the other two matters which came to light were, first of all, the income from bloodstock interests which was completely disclosed at the time of the Price Waterhouse investigation and, finally, that sum of £1.3 million derived from owners' betting over the years. The nature of that disclosure, or perhaps I should say non-disclosure because it did not come to light until after the draft report of Price Waterhouse had been produced, requires explanation.

My Lord, may I turn to those two matters, the bloodstock interests and owners' betting. I will take the bloodstock first. To some extent it is right to say that this does overlap with that sum of £1.3 million. My Lord, what happened was this. During the 1960s, I am going back now to that period, Lester Piggott was riding frequently in Ireland as a result of his arrangement with Mr O'Brien. In 1969 through one of Mr O'Brien's owners he received the present of a nomination in respect of a famous stallion called Sir Ivor. Therefore he bought a mare to make use of that nomination and as a result his bloodstock interest started from that time, back in 1969.

By 1972 he had four or five mares and various other interests, whether it was a share, an ABR or a nomination does not really matter, he had various other interests in other stallions. My Lord, stallions then and now, as I understand it, nearly always stand abroad, offshore, outside the UK if for no other reason than nowadays it means it is not subject to VAT, but historically stallions have always stood outside this country. It therefore has been an invariable custom in the racing world for all bloodstock operations to be conducted on an offshore basis.

By 1972 in circumstances which I will detail in just a moment when I come to the owners' betting, owners particularly in Ireland had begun the practice of giving their winning bets on their horses to the jockey or part of it. Because he required a bank account for his bloodstock business which was slowly beginning to build up he opened an account in Dublin at the Allied Irish Bank in the name of Lambay, the offshore company in whose name his bloodstock was perfectly properly registered.

The intention at that time was to have that account in Ireland in order to make payments out of it in respect of his bloodstock interests, which at that time were largely in Ireland. The bloodstock income as distinct from payments was largely being credited, as you have been told, to the Lambay account which was offshore, originally in the Bahamas. In the result, because the Dublin account, in order to make the payments in respect of his bloodstock interests, needed funds, it started by being funded as a result of the cash payments he was being given from owners' betting. In fact there were comparatively little bloodstock payments to be made in the 1970s, the income being derived largely from selling nominations that he had been given and a few sales of yearlings that he had bred.

My Lord, I can probably deal with this very shortly and simply. If one takes the period 1972 to 1980 the profit and loss on his bloodstock dealings at that period more or less evened out over those eight years. Sometimes they made a profit, sometimes they made a loss. The substantial profits really started to arise as from 1981. That appears to be borne out by a schedule which one can find at page 23 in the Price Waterhouse report, but to which I do not think it is necessary for me to refer.

My Lord, in that period up to 1981 the income continued largely to go offshore to the Lambay account and was used in various ways by those looking after that money abroad, including dealing in property. Over that period £500,000 – Mr Hidden made reference to this – was repatriated to this country into the Leadenhall account in the Isle of Man to purchase the land and build property in Newmarket for the training establishment he was preparing for his retirement as a jockey. He bought that land, he built the stables, got the land next door which already had some buildings upon it and then managed to buy the freehold. All that was done over a period of ten years. The outlay was approximately £500,000.

My Lord, that was the position when the 1981–2 enquiry started. In that enquiry there was – I think this was mentioned by Mr Hidden this morning – no detailed investigation into the accounts, particularly the Lambay account abroad, although the existence of that account, the fact that it had funds and the fact that £500,000 had been repatriated, was all known and apparent to the Revenue at the time of that enquiry. Ultimately tax was assessed and agreed, but the question of the source of that income and the full amount of that income into the Lambay account abroad, the source being partly from bloodstock, that never specifically arose as a question in the course of that enquiry, although I accept of course that it was never volunteered. The fact that it was income derived from bloodstock operations was never made known to the Revenue.

My Lord, it is right that I should say this. There was absolutely no secret that Mr Piggott had his bloodstock operations under way. They were well publicised, including the fact that he bred a horse [Cavo Doro] which came second in the Derby. That was well known and featured publicly that it was a horse which in fact he had bred. It is also right that I should say that certainly up to the time of the 1982–3 enquiry Lester Piggott had always understood that the fact that these matters were offshore, and as everybody else, as I understand, was of that view at the time as well, this was legitimate tax avoidance and was being done for that purpose. Your Lordship will note that there is no suggestion in this indictment that there was any evasion in respect of these matters prior to the 1982 enquiry at which time he was told to bring his offshore operation onshore.

My Lord, it is right to say, though, that thereafter in so far as his bloodstock income was concerned, and unhappily it was as from that moment that it escalated, matters were allowed to remain the same and the man Ashenheim whom your Lordship has heard mentioned who had been looking after these finances abroad since 1979, continued to receive the bloodstock income, the bloodstock now having been registered, because it had to be registered in a name, in the name of Western Agency. The income which in the last two years became substantial was largely as a result of a very valuable interest in the stallion Roberto which was standing in the United States, the nominations for which he was entitled to he was in a position to sell. It was not until the 1986 enquiry was instituted that full disclosure of those two years subsequent to the 1982–3 enquiry was made known to the Revenue.

My Lord, I said the bloodstock was to some extent tied up with count six, the omission of the income which had built up over a period of nine or ten years as a result of owners' betting. It is quite clear in our submission that this count in the indictment, count six with that very large figure is really the catalyst of this whole matter. There is no doubt that it was the non-disclosure of the Allied Irish accounts to Price Waterhouse into which the receipts from that source went and the resulting non-disclosure to the Inland Revenue that caused the Commissioner to prosecute rather than to compound.

The Price Waterhouse report was commissioned in February 1986 and produced the following autumn, but of course the Inland Revenue 1985 enquiries which led to the enquiry being started openly against Mr Piggott and the employment of Price Waterhouse had caused them to believe that there was an account at the Allied Irish Bank and, when no such accounts were disclosed in the report, notices were served which caused Mr Piggott then to divulge.

Of course, that looked very bad, let me say that at once, but before I come to the explanation, as I hope to persuade your Lordship that there is one which is at least understandable in the particular circumstances, could I just say a little bit about the Allied Irish accounts themselves. This I think does bear saying so that your Lordship really appreciates the extent of these accounts.

My Lord, as I have already explained, these accounts started when one account was originally opened in Dublin in 1972 for the purposes of his bloodstock. Thereafter during the 1970s it was used principally, as I have already explained, not for the receipt of bloodstock income which was going abroad, but was funded in order to make the bloodstock payments from the cash payments he was receiving out of owners' betting. That was a source which escalated during the 1970s from the time that first account was opened in 1972.

My Lord, it might be helpful while I just deal with these accounts to have in front of your Lordship the schedule that Mr Hidden referred to. I think it is page 14, exhibit 34. One can see straightaway if one looks at that, that until 1978–9 the only accounts which were being operated were one current account, the very last one in the list, the Lambay external account, and the two above it, two deposit accounts. The only accounts which were being operated were those in Dublin. Throughout the whole of this period, I will look very shortly at the picture in a minute but could I make this point at once, the only other current account that there is in the 17 is the second one on that list, the Lambay current account in London. All the rest of the accounts are deposit accounts either in London, the Isle of Man, the Channel Islands or in Eire.

By 1979 there was a substantial amount of money on deposit in Dublin, and on the advice of the bank manager in Dublin he then opened accounts in London partly because of the concern in relation to currency, which was a concern voiced to him and he was made aware of by the manager of the Dublin bank, and partly for convenience because by now he was spending much less time in Ireland and much more time in England. So it was not until 1979 that the London accounts were opened because one sees some figures appearing in them for the year 1979–80. Thereafter he took the advice not of his Dublin bank manager but of his London bank manager at the Allied Irish Bank. It was on his advice that further deposit accounts were opened in the Isle of Man and in the Channel Islands.

As I have indicated, throughout the whole of this period there were only two current accounts, the rest were deposit accounts and the money on the advice and solely on the advice of the bank manager or managers was in fact being transferred and juggled between these various deposit accounts so that the maximum interest and possible currency gains could be made. It has been pointed out, and I cannot complain, that five of these accounts were in false names. My Lord, the false names or allegedly false names are the five accounts either in the name of K. and S. Day or K. Armstrong. I suppose it would be correct to say that strictly speaking they are in false names, but there was in fact no ulterior motive in those names. All the other accounts as one can see there, Lambay and Zeus, were directly capable of connection with Lester Piggott. The other accounts had to be given a nomination, and what he did was to choose the name of Armstrong which was his wife's maiden name, and the name of Day, who was an ancestor of his and apparently a very famous trainer in the middle of the last century. That was the extent to which it can be said that there was falsity in the nominations of these accounts.

My Lord, what he did, so I am instructed, is that really the movements of these monies which one can see there, were entirely at the suggestion and on the advice of his bank manager. He would go to the bank once or twice a month, pay this money in which he had been receiving from the owners and effectively did what he was told. The fact that he was advised in this sort of way is really confirmed, we would submit, by what the prosecution have said first of all in the summary of the facts which your Lordship will have seen at the top of page 25, and indeed also from what Mr Hidden has told your Lordship this morning.

There came a time when he was asked by the London bank manager to sign an Inland Revenue form to say that he was non-resident so that the bank did not have to declare the interest on these accounts to the Bank of England in the normal way, when the bank manager knew perfectly well he was resident in England and indeed suggested to him, as he did, to give his overseas address as the bank's address in Dublin. My Lord, I say that and point it out merely, as I hope your Lordship will agree that I am entitled to say, that this is an example of really how badly he was served and ill-advised by his professional advisers, or at least some of them.

Those accounts, as your Lordship knows, were finally closed in 1986 and the funds were transferred to Mr Ashenheim offshore. That goes to make up the figure about which I will be telling your Lordship in a moment when I come to the asset position which is now held by Mr Ashenheim on the basis of cash.

My Lord, having said that in relation to the Allied Irish accounts, may I now come to the reason, at least the explanation, for the non-disclosure of these accounts and particularly the non-disclosure at the commencement of this enquiry at the beginning of 1986.

My Lord, the source of the revenue in those accounts was the proceeds of owners' betting, and perhaps I should explain that so it is not misunderstood. It is also highly relevant to the explanation. Betting by a jockey himself is absolutely prohibited by Jockey Club rules, it is a cardinal sin and if discovered would be severely dealt with by disqualification no doubt, and probably quite rightly. That applies to any betting by a jockey even though riding the actual horse which was the subject of the bet. On the other hand there is nothing in the rules which appears to suggest that owners shall not give a percentage of their betting wins to the jockey who rides their winning horse, although in reality that is really just another way of funding a bet for the jockey and placing it on his behalf. It has become a very common practice, certainly in regard to top jockeys, although owners would never broadcast the fact and sometimes would not even tell the jockey concerned until after the event.

It was usually done by owners obviously who bet themselves and substantial bets for jockeys were really quite commonplace. Of course your Lordship will readily appreciate that the dividing line between defining such a bet as a jockey's bet or an owner's bet resulting in the jockey receiving a cash gift from the owner's winnings might be very indistinct indeed, and that an owner's bet for a jockey might easily be construed as a jockey's bet for himself. Not only might the bet be difficult to construe in regard to the rules, but in addition at that time the whole position regarding any tax liability on such a payment to a jockey was an undetermined grey area and remained so.

I was touching upon this before, but, my Lord, may I just elaborate for a moment. If the owner, a jockey or any person placed a bet for himself, no income tax would be payable on the winnings, except of course betting tax, but if an owner funds a bet for a jockey what is the position then? Is the stake a gift and taxable? If so, does it make any difference if it is a winning bet or a losing bet? If a winning bet, stake or otherwise, is taxable, is a losing bet deductable? Are the winnings, as distinct from the stake, taxable on the basis that they in fact constitute a gift in relation to his riding?

My Lord, as I have already indicated – and I hope I made this clear because it may be that I did not – although way back in 1973 owners' betting had been raised by the Inland Revenue, in the circumstances which I outlined to your Lordship, following upon Mr Piggott's written voluntary admission, it had been left in limbo and never definitely resolved. Your Lordship will remember I said that his then-accountant had taken the view that maybe the winning portion of the bet, as distinct from the stake, was not liable to tax. That was his view, but it had never been put to the test and certainly not agreed by the Revenue.

In those circumstances, my Lord, I would just like to make it clear because it could radically affect the overall situation in respect of these charges in so far as amounts are concerned, that although of course it is accepted that all those monies referred to in count six which had built up over the years to £1.3 million should have been declared and were omitted from Mr Piggott's return, hence his plea, and maybe that the stake at least is taxable, it is not necessarily accepted that the winning part of those bets is. I understand that this is a matter upon which the courts may have to adjudicate in due course, because this will be disputed, so I am informed, by other jockeys into whose tax affairs enquiries have been and are still being made, particularly in respect of similar sources of revenue.

I say this because although, as I have indicated, the omitted figure is £1.3 million and that should have been declared and was not, the amount of tax alleged to have been evaded thereon may well be an inflated figure which in due course could come to be substantially mitigated. My Lord, I cannot put it any higher than that, but I do put it in that way and I invite your Lordship to bear that well in mind.

My Lord, following 1973 when this matter was not pursued, Lester Piggott continued as before, and that source of income escalated and built up during the 1970s. One only has to look at the prosecution schedule to see in that bottom line the figures increasing year by year until we arrive at that total of £1.3 million at the end. It was nearly £1 million by the time this enquiry started, that was the 1982–3 enquiry, in the Allied Irish account which had built up virtually untouched. You can add those figures up as you go along because there is not a continuing balance on that schedule. If you add them up you arrive at the end almost exactly with the figure of the total. That shows that it was virtually untouched over a period of ten years.

Of course that resulted in another problem with which he was faced when the 1982–3 enquiry came round. Something which just happened following the advice of his bank managers. This was that interest was being earned year by year which compounded year after year. Of course if the income is not being disclosed then neither could the interest because they do flow together, hand in hand. That was the position in 1982 when he failed to disclose these accounts. He failed to do so quite simply because he had two major worries. The first was that the sum in this account had grown from 1972 when it was a few hundred pounds until by this time it was just about £1 million, the figures one sees in that schedule with the exception of the last year.

On top of that, of course, was the interest and his worry was that if this large sum was in fact taxable, as he feared it might be, together with the interest which certainly was, he was very concerned, indeed frightened, I think would be the right word to use, as to the consequences of then disclosing it, it having grown into such a huge sum of money. He was equally concerned at the view that might be taken by the Jockey Club as to that source of income which he feared could, he would have been wrong, have jeopardised his whole future in racing if those large amounts of betting came to light. In fact may I say at once when I say he was wrong, the sadness is that in fact his worry about his professional body was apparently misplaced because it is now understood that that would not be considered contrary to the *Rules of Racing*.

MR JUSTICE FARQUHARSON: Would the Jockey Club have objected about the non-disclosure of retainers at Weatherbys?

MR MATHEW: My Lord, yes.

MR JUSTICE FARQUHARSON: I rather get the impression from what you were saying a few minutes ago that they would not have objected.

MR MATHEW: My Lord, no, that is certainly not so and if I have given that impression I would not seek to do so. I say that for this reason. The only action that was taken against Mr Cecil, and there was action taken against Mr Cecil as I understand it by the Jockey Club, was a disciplinary hearing at which it was suggested and found to be proved that he had not registered at Weatherbys the illicit arrangement that he had with Mr Piggott. I think he was fined a sum of £2,000.

MR JUSTICE FARQUHARSON: I do not want to trouble you with the details.

MR MATHEW: My Lord, I did not want it to be understood that the Jockey Club would have officially approved of this sort of arrangement of not being registered at Weatherbys, but as I have indicated, if we face the realities of this matter it is quite clear that they must have appreciated that this was the situation in so far as Mr Piggott and other jockeys were concerned.

MR JUSTICE FARQUHARSON: They must have done, look at these documents.

MR MATHEW: My Lord, precisely, but at the time before these documents came to light.

MR JUSTICE FARQUHARSON: I fear I may have taken you off your submission, because I am very anxious to hear about the non-disclosure of these bank accounts, or at least the reasons you are now developing.

MR MATHEW: My Lord, I can put it now absolutely simply. The history I have explained. Nothing really much had happened in 1973. He continued placing these monies in the original Allied Irish Bank account which had been started on his bloodstock income. Over the next nine years it built up in an amazing way to this sum with the interest compounded into the sort of interest amounts that your Lordship sees in the other two counts. Because of that, when the 1982–3 enquiry commenced, his worry, concern and fright was that that sum of money might put him in a situation with the Inland Revenue, the like of which he is in now before this court.

If that be the position in 1982–3 when he stupidly for those reasons allowed those factors to prevent him from disclosing, by 1986 it was even more difficult for him so to do. Not only had the amounts further increased, both the amount from just under £1 million to up to £1.3 million in the accounts themselves, but the failure to disclose in 1982, not having disclosed to the Inland Revenue in 1982 would be a further aggravating feature if he did in 1986. Stupidly he decided that it would be better to put his head in the sand. The Inland Revenue in fact knew about these accounts from their own sources of information no doubt, and as a result of the enquiry which was then made he was prevailed upon by Price Waterhouse to disclose and so he did.

My Lord, those matters are now fully before the court. Of course he appreciates that they should have been in 1982–3. Of course he appreciates his position. He might not have even been in this court today if it had not been for that disclosure in 1986 and his punishment for so doing has been extreme.

My Lord, what I want to do now, I hope, is to try, and it is not easy, to answer the question of why did he continue to do this. Why, following the 1982 settlement, did he still fail to return his full income from riding? Why did he not learn the lesson when the warning bells had so loudly been rung?

Well, the fact is he just does not know himself, and, I hope he will forgive me for saying so, in his inimitable, uncommunicative way it has really been impossible for him to give an explanation. Perhaps there is none. I have already stressed to your Lordship that he did not need the money. I have already stressed to your Lordship that he never spent the money. The only thing he ever wanted was to prepare the ground and build up a training establishment in Newmarket where he could train when his career as a jockey was over in order to keep within the racing scene. This he did by buying part of the land originally in 1970, built upon it slowly year by year the stables which stand there now and are occupied by 70 horses, building the house in which he now lives next door and the house which he built for his aged mother and father in the corner of the property.

My Lord, it should have been shown that was the £500,000 which came back from offshore to Leadenhall, which is almost exactly the sum of money which has been spent to purchase that training establishment and home. He could easily have afforded to do so with the earnings he was accumulating over these years out of his net income. The real fear that he had was, if he finished as a jockey, and he expected to have to finish much earlier than he did, he would cease to be a part of the racing world, because when he asked himself, 'Is there life after racing?' the only answer he could find was: 'Yes, but only if I am a successful trainer.' He knew that past history is littered with the failures of jockeys who retired and set out on that course.

My Lord, did he fear that failure and the need for the comfort of a financial cushion? Did that play a part? Did his character of secretiveness, thrift and apparent compulsion to hoard play a part? Did the nature of his physical disability from birth play a part, or was he then unthinking in his own isolated way, unable to appreciate the disastrous consequences which might accrue which can only be described in this way of acting, a 'quirk' because it was being done so openly and blatantly and for no obvious reason? As a result one wonders whether he can be judged by normal standards, but one thing is certain and that is that this was not a calculated dishonesty for the purposes of personal greed, to have money for his own indulgence or even the indulgences of others.

My Lord, what is the position now? Right at the outset I touched upon the financial position but, my Lord, it is only right I should give your Lordship a little more detail. The tax evaded, I do not say allegedly because he has pleaded guilty, in respect of the matters in the indictment which covers all the matters which the Crown allege are the subject of dishonest evasion, there is nothing else, amounts to £1.7 million. The taxed interest amounts to £1.1 million, making £2.8 million, his liabilities in respect of the matters in the indictment.

My Lord, he has now paid, these figures are agreed, just over £3 million so far. It was paid because it was initially apportioned to the counts in this indictment. If you apportion the two counts in this indictment, he has about £250,000 in hand. This money was available and this money has been paid but, having said that, there are further substantial amounts of tax due. There is further tax due not the subject of any evasion otherwise they would be matters in the indictment.

There is further tax due for the years prior to 1984, for the last three financial years, his last year racing and his two years as a trainer. Perhaps we can forget about his two years as a trainer because, successful as he was, the profits were minimal certainly compared with his riding.

Therefore, there is pre-1984 and post-1984 tax still to be paid to make his position correct with the Inland Revenue. The fact is that tax under those two headings will not be less than £1.5 million and it looks as if it may be considerably more; it could be considerably more, I perhaps should say, because unfortunately £1.5 million has already been offered in full settlement and has been refused at this stage. Therefore I am not in a position to tell your Lordship precisely what the tax ultimately will be under those two headings, but I think I would be right to say it certainly will not be less than £1.5 million and it could be considerably more.

Having said that, could I interpose to make a point which I hope will commend itself to your Lordship. I have of course already indicated to your Lordship from some of the letters which I have submitted today that certainly in some degree he was not truly served by his advisers, both lay and professional, and there really does not seem to be any doubt about that. If he had had proper and expert tax advice there were any number of lawful ways, settlements, insurances and pension schemes and so on in which he could have mitigated these enormous tax liabilities by a very, very substantial amount. The sadness is that he took no expert advice. He certainly did not receive any expert advice, and if he had and had made full disclosure he would be a very much richer man today even if these matters had not come to light.

What are his assets now? I can deal with them in three headings. I said a short time ago that when the Allied Irish Bank accounts were closed in August 1986 the balance in them went to Mr Ashenheim off-shore. Such cash as he has is in those hands, in safe hands. It is available, the cash held offshore, and it is really the totality of the cash available immediately which is £2.2 million. I am dealing in round figures but that is as accurate as one can be. Of course that is the only sum immediately available from which these further taxes of not less than £1.5 million, will have to be paid. Therefore, depending upon whether that is the figure, or more after the final meeting of those liabilities, it appears there will not be a great deal of money, if any, left in the form of cash.

The second heading on his assets is bloodstock, his interests in stallions and so on. That is a very difficult figure to assess. We have tried to get expert advice upon it. It is a figure which changes very often over short periods depending on the capacity of the stallion. All one can say is it would probably be about half a million pounds, but they are not readily realisable assets. Indeed, it is his bloodstock interests that keep the training establishment together at this particular time.

The third heading is property, the house, stables, training establishment in Newmarket and the flat in London. He has a flat in London which is worth probably, it was until a few days ago, £200,000 or thereabouts. The training establishment which is his livelihood and his home, again is very difficult to value. It is not like a private house where there is a ready market. There will not be a great many persons who want to take on 15 acres, two houses and something in excess of 100 stables unless there is somebody who particularly wants to move their training establishment or has a great deal of money to start one up from scratch. Therefore the amount depends entirely upon the sort of purchaser. It is a very difficult property to value and the best one can do is to say it will not be worth less than £1 million and could be worth considerably more.

Allied to that establishment there is of course another intangible asset and that is Lester Piggott's training ability. I think I have already pointed out the difficulties there are for jockeys who seek success as a trainer. Lester Piggott was, needless to say because of the nature of the man, beginning to demonstrate that he was to be the exception. In his first season last year he trained 30 horses, including the winner of a major two-year-olds' race, which by any standards, I am led to believe, is a unique achievement. As a result, this year the number of his horses increased by well over half. By late summer, August or thereabouts, he had already achieved another 30 winners, but in the last few weeks they have not been so successful. There is no doubt, and he is the first to admit it, that the strains of this impending trial had finally affected even his dedication and concentration. Now of course his future as a trainer is dependent upon the outcome of this case today. One thing is certain. His training career cannot survive regardless of any view the Jockey Club may take unless he is in a position to be in personal control at the beginning of the next season in six months' time.

My Lord, I have to approach this matter realistically on his behalf. He now, and I stress that word 'now', appreciates the danger in which he stands. He had the warning. Those large sums arise really because of his immense determination to be the best, which he became, and, since he never spent it, large amounts of compound interest accumulated. That is why the figures are so high in this case. A less successful person who was therefore a lesser earner but whose conduct was nevertheless identical, would have lesser amounts in the charges to answer for, but his culpability would be the same. I do invite your Lordship to look, therefore, at the conduct rather than the amounts, conduct which is never going to happen again. Now he is in the hands of the best possible advisers.

My Lord, of course it is unnecessary for me to say anything as to the consequences of a custodial sentence upon him which was immediate, the consequences not only on him but on his new career and on his family, which would spell the end of everything that he has striven for all his life. I know that your Lordship will bear that in mind. One is dealing with a person who sits there with 40 years of determination and self-denial written into his face. One is dealing with a person for whom the guillotine must fall in a time of his life when he can never achieve higher than he has. It is unnecessary also for me to itemise the inevitable burden that he and his family have carried for the past two years and in regard to which he has stayed within the jurisdiction to face.

At the end of the day, perhaps the predetermined feeling, as Mr Hidden said, which prevails is one of sadness that such an admired and public figure who has given so much pleasure to so many people should now be suffering this public disgrace. He is certainly sad not only because of the suffering, the sorrow and the contrition which he genuinely feels, not only because of the unhappy attention he has caused to be focused on his beloved world of racing, but also because he knows, and he has told me this with conviction, that for him there is no life after racing. He has no other life and therefore he is now literally standing with his whole life in the balance. My Lord, is he not entitled to say through me: I have served my country as an ambassador abroad and I have served the public with dedication all through my racing life which is now over, and to ask your Lordship, have I not built up sufficient credit to stand me in good stead at this moment?

My Lord, I invite your Lordship to say that this is a case which in many ways is an exceptional case and therefore it is possible to deal with in what to some might seem to be an exceptionally lenient way. My Lord, that is all I say unless I can help your Lordship further.

And so ended Mr Mathew's submission. No sooner had Mr Mathew returned to his seat than Mr Justice Farquharson asked him if Piggott would be able to hear what he had to say in passing sentence. After Mr Mathew told the judge Piggott would be able to hear if he was addressed directly, Mr Justice Farquharson turned to Piggott, now, after all the court had heard, a sad figure standing alone and about to bear the ultimate responsibility for his actions, and began his summing up.

This is what he said:

MR JUSTICE FARQUHARSON: Lester Keith Piggott, I suppose that the arguments in your favour could scarcely have been put more attractively than they have during the course of the afternoon and, indeed, during the course of the day because the prosecution have spoken so well of you in your career, having regard to your fame. I take that very much into account.

Perhaps more than anything, I take into account the substantial repayments you have made to the Inland Revenue including the amounts covered in this indictment. I, of course, pay attention to the fact that you have admitted these offences which I emphasise are offences of dishonesty. It is right perhaps also for me to recognise that a lot of the dishonesty in which you have engaged in your failure to own up to the Inland Revenue as to your various assets, has taken place in a climate where cash payments are not infrequent and often not accounted for. I repeat, those matters are very much in my mind.

On the other hand your fame has resulted in you having a quite enormous income. Tax-gathering must depend, must it not, on the honesty of all of us when the demands come in. Up and down the country those who only have a tiny proportion of what you enjoy pay up, loyally meet their obligations. So how can I pass over your case when you had the resources to meet the heavy demands that no doubt would have been made upon you and still have a large amount of money to look after yourself and your family? One might have been able to accede to the submission made by Mr Mathew if, when the matter really came up to the boil in February 1986, or April 1986, you then revealed all those bank accounts and the monies that they held, but not only did you not reveal them to the Revenue, you did not even tell your own professional advisers until finally it was forced out in December of last year.

If I were to pass over this it would be an invitation, I feel, for other people to be tempted to dishonour their obligations and try and cheat the Revenue.

In the result, I am going to impose terms of imprisonment upon you on counts six, eight and nine, amounting to three years. On the remaining counts of the indictment there will be sentences of two years; all those sentences will run concurrently. You must pay the costs of £34,000 of the prosecution and there will be a fine which, in the circumstances, is a nominal one of £5,000 on each of those counts with which the Company is also indicted, that is, counts three, four, five, six and ten. The Company itself will be fined the sum of £100 on each of those counts.

On announcement of the judge's sentence, all eyes in the courtroom focused from the judge on to Piggott. But the face was as millions of people have seen it before, set in a stony stare. As he was led from the room by the prison officer, without glancing at his wife, Susan burst into tears and for several minutes was comforted by a female usher until solicitor Jeremy Richardson arrived at her side.

As some reporters raced from the court to find the nearest telephone and announce the verdict to their newsrooms, others stood in groups debating the outcome. The barristers began packing up their papers and files, the court slowly emptied, and, within five minutes, it was empty once more except for a court usher who checked the benches for anything left behind.

Susan Piggott was taken down to the cells with Mr Richardson where she spent a short time with her gaoled husband. By the time she emerged from the rear of the court to make the journey back to Newmarket, Susan was much more composed. Mr Richardson made a short statement to the waiting journalists, saying that Piggott would not appeal against the sentence.

Piggott himself emerged a little later handcuffed to another prisoner and boarded the prison bus bound for Norwich goal where he would spend the next few days before being transferred to a more comfortable open prison. He managed a rare smile inside the bus, no doubt his sense of humour briefly restored by the wisecrack of a fellow prisoner.

Now, there would be plenty of jokes cracked about Her Majesty's former jockey turned Royal guest at one of HM's prisons. Piggott would serve a year of his sentence; twelve months faced him of a life he had scarcely imagined.

17. Repercussion and Recrimination

Lester Piggott had not yet arrived at Norwich Prison before the media was telling the world of the outcome to the trial. By the time he had gone through the humiliating procedure of registration at the crowded Victorian gaol, public reaction to the sentence was already being voiced: a debate that will continue for many years. Initial reaction was one of sadness and sympathy and there were few other than the stone-hearted who felt neither for the predicament now facing Piggott and his family. But while racing's name was still wet from the mud it had been dragged through in that Ipswich courthouse, some of the industry's leading lights did little by their ensuing hysteria to paint a picture of horseracing as other than a small, insular world, naïve at best.

People put the blame on Piggott's advisers, others thought he had put so much into racing that a prison sentence was beyond imagination. The consensus was that as Piggott had not raped or mugged anyone he should not have been sent to prison. Of course, the loss of a dear friend, no matter how temporary, is a time of sadness, in this case, shock. Perhaps with hindsight, and more importantly, in full knowledge of the facts, however, the outbursts that greeted the sentence would not have been as severe.

But was Piggott treated harshly by the court? According to one of the country's leading criminologists, Dr Michael Levi, of the University of Wales, College of Cardiff, a leading authority on tax frauds, the answer is no. Dr Levi cited several cases to prove the point: a roofing contractor gaoled for six months for evading £965 VAT (upheld on appeal); a man who pleaded guilty to receiving stolen Inland Revenue vouchers involving £116,000 who received a seven-year sentence, reduced to four years on appeal; a driving school proprietor who failed to get his 12-month sentence reduced by the appeal court for defrauding VAT of between £26,000 and £41,000; and the case of a gambling accountant whose sentence for a £3.25 million non-tax fraud was reduced on appeal from fourteen years to eight.

Perhaps Britain needs a major review of the punishment for non-violent 'white collar' crime when the alternatives to a prison sentence can be thoroughly debated. That subject, however, is for the future, not as the law stands today.

It could, of course, be legitimately argued that Piggott had indeed tried to mug society itself. Had he successfully evaded that multi-million pound tax debt, how would society have quantified the loss? Would those millions have paid for new kidney machines to keep alive those patients who would otherwise die because of the shortage of such apparatus, or would it pay for the training of nurses so desperately needed for the treatment of post-operative heart-surgery babies? Would the money have gone into education, provided old people with extra winter warmth, or even installed miles of motorway crash barriers? As idealistic as this all sounds, is there not a case for arguing that in a democracy such as ours, society and its millions of ordinary and honest taxpayers should work on such assumptions: that what they pay in taxes does keep Britain working despite its faults?

Piggott's only crime, said one racing figure, had been the unpardonable one of being caught. Another said that tax fiddles had always been part of racing, while a racing commentator said the transgressions had only been on a very minor scale. At a stroke, comments such as these erased the many decent and laudable aspects of horseracing from the minds of the general public. To them, it might have seemed, racing had always been bent, run by crooks for crooks and now their suspicions were only being confirmed. Members of the Jockey Club, that institution which for years had been carefully nurturing a modern and progressive image of racing, must have winced. For the Lester Piggott affair had cost them dear in lost prestige and had set them back years.

Of particular concern to racing's rulers was the area of bets for jockeys or, as Piggott's counsel, John Mathew, put it, the question of owners funding a bet for a jockey and placing it on his behalf. As Mr

Mathew pointed out, betting by jockeys is a cardinal sin and would be dealt with severely under the *Rules of Racing*. But, he said, there was nothing in those rules which appeared to suggest that owners should not give a percentage of their winning bets to the jockey who rides their winning horse. It had become a common practice certainly in regard to the top jockeys, although owners would never broadcast the fact and, sometimes, would not even tell the jockey concerned until after the event. The practice was carried out by owners who obviously bet themselves; substantial bets for jockeys were really quite commonplace. Piggott's counsel went on to say that the dividing line between defining such a bet as a jockey's bet or an owner's bet, resulting in the jockey receiving a cash gift from that owner's winnings might be very indistinct indeed. Therefore an owner's bet for a jockey might easily be construed as a jockey's bet for himself.

Mr Mathew's argument was that if a jockey received a sum of money as the proceeds of an owner's winning bet, then betting tax would have already been paid by the owner on his winnings and no income tax would be due. So what was the position with the 'gift' element of his winnings to the jockey? Were the winnings, as distinct from the stake, taxable on the basis that they constituted a gift in relation to the jockey's riding?

The Inland Revenue, of course, consider such gifts to be taxable. Consider the implications otherwise: the winning owner buys a bottle of champagne from his winnings and tips the barman or waitress, he tips the taxi-driver on his way back to the station, tips the doorman at his hotel (all tips, of course, being declared income). Flush from a touch at the races, the householder pays the plumber in cash from his winnings. Indeed, the permutations for all beneficiaries to avoid paying tax are endless and one suspects that if, as has been reported, jockeys do ever challenge the ruling in the High Court then they would receive short shrift from a judge.

In reality there are many owners who never bet at all. There are lots more who do bet but never back their own horse and instead perhaps back what they consider to be the danger. In other words, there are a considerable number of horses that win races and go unbacked by the owner. But what happens when these horses win? Do owners tell the jockeys they never had a bet and therefore they must whistle for their present? No, of course they do not. Jockeys still receive their cash gift from the owners out of the owners' prize money as it were, and this is the spirit in which the present was given and which forms the basis of the Jockey Club's allowance of the practice. This goes back to the days when jockeys did not receive a percentage of the winning prize but instead had to rely on an owner's generosity for a present to supplement their riding fees. Whether the winning owner had had a bet or not was of little concern to the rider – the present was simply his share of the prize money he had just earned for that owner. To suggest that substantial bets for jockeys were quite commonplace must have had the Stewards of the Jockey Club choking on their port. Another comment at which racing observers must have been slightly mystified was the reference to British bloodstock operations. Mr Mathew said that, as he understood it, stallions have historically always stood outside this country. Talking about Piggott's bloodstock interests which dated from 1972, he told the court that stallions then and now always stood abroad if for no other reason than nowadays it meant they were not subject to VAT. No doubt the owners of the 1,000-plus stallions registered in Britain in 1989 would disagree.

So alarmed were the Jockey Club about matters arising from the Piggott trial that they immediately set in motion a major review of Rule 62(ii), which prohibits jockeys betting. It was in the December of 1987, nearly two months after Piggott was jailed, that the Jockey Club announced the move in a document released from their headquarters in Portman Square entitled: 'The Lester Piggott Affair'.

In a statement they said: 'The Stewards are anxious that if a case of a jockey betting is discovered, the rules should be sufficiently comprehensive to cover a wide variety of situations. To this end they are broadening the rules to incorporate other persons betting on behalf of jockeys.'

The reference to 'other persons' meant that the new rule would include owners, friends and jockeys' own 'punters', in an effort to repair the damage to racing's image brought about by the publicity in the wake of the Piggott trial.

It was another three months before the changes were announced. The addition to the rule now made it an offence for a jockey not only to bet himself but also to instruct any person to bet on his behalf or (and this is where they were putting the emphasis) to receive knowingly the proceeds of any bet. Fundamentally, of course, there was little in the new rule which was not covered by the old one; it was just that the Jockey Club were tightening up the whole area and literally spelling out what jockeys could not do – not that the previous rule allowed them as much. Despite this move, there would be little the Jockey Club could do to enforce it. A jockey now receiving a present from a grateful owner could warily ask if the cash had come from the proceeds of a bet and presumably refuse if it had.

Then again, an owner could say the cash came from his left-hand pocket and not the newly acquired wad of notes in his right-hand pocket which he had just picked up from the bookmaker. Even so, the reiteration of the perils for jockeys who bet or receive money from bets is a sobering reminder to anyone who might want to continue the custom that netted Lester Piggott so much money.

As if to emphasise how seriously the Jockey Club were viewing the Piggott situation they had stated that enquiries into allegations of possible breaches of the *Rules of Racing* by Lester Piggott were continuing.

There was another rule change at this time too, one which had prompted the Jockey Club to hold consultations with the Inland Revenue and Customs in an effort to solve the question of a jockey's retainer, his taxable income and allowable expenditure. This had been the area most directly affecting the men from Portman Square, some of whom had been owners with Henry Cecil and had received the now-infamous letter requesting cash payments for Piggott (this was in force for the seasons 1981–4).

According to Mr Mathew, during the trial, the Piggott cash retainer arrangement which, he said, had been drafted after legal advice (and which was later held to be contrary to Jockey Club rules) was circulated to Cecil's owners of standing in the racing world, including members of the Jockey Club and at least one Steward of the Jockey Club.

He told the judge: 'I did not want it to be understood that the Jockey Club would have officially approved of this sort of arrangement of not being registered at Weatherbys but, as I have indicated, if we face the realities of this matter, it is quite clear that they must have appreciated this was the situation in so far as Mr Piggott and other jockeys were concerned.'

To that, Mr Justice Farquharson retorted: 'They must have done – look at these documents.'

In their 'Lester Piggott Affair' statement, the Jockey Club virtually cleared those involved although a final paragraph 'regretted' that effective and more positive steps had not been taken at the time. The statement said:

The then senior steward, Captain John Macdonald-Buchanan, has stated that early in 1981 when he had a horse in Mr Cecil's yard, he received a letter from the trainer requesting some additional requirements over and above the amount due for Lester Piggott's retainer registered with Weatherbys.

After consulting with both Mr Louis Freedman, the deputy senior steward who also had a horse with Mr Cecil, and Mr Simon Weatherby, secretary to the Jockey Club, Captain Macdonald-Buchanan decided to take immediate action personally.

The senior steward visited Mr Cecil and pointed out to him the implications of what he had written and warned him that his actions were likely to be in breach of the Rules of Racing. He further stated that Mr Cecil should withdraw the letter or register it fully in accordance with Rule 75 (that all agreements must be registered at Weatherbys).

Captain Macdonald-Buchanan considered this was understood and accepted by Mr Cecil and, as a result, he believed he had acted promptly to prevent any breach of the Rules of Racing. His horse retired to stud and between 1982–6 he had no horse in training with Mr Cecil.

Captain Macdonald-Buchanan left office in June 1982, and Mr Simon Weatherby died in January 1983. There were no records of the advice given or action taken over this incident.

Captain Macdonald-Buchanan has emphasised that he takes full responsibility for the action taken in 1981 regarding the 'Cecil letter'.

Between 1981–3, Mr Louis Freedman was a steward of the Jockey Club and also had horses with Mr Cecil. In connection with the breach of Rule 75 by Mr Cecil, Mr Freedman states that prior to the 1983 season he received a computer print-out from the trainer making a similar request for cash payments and that he immediately wrote to Mr Cecil stating he would have nothing to do with the proposed agreement and also spoke to him about it.

Mr Freedman further states that Mr Cecil assured him that the print-out had been sent in error and that he then assumed that appropriate action had been taken to register the agreement properly. He was supported in this view by the fact that deductions made from his account by Weatherbys in 1981 and 1983 appeared to be consistent with the full retainer.

When Mr Cecil's breach of Rule 75 became apparent following a newspaper article in 1985, the Jockey Club took prompt action. The

Disciplinary Committee held an inquiry and, as a result, Mr Cecil was fined £2,000.

The stewards very much regret that the action taken on the Cecil letter between 1981–4 was not effective and accept that the interests of all concerned would have been better served if more positive steps had been taken at the time.

That last paragraph, from the Club that runs racing with a rod of iron born from a supposedly strict military precision and discipline, needs very little comment. The rule requiring retainer agreements between a jockey and his trainer or owner was correspondingly dropped. Now it is no longer necessary for a jockey to reveal the financial details of his retainer to Weatherbys – this is a private matter and only declarable to the taxman – although the other information about his retainer still has to be notified to racing's administrators.

Lester Piggott began the New Year of 1988 in surroundings far removed from the sunny luxury of his past winter haunts; Highpoint Open Prison in Suffolk has a softer régime than Norwich Gaol to where he was initially sent, but in his small, shared room in the prison's North Wing, the strain of his incarceration was beginning to tell. Piggott's personality was not suited to prison life; its 'social' environment, psychologists say, leaves those possessing an outgoing quality better able to cope with the rigours of a daily routine which, at best, is daunting. It was this fact, and what some prisoners saw as a somewhat privileged existence (Piggott had one cell-mate while other inmates were four to a room) that led to resentment among many of them. Some thought him standoffish, snooty, perhaps a view they would have of anyone with introversion woven into a character 'sheltered' by the confines of a life where horses, not people, were of the prime concern. Here, in Highpoint, he would be expected to mix with his fellow cons, crack a few of those famous jokes, maybe relive some of those magic moments of the turf. However, shunning other prisoners as he often would the prison food, Piggott found it hard to come to terms with this new and enforced alien existence.

At Piggott's Newmarket stables, Susan Piggott was trying to maintain normality in running the yard and supervising the loyal staff. Susan had been granted a temporary licence to train the horses as soon as Lester was imprisoned, sending out her first winner, Turbine Blade, at Nottingham, with just three weeks of the 1987 Flat season remaining. But now, with the start of the 1988 season less than two months away, Susan applied to the Jockey Club's Licensing Committee for a full licence and this was granted at the end of January.

Piggott's misery, however, manifested itself before the licence was issued to Susan on a permanent basis, for that same month, prison warders found him unconscious in his cell. After warders had given Piggott the kiss of life in their efforts to revive him from what they thought was either a heart attack or a drugs overdose, he was taken by ambulance to hospital at Bury St Edmunds and subsequently transferred to the hospital wing back at Norwich Gaol until his recovery a week later. Such was the strain of life behind bars that a combination of circumstances led to nervous exhaustion and blackout.

When he was eventually returned to Highpoint, Piggott was switched to the better-equipped D-wing. One of his tasks was as teaboy in the prison workshop. Occasionally he was given other menial jobs such as storeman, sweeping or gardening, and at one time he helped out in the laundry. In D-wing, too, Piggott began to eat better and build his strength, watching the televised racing at every opportunity, tipping the odd winner like the Grand National winner Rhyme' N' Reason. But the bad days outnumbered the good. He was once allowed home to visit his father who had suffered a heart attack, a visit on compassionate grounds to an old man devastated by his son's imprisonment.

As if to endorse the armchair philosophy that negativity breeds more of the same, another blow to Piggott came on 6 June, with the announcement in the *London Gazette* that he had been stripped of one of his most prized possessions, the Order of the British Empire. Piggott had received the OBE from the Queen in the 1975 New Year's Honours List for his services to racing. Sadly, the awards are also made to honour good citizenship, and Piggott's criminal conviction made the loss of the honour a certainty. Now it meant that not only had he thrown away the chance of a knighthood, but he had joined the disgraced ranks of others stripped of their titles – men like traitor Anthony Blunt and former raincoat magnate Lord Kagan.

Predictably, the stripping of Piggott's title, which had been endorsed by Buckingham Palace on the recommendation of the Prime Minister, brought bleats of protest from some prominent racing figures which showed, if nothing else, that when the blinkers of life and society in general are produced, they fit perfectly on some sections of the racing game.

Susan Piggott had been maintaining a dignified silence throughout this period, instead concentrating on the job in hand, that of sending out as many winners as possible from Eve Lodge. Although the number of winners was down on the previous season, by mid-August Susan had been responsible for 17 winners, when tragedy struck on the early-morning gallops. Her faithful 'pony', Pepe, stumbled, crushing Susan underneath, fracturing her skull, her collarbone, and breaking ten ribs. So serious were the injuries – her skull was doubly fractured from ear to ear – that there was grave concern for her life and she was placed on a ventilating machine in intensive care at Addenbrooke's Hospital in Cambridge. She was given paralysing drugs to prevent her body fighting the discomfort of the ventilating treatment. Unable to eat or talk, everyone's hearts went out to hope for a speedy recovery while, once again, attention was focused on Piggott and his plight in prison.

It was a cruel blow to a family that had rallied in the face of adversity. With Susan incapacitated, eldest daughter Maureen was immediately granted a temporary licence to handle the day-to-day running of the yard. By the end of the season, some two months later, she had coped admirably, sending out six winners and proving a credit to her parents.

Six days after the accident, Piggott was allowed out of prison to visit his wife. In all his career in the saddle he had suffered serious injury but none quite as bad as this. By now, doctors were a little happier with Susan's condition although the left side of her chest had been crushed and had collapsed. But if the world needed to know that the woman behind Lester Piggott was made of strong stuff, Susan confounded doctors by walking unaided from the hospital only four weeks later and just days after coming off the ventilator machine. With her as she left the hospital gates was Maureen, smiling this time in contrast to her horror exactly a month to the day at finding her mother lying crumpled and unconscious on the gallops of Newmarket Heath.

With fears for Susan's health allayed, Piggott was anxiously awaiting news of his possible parole. At this time, too, there were reports that Piggott faced a new tax investigation and could be faced with a bill of around £1.5 million. In reality the Inland Revenue were continuing their negotiations with Piggott over legitimate tax affairs prior and subsequent to the years which were the subject of his indictment. At the time of his trial Piggott had offered the Revenue £1.5 million (on top of the £3 million he had already paid because of the fraud) but this sum had been refused and the eventual amount was considered to have to be considerably more.

As to his parole, it had been readily accepted that, in line with normal procedure, a model prisoner could quite confidently expect to be allowed out of prison on licence after having served a third of his sentence. The problems of being a sporting superstar are double-edged, however. Piggott's parole was a subject causing division among members of the Parole Board and, indeed, the Home Office itself.

A minority of Parole Board members took the view that to release Piggott at the first possible moment might lead the general public to believe that Piggott was receiving favoured treatment. Home Secretary, Douglas Hurd, who took an interest in Piggott's plight, came down on the side of 'clemency' and recommended Piggott should be released. And so, on the morning of Monday 24 October, he walked out of Highpoint a year and a day after his sentence to be greeted by Maureen who drove him the twelve miles back to Newmarket. Once in the outside world, Piggott rounded on the media who, he said, had made life in prison much harder for him by the many wild and inaccurate reports about his lifestyle inside. Such as champagne dinners, parties and pornographic film sessions. Conversely, there were inmates at Highpoint who felt a relief at Piggott's freedom – because, they claimed, he had made their lives more difficult!

At home there was a warm welcome from Susan, still recovering from the accident. A little later the Jockey Club were to make it compulsory for all trainers to wear safety helmets when out at exercise, thereby answering a call – belatedly, some felt – from the more sensible sections of racing that had gone unheeded for years. For it was undisputed that, had it not been for the safety helmet Susan chose to wear, albeit a badly dented one, she would not have been waiting on the front step to greet her husband home.

There was good news, too, for Piggott in the form of a statement from the Jockey Club saying that they would not be taking any further action regarding the likelihood that Piggott had, by his offences, brought racing into disrepute, a charge that could have affected his re-applying for his licence to train. There would be no action either on the Maurice Pitt tape which had been authenticated in a voice test by Dr John Baldwin of the linguistics department of London University.

The Jockey Club statement read:

In their statement issued immediately after Lester Piggott's conviction, the Stewards of the Jockey Club announced that they would examine records of his trial to decide if the Rules of Racing *had been breached.*

At their meeting on 12 September 1988, the stewards discussed what action should now be taken. In their view, and in the view of their legal advisers, the evidence produced at his trial indicates that Lester Piggott may have committed acts liable to cause serious damage to the interests of racing which would be a breach of Rule 220(iii) as it stood at the time.

However, taking into account the fact that he is, in effect, already serving a period of disqualification by being imprisoned for a tax offence, and mindful of his past services to racing, the stewards have decided to take no further action in the matter.

Should Lester Piggott decide to make an application for a licence to train, it will be considered by the Licensing Committee in the light of all the facts available at the time.

The stewards have also received a full report of investigations undertaken by their security department into press allegations that in 1971, when he was a jockey, Lester Piggott had been involved in betting transactions contrary to the requirements of the Rules of Racing.

After taking legal advice on the evidence which had been obtained against a background of events which took place 17 years ago, the stewards decided that there was insufficient evidence to warrant holding an enquiry.

Slowly, the world of horseracing began to recover from the affair and all its implications. Operation Centaur, no doubt, had been a blessing for the sport. Racing's wayward course had been corrected by its impact; a short, sharp shock delivered with the sting of that famous Piggott whip. To some insiders, though, Lester Piggott's actions had not only brought shame on racing but were prompting repercussions that brought problems to the already-difficult job of training racehorses, particularly some of the smaller stables. Indeed, for some months after Piggott's release, one well-known Northern trainer was still doing battle with the taxman who wanted to charge him tax on the training fees he did not charge himself for the few shares of horses he owned in his stable. As these were shares in moderate horses the trainer had been unable to sell to owners, he was understandably feeling aggrieved. This, however, was only one small manifestation of the stringency the Inland Revenue were now applying to their dealings with all involved in the sport.

The Jockey Club, thankfully, have now taken steps to put an end to practices it knew were prevalent. The only regret is that it took the outside agencies of the Inland Revenue and Customs and Excise for this to happen.

For Lester Piggott, life has taken on a new meaning, thrown down a fresh challenge. He must put the humiliation behind him and begin to pick up the pieces, knowing that his name and reputation will always be tainted by that fall from grace because of greed.